# The land without musi

**Music and society**

*Series editors*    Peter J. Martin and Tia DeNora

Music and Society aims to bridge the gap between music scholarship and the human sciences. A deliberately eclectic series, its authors are nevertheless united by the contention that music is a social product, social resource, and social practice. As such it is not autonomous but is created and performed by real people in particular times and places; in doing so they reveal much about themselves and their societies.

In contrast to the established academic discourse, Music and Society is concerned with all forms of music, and seeks to encourage the scholarly analysis of both 'popular' styles and those which have for too long been marginalised by that discourse – folk and ethnic traditions, music by and for women, jazz, rock, rap, reggae, muzak and so on. These sounds are vital ingredients in the contemporary cultural mix, and their neglect by serious scholars itself tells us much about the social and cultural stratification of our society.

The time is right to take a fresh look at music and its effects, as today's music resonates with the consequences of cultural globalisation and the transformations wrought by new electronic media, and as past styles are reinvented in the light of present concerns. There is, too, a tremendous upsurge of interest in cultural analysis. Music and Society does not promote a particular school of thought, but aims to provide a forum for debate; in doing so, the titles in the series bring music back into the heart of socio-cultural analysis.

*Further titles are in preparation*

Andrew Blake

# The land without music

Music, culture and society in twentieth-century Britain

## Manchester University Press
Manchester and New York

Distributed exclusively in the USA by St. Martin's Press

*Published by* Manchester University Press
Oxford Road, Manchester M13 9NR, UK
*and* Room 400, 175 Fifth Avenue,
New York, NY 10010, USA

*Distributed exclusively in the USA by*
St. Martin's Press, Inc.,
175 Fifth Avenue, New York, NY 10010, USA

*Distributed exclusively in Canada by*
UBC Press, University of British Columbia,
6344 Memorial Road, Vancouver, BC, Canada V6T 1Z2

*British Library Cataloguing-in-Publication Data*
A catalogue record for this book is available from the British Library

*Library of Congress Cataloging-in-Publication Data*
Blake, Andrew.
    The land without music: Music, culture and society in twentieth-century Britain
Andrew Blake.
        p.   cm.—(Music and society)
    Includes bibliographical reference and index.
    Contents: A British classical music?—A story of British pop—
The romanticism of rock—The landscape with music—The muse of
diversity.
        ISBN 0-7190-4298-4 (cl).—ISBN 0-7190-4299-2 (pb)
        1. Music—Great Britain—20th century—History and criticism.
    I. Title.    II. Series: Music and society (Series)
    ML285.5.B55    1998
    780'.941'0904—dc21                                                      97-2600

ISBN 0 7190 4298 4 *hardback*
    0 7190 4299 2 *paperback*

First published 1997

01  00  99  98  97        10  9  8  7  6  5  4  3  2  1

Typeset in Great Britain
by Northern Phototypesetting Co Ltd, Bolton
Printed in Great Britain
by Bell & Bain Ltd, Glasgow

To John Surman
whose music has been a source of inspiration for thirty years

# Contents

# List of figures

# List of tables

# Preface

Early in 1995 Nick Kent, a government education adviser, announced grandly that Schubert was better than Blur, and that children ought to share this insight. In other words, they should be informed that the music of an Austrian who died poor, known only to a small circle of friends, in 1828, is better than the music of a British band who have attained international success in the 1990s.

Kent's value judgement fits eerily alongside an earlier piece of propaganda. In the early months of the First World War, German author Oskar Schmitz dubbed Britain 'Das Land ohne Musik' – the land without music.[1] The insult should really have been translated as 'the land without composers'. There was in fact a great deal of musical activity in Edwardian Britain – privately performed parlour songs, and the public music of festivals, the brass band and choir competitions, music-hall, classical concerts and opera. But, Schmitz implied, there was not, as in Germany (and Italy, Russia and France), an orderly sequence of 'great' British composers.

Strictly speaking, Schmitz's put-down was too late, if only by a generation. Edward Elgar's music had been conducted and praised by Richard Strauss, arguably the last member of that German tradition of composition. Many younger composers had growing reputations: Cyril Scott and Ethel Smyth, both German-educated, had written operas for Continental houses; Ralph Vaughan Williams, who had studied with Ravel in Paris, had begun his long career as a symphonist. In the eighty years since Schmitz wrote, Britain has become the land *with* music. Music is one of the comparatively few success stories of late twentieth-century Britain: in the 1980s, London could (and did) call itself the music capital of the world.

In classical music, since the rise to brief European prominence of

Elgar 100 years ago, there have always been British composers to fill that German gap. Some, like Vaughan Williams and Delius, have an honoured place chiefly as national composers. Others, such as Britten and Tippett, have achieved real international eminence. There are current British composers who write in many styles – from the complexity of Brian Ferneyhough and James Dillon to the rock-related minimalism of Steve Martland and Michael Nyman – and who are respected world-wide.

Similarly, British pop, once in thrall to American popular music, has had world-wide success since Merseybeat's rise to eminence in the early 1960s: British pop has consistently made its mark internationally, from the r'n'b (rhythm 'n' blues)-derived music of the Rolling Stones from the 1960s onwards to the knowing impishness of Pulp in the 1990s. There is no more successful light music composer than Andrew Lloyd Webber, whose musicals are as popular on Broadway in New York as in the West End of London; Lloyd Webber's company has built theatres in Germany and Japan specifically to perform his works.

The less well rewarded work of British jazz musicians (from the relatively conventional blowing-over-changes of Tony Coe to the free improvisation of Evan Parker) is also respected world-wide. The British folk scene, nurtured in the 1900s by middle-class musicians desperate to preserve what they felt was a vanishing heritage, then revived in the 1950s by communists who dreamed of a music created outside the class and commercial imperatives of other forms, has been served by dedicated enthusiasts who have continued the act of preservation, but have also played an important part in the remaking of the relatively closed world of folk into the more inclusive 'world' roots music movement.

As the latter indicates, all this has been accomplished through the interaction of British musicians with music and musicians from elsewhere in the world. Britain (especially London and the other big cities) has been a hub of musical interchange and development. A recent example is Bhangra, a traditional Punjabi folk music, which has been reworked in Britain to become a contemporary dance idiom. Again, rave music (using this term to refer to musics developed during and since the 'acid house' dance scene of the later 1980s) has grown in Britain as young people seek to unite the pleasures of technology, the body and the mind, and to transcend the limits of their parents' culture. In these ways the whole meaning of

music is being redefined through cultural and generational interchange.

This book explores some of the trajectories, linearities and paradoxes which have constituted contemporary British music. Like all
histories, it is an account of the present, telling how we got to the
here and now of the late 1990s. It is also an intervention in a set of
arguments about who 'we' the British are, and what 'our' culture is.
I attempt to show that culture, including tradition, is always constructed and always contingent; that it can and must reshape itself
continuously; and that the various searches for an authentic
national musicality (through folk revivals, pastoral symphonies or
Britpop) are part of a culture which has been massively reconstituted several times during the century.

One such reconstitution currently working through involves the
conceptualisation of Britishness. A great deal of attention was paid
to 'Englishness' during the 1980s. In the 1990s, as local nationalism
revived in Wales and Scotland, as the communities of post-war
immigrants began to articulate their presences more powerfully and
as the question of British–European relations began to loom larger
on the political horizon, this concern, however multivocally Englishness was constructed, seemed inadequate. 'Britain' and 'Britishness', explored historically by Linda Colley in her 1992 study
*Britons*, seemed a clearer point of reference, even as some constituent parts of Britain signalled their unwillingness to remain so.
Though many of the musics and musicians mentioned in this book
thought of themselves as, for example, English, or Scottish, and
dealt quite ostentatiously with Englishness or Scottishness, as many
did not. Cultural identities have always been open to those with the
will to adopt them. Early in the century the quintessentially bourgeois Englishman Sir Arnold Bax constructed a Celtic identity for
himself, partly through his symphonies; at its end another English
symphonist, Sir Peter Maxwell Davies, has done the same, living in
the Orkneys and writing music increasingly inflected by Celtic
sources. One such composition, 'The Beltane Fire', was shortlisted
for the 1996 Mercury Music Prize – at about the same time as the
quintessentially bourgeois English rock musician Mike Oldfield's
latest CD, *Voyager*, described in his record company's publicity as
'An inspirational Celtic journey', entered the album charts. Through
their work, all three have reinvented themselves as British.

There are, then, important continuities in the story of the land without music. Their presence will help to orient a path through a very complex set of lineages, not all of which point forward: as much has been invested in the making of traditions as in the future of British music.

My own orientation has been helped by many friends and colleagues. This book originates in a chapter written for *Modern Times*, a book collectively produced in my former workplace, the Department of Cultural Studies at the University of East London.[2] Taking as our starting-point Marshall Berman's *All that is Solid Melts into Air*, we debated and explored the physical and psychic structures of Modernity. The sessions which argued through the various chapters of this project were among the most intellectually stimulating of my life, and I remain grateful to all those who took part in them: Sally Alexander, Peter Horne, John Marriott, Mica Nava, Alan O'Shea and Bill Schwarz. For specific moments of help and encouragement, I should like to thank Alan Durant, Rory Forsyth, Colin Graham, Gillian Moore, Anita Roy, Errollyn Wallen, John L. Walters and Ben Watson. In more general terms, I owe a debt to the students on the popular music course which I taught at UEL for eight years, and to Ashwani Sharma, with whom in the latter stages I taught it. Special thanks to postgraduate students Jeremy Gilbert, Rupa Huq and James Ingham, whose insights have informed my work. I look forward to their contributions to the future of music in Britain ...

## Notes

1  This is discussed in chapter 3 of R. Stradling and M. Hughes, *The English Musical Renaissance 1860–1940: Construction and Deconstruction*, Routledge, 1993.

2  A. Blake, 'Re-Placing British Music', in M. Nava and A. O'Shea, eds, *Modern Times. Reflections on a Century of English Modernity*, Routledge, 1995, pp. 208–38.

# Introduction: re-placing British music

Confidence seemed high in the land without music in the summer of 1995, as this book was first drafted. Britain had never been more musically sure of itself. Radio Three, the BBC's classical music station, was half-way through 'Fairest Isle', a year-long celebration of British music. Focused on the tercentenary of the death of the composer Henry Purcell, this year saw first performances and new interpretations of works from England, Wales, Scotland and Northern Ireland. The climax of the celebration was the premiere of a new piece for alto saxophone, drumkit, and wind instruments by Sir Harrison Birtwistle. This rebarbative piece (aptly named 'Panic') was given its first performance during the second half of the Last Night of the Proms, which is usually an occasion noted for its Heritage Culture conservatism – and its raucous audience participation. This aspect of the evening was underplayed, as Sir John Drummond, the director of the festival, announced that the audience would not be permitted to bring with them the usual klaxons, horns and balloons. Instead, they were enjoined to witness in appreciative silence the work of a great, living, British composer.

This unusual event, allying British Modernism with an attempt to reconstruct British decorum, followed on the heels of a well-publicised contest in the pop world. Two bands on the up and up, Blur and Oasis, released singles on the same day in an ostentatious competition for the number one position in the national sales chart. The media hype accompanying the contest was enormous. In the broadsheet papers, a crucial aspect of both bands was seen to be their relation with previous generations of British pop songwriters and performers. Much of the press argued that the two bands were only the forefront of a new wave of 'Britpop' – bands such as Pulp, Elastica and Echobelly – whose success would mean that popular music in Britain was at its healthiest for a generation.

And yet behind all the celebration the indications are that music in Britain has reached a point of crisis. There have been various changes in the role of the state – in the law affecting copyright; in the criminal law restricting the 'right to party'; and in patterns of arts funding. Partly as a result of new state policy, there have been changes in the place and nature of the broadcasting industries, which have introduced, among other things, American-funded MTV on satellite and cable, and new genre-specific local and national radio stations, which have in turn produced defensive changes by the established broadcasters. State policy has also changed the nature and role of education, in music as elsewhere in the curriculum. These changes have all had acute short-term effects, but they have also had medium-term impacts on the production and use of music in Britain; the long term promises little that is positive.

The word 'crisis' may seem sensation-seeking; a few examples of recent developments may clarify my meaning. Late in 1993 the Arts Council, the body charged with the distribution of government funding for the arts, tried to cut the number of state-funded orches-tras in London. The Council had been trying to do this for at least twenty years,[1] but had never had the courage to face up to one of the few efficiently unionised areas of the entertainment industry. Deftly avoiding the decision-making for which it was set up, it asked a high court judge to make this decision for it. The judge led an inquiry, but his report was a fudge, in the grand tradition of Arts Council 'decisions': no orchestra should be denied funding alto-gether, but none would get quite what it wanted. One member of the Council's music panel, Priti Paintal, a composer who had cham-pioned the exercise because she believed that it would free money for the support of musics from outside the European-composed tra-dition (such as her own), resigned from the panel. In mid-1995 two of the remaining underfunded orchestras announced that they were going to merge anyway, but talks between managements broke down when they could not agree on 'cost savings' (i.e. redundan-cies). Meanwhile similar negotiations, on the basis of similar ill will, took place in Scotland as attempts were made to close the orchestra of Scottish Opera and replace it with an *ad hoc* group based on the Scottish National Orchestra.

While the Arts Council was egging its own face, an action was brought in the high court by the singer George Michael, demanding freedom from what he characterised as the 'slavery' of his record-ing contract with Sony, the Japanese multinational which had bought CBS, the record company with which he had actually signed. Michael was concerned that Sony were resisting his attempts to portray himself as a mature and serious musician, able to appeal to the over-25s who buy most CD albums, rather than to the single-buying teenybop audience of his early 1980s pop duet Wham! Michael, it seems, wanted to develop a long-term career; Sony wanted a product they could sell easily to a precise market. After a long trial, Sony's ownership of all Michael's intellectual property for the next ten years was upheld, on the grounds that Michael had been a free party to the signing, had already renegotiated the terms, and that he had been paid an advance of £11 million. Michael's alternatives were to make music for Sony, or to make no new music. There was then an eighteen-month negotiation to free Michael from Sony, whose compensation included percentage points on any material he made for his new label, Virgin.

Meanwhile, Irish rock band U2 were locked in a legal wrangle with the Performing Rights Society (PRS), an agency which collects royalty payments for the performances of music, and having taken a cut, passes them on to the artists, their agents and publishers. The PRS, claimed U2, were dilatory and inefficient in this process, and had lost them (among the richest musicians in the world) millions of pounds. U2 wished to collect their own royalties. The PRS's defence was weakened by the news that they had spent over £10 million on a new computerised database, intended to speed up the process of payment for performance. The system had been so badly designed and developed that it was abandoned without being run. In the royalties industry, now the centre of the music business, the machinery was not working.[2]

Perhaps these legal and financial wrangles were a symptom of a growing sense that the milch cow of British music, pop and main-stream rock, was losing its place in an increasingly American-domi-nated market. Britpop is one defensive reaction to this tendency. At the BRIT (British Record Industry Trust) awards ceremony in 1993, there was panic as it was realised that there was no new British act with even the potential for world-wide success on show (but plenty of Americans): hastily the band Suede were pressed into service. The following year Suede were there again, and the British band-

leader and singer/songwriter P.J. Harvey and the Icelandic singer/
songwriter Björk were the stars of the show, the two women performing together in a surprisingly spontaneous way for this over-
rehearsed ceremony – but the sense of panic remained when it was
revealed that approximately three million viewers had channel-
hopped during their duet. These worries reinforced the industry's
more general gloom, heightened when influential cultural critics
such as Simon Frith and Greil Marcus started proclaiming the
'Death of [Anglo-American] Rock', and falling sales, especially of
singles, seemed to confirm the prognosis.[3] But the Americans, whatever the eventual fate of 'grunge' rock after the death of its leading
exponent, Kurt Cobain, could immediately put the vigorously controversial rap, and a country music revival fronted by the homely
Garth Brooks, in its place, while Brits could only counterpose the
fluid and heterogenous, but relatively popstarless, dance music.[4]

Thus the press hysteria over Blur, Oasis and the other young
exponents of Britpop was a response to this nagging sense of crisis:
here were stars, who wrote songs with lyrics and hooks. Just like the
good old days. Britpop is located in a culture of nostalgia and redis-
covery, one which has affected many levels of the music business. At
the end of 1995 two actors, Robson and Jerome, covered 'I Believe',
a song made popular in early 1960s Britain by the Bachelors. Produced by 1980s pop svengalis Stock and Aitken, the single sold to
people of all ages. Almost immediately the charts were topped by a
cover version of 'Wonderwall', an Oasis single which is itself a pastiche of 1960s pop, by the Mike Flowers Pops, an outfit claiming to
be a re-creation of the 1960s metagenre known as 'easy listening'.

So the newer bands' success owed a great deal to their use of earlier models – indeed, Elastica were successfully sued by the Stran-
glers, who argued that their 1977 song 'No More Heroes' had been
stolen in tempo, melody and harmonic structure. This piece of bor-
rowing was the exception only in its turn to the music of the 1970s:
by and large the 1960s provided the models, and Britpop's fans,
whatever their ages, wallowed in nostalgia for the days when the
Kinks wrote about Waterloo sunsets, the sixties were swinging and
all was right with the world. Likewise, Drummond's insertion of
Birtwistle's 'Panic' into the Proms was both an attack on the Last
Night's carnivalesque nostalgia for Edwardian patriotism, and its
replacement with yet more nostalgia for the 1960s. For upper-middle-class men of Drummond's generation, British Modernist music

was itself part of the heroic culture of the 1960s, during which a self-proclaimed radical avant-garde forced its way into the Establishment: administrative careers like Drummond's were built on the changes wrought at this moment.

Viewed from mid-1990s Britain, this retrospection seems dangerous, whatever the attractions or otherwise of the music. British Modernist composition, the music of an elite, relies on state subsidy. In the newly privatised Britain of the post-Thatcher era, this is an anachronism as severe as the musical language itself, as deep a product of the 1960s as anti-Vietnam War demonstrations and the decline of the British car industry – as is the musical language of Britpop. Perhaps more importantly, sixties Modernism and Britpop shared a notional 'whiteness'. Almost all composers of experimental classical music are white men. Though many of Britpop's exponents are not white, and the bands are more gender-mixed than in the sixties themselves, the retro-created 1960s are a vision of a comparatively unicultural, white Britain. In a multicultural and postcolonial 1990s Britain whose vibrant musical forces included jungle and bhangra, this celebration of the songs and performing styles of the 1960s seemed to some observers to verge on racism. Certainly as Britain worried about future relations with Europe, the retreat to an Anglocentric pop too often carried with it a xenophobic tinge.[5]

Meanwhile – as if to underline the point – artists, journalists and promoters associated with black British music, arguably in its healthiest state ever in commercial terms, with soul acts like Des'ree, Gabrielle and Seal, a strong reggae/ragga culture, and the burgeoning of jungle, felt so concerned at what they saw as a lack of investment and appreciation of black British talent by the major record companies that early 1995 saw the launch of a r'n'b chart specifically for black music, to underline its presence and its continuing importance to the British music scene.[6]

'Rock', however, in the sense of music played in sports stadia by middle-aged white men, obstinately refuses to die. *Bat out of Hell II*, an album by Meatloaf, topped the British chart in the autumn of 1993, and the chief so-called dinosaurs, the Rolling Stones, postponed their extinction yet again by releasing *Voodoo Lounge*, an album of new material, in the spring of 1994 – which sold well, as Messrs Jagger and Richards cranked their limbs into touring mode once more then and in 1995, when they released *Stripped*, a live album of classic tracks; another album of new material was to be released in 1997. Not to be outdone, Dire Straits went round the world in a year and a half, while Pink Floyd toured the stadia in the autumn of 1994 to promote their new album *The Division Bell*.

If the death of rock, or the single, or classical concerts, or state-subsidised Modernism, or any other aspect of music has been exaggerated, the sense of crisis in music as a whole remains. It is likely that the late twentieth century is witnessing the death of music as an autonomous, abstract entity. Music is increasingly being used as an (important) adjunct to other forms of entertainment, rather than as entertainment in its own right. Hi-fi systems designed to decode cinema sound are on sale. That Rolling Stones live album, *Stripped*, contained material for CD-ROM; Peter Gabriel, David Bowie, Whitesnake and others have released material on allegedly interactive CD-ROMs;[7] Nintendo and Sega games, and their PC and Mac equivalents, have to some extent replaced items which offer their purchasers music and nothing else – and they were outselling singles in the early 1990s. Music sales, even genre revivals, are often generated by television advertising or by film sound-tracks. Recent British films following this practice include the upper-middle-class comedy *Four Weddings and a Funeral* (1993), with pop sound-track; *Shopping* (1994), an everyday story of ram-raiding folk, used contemporary dance music; a movie released in early 1996, *Trainspotting*, an adaptation of a novel about Edinburgh junkies, was tied into a Britpop/dance sound-track. The musical and the visual were intertwined in these commercial ventures.

The trend away from pure sound was not confined to pop. In August 1994 the management of the Royal Philharmonic Orchestra announced that it would combat falling audiences for classical music (which have been in decline since the early 1970s) by hiring the Royal Albert Hall, using video and laser effects along with the music, and offering the resultant product to subscribers on cable television. The reaction among commentators and traditional concert-goers was one of panic.

Crisis, then. Yet a language of crisis needs the historical comparison which this book aims to provide. There has *never* been a moment in which an established national musical tradition existed and reproduced itself unchallenged. It can be argued that the history of British music throughout the twentieth century has been one of *continuous* crises, as changing patterns of musical education and training, marketing and distribution, performance and reception have interacted. As the conjuncture of Birtwistle and Britpop seems to demonstrate, however, there is one comparative constant: the *search* for a definitive national musical identity. This book attempts to address the origins of the present crisis through a cultural history which charts the developments and changes in British music through the twentieth century as a search for a settled and defined national music, a literally essential sound. But there is nothing purely musical about this endeavour; it is simultaneously textual, a product of criticism and journalism, and this journey must begin with the paradox confronting words about music.

### Music heard, faintly, through text

We all approach music through speech and writing. Concert programmes, CD sleeve notes, reviews of gigs and albums; writing about music is everywhere. There are dedicated magazines: for followers of particular genres (e.g. *Folk Roots*), or particular forms of listening (*Hi-Fi News*), or users of specific musical instruments (*Guitarist*) and recording devices (*Sound on Sound*).[8] Many of these journals provide vital operational information; others offer interpretations, guiding our ears as we listen for pleasure.

The texts of music have always guarded against, and in many cases prevented, the radical implications of the act of listening. They have mediated the biological action of the human body's and mind's responses to pressure changes registered by the ears (and the gut, if they are powerful enough) as sound. They have prepared the listener before the experience of listening, guided the listener during that experience, or enlightened (or consoled) him or her after the event, thereby helping to structure that listening, taking it from the 'natural' physicality of sound to the 'cultural' state of sounds endowed with human meaning. And they have performed similar operations in regard to the performing and creating of music. Before this text provides its own mediation of the listening and performing process, it will delineate aspects of this mediation itself, firstly by commenting on the ways in which texts create music in British culture.

### Music in writing: approaches

To begin with a familiar straw man. Of all the arts, music remains the least open to cultural analysis. The textual study of sound is one whose richness is too often refused by those who have re-created music as a certain type of text – the score – and just as often refused by those for whom the attempt to describe sound as meaning-giving is impossible, and who therefore interpret words, rather than sounds. Musicology and musical analysis, on the one hand, hide music's meaning (even for many of those who create, perform and listen to it), going beyond the score and breaking it into component parts within a jargon-rich environment addressed only to a small academic circle. Western musicology, though still in some quarters ready to defend to the death notions of value and hierarchy, can find no place for the consideration of the wider hierarchies of class, ethnicity, sexuality and gender, or the political economy of musical production and consumption. Instead, in the appreciation of a given musical canon, certain works are deemed worthy of a complex form of 'analysis' in which attention is given to the details of the score, but not to their context beyond a certain biographical commentary. Popular musics, on the other hand, are routinely celebrated or reviled without adequate cultural or musical analysis. Biographies of stars and bands, and histories of popular music, seem usually to have been produced in a vacuum without theoretical models or all but the most immediate traces of history.

But this straw man has already been lit; indeed, the fire is burning brightly. These restrictive attitudes are changing, and in terms of accepted hierarchies of value, the changes have been led from the bottom up. The explosion of academic work on popular culture, and the related rise in 'cultural studies' as a critical, interdisciplinary approach to all representational forms, has transformed the study of popular music. There are now abundant books, journals and courses in popular music performance, in music technology and in the cultural study of popular music on undergraduate and postgraduate cultural studies and media studies courses.

Many writers with a background in traditional Western musicology but a love of popular music in one form or another have begun the difficult process of addressing popular music as sound, and thereby perforce transcending the limits of musicological discourses which have fetishised harmony as the principal content of all music (and thereby ignored or dismissed music in which large-scale harmonic processes are not the most important element).[9] At the same time we have seen the emergence of a popular music journalism informed by cultural theory, and sometimes practised by academics: Simon Reynolds blissed out on Barthes and other French theorists, Jon Savage gloomed out on the same writers, Greil Marcus producing eclectic history one minute, writing for the academic journal *Common Knowledge* the next.[10]

So 'popular music' is now a flourishing academic and journalistic industry, an object of study in all its complexity: a mass producer of text. Things are not so positive in the academic study of 'classical' music, although there have been important developments. As Susan McClary's essay title 'The Blasphemy of Talking Politics during Bach Year'[11] indicates, there remains a great deal of resistance to the treatment of Western composed music as a historically situated product, especially if this threatens established hierarchies of musical value. McClary herself has been the object of vilification, and her publishing profile is slight, arguably because she represents such a threat to established musicology. There are, however, an increasing number of exceptions to this silly rule. McClary and Richard Leppert's collection *Music and Society* tries to cross boundaries, including essays on both classical and popular music. McClary's *Feminine Endings* proposes a feminist aesthetic, reading most romantic music as masculine in character and arguing for a feminine music which does not reflect what she sees as the periodisation of male sexuality.[12] Gay and feminist studies threaten to transform musicology in the USA in the next generation (though they also threaten to throw back the study of music into a 'reconsideration' of the usual canonic work).[13] Musicology (the scholarly assembly of scores), and analysis (the score-based analysis of musical texts), though both are too little concerned with unwritable aspects of music such as timbre/grain, can be insightful, of course.[14] But Western musicology remains shy and introverted; not enough informed by history, let alone by sociology, anthropology and cultural theory (where it has strayed into the anthropological, in ethnomusicology, there is a different set of problems to be addressed).[15]

There is a bigger issue, which may be approached through a favourite metaphor. I like to think of music as a landscape, in which fields of similar endeavour are rather arbitrarily divided by high hedges. Far from being convinced that the grass is greener on the other side, some people are head-down grazers on their own patch, resolutely uninterested in seeing into the next field. While some of the recent work on popular music makes continuous, and illumi-

nating, reference to the world of classical music,[16] there is less traffic in the other direction. Books that cross these barriers, or refuse
to recognise them, still cause critical confusion. The hedgerow
problem remains, obscuring the view for those on both sides.

### Problems of music in theory

Musical culture can be approached through discussion of the problems, potentialities and pitfalls of a theorisation of music which is,
as yet, struggling towards birth. This will happen at different stages
throughout the book, but some general points can be made here.
Cultural theory has been applied less to music than to the other arts.
Theoretical work based on the various French arguments against
existentialism (the work of Foucault, Derrida, Lacan, Kristeva and
Cixous, among others), and using poststructuralist linguistics and
psychoanalysis, has illuminated the study of literature, art and film.
Though there have been influential treatments of music within this
body of work, by Barthes and the prolix Jacques Attali,[17] music
remains at its margins. There is one particular problem.[18] Film theory has almost nothing to say about music; most writing about film
or television discusses the visual while ignoring the sonic.[19] Music is
a crucial part of film, even if we don't listen to it as such; but then
we don't listen to much of the music which surrounds us.[20] In the
age of mechanical reproduction, the era of the car radio, concourse
Muzak, the juke-box, and the walkman it is a virtually ever-present
component of everyday life in the late twentieth century; music has
a fairly continuous subliminal place in our lives, as well as in most
cases a more deliberate one, and any theory of music will have to
take account of those two very different musical presences.

  If much music is hidden from our immediate perception, and
therefore hidden a long way from our knowledge, hidden even from
the sophisticated discourse of film theory, are there any ways forward into a general theory of music in contemporary culture? If
most music today is indeed a merely subliminal presence on or
below the threshold of consciousness, can we usefully talk about it?
In what ways can it be said to exist? I believe that there are in fact
one or two useful theoretical positions which can act as a starting-
point, raising questions, and there are a few specific pieces of work
which already provide answers – among others Barthes's argument
about the pleasures of the body in musical performance and Julia

Kristeva's (and others') theorisations of *écriture féminine*, a mode of writing which places non-linguistic sounds in the 'semiotic order' against the 'symbolic order' of patriarchal language (which leads to McClary's argument for what could be called a *'musique féminine'*).

Theorisations such as these psychoanalytic constructions carry the danger that they leave us with an ahistorical nothing, the supposed 'bliss' of an infinite regression to gurgling babyhood as the only way out of our current malaise (i.e. since this can't happen, none). Since we are aware of movement through time, we must also think of change, of history and the part music has played or can play therein. How can we generalise about music in society? Can we, for instance, construct a tradition, or several traditions, of musical/cultural interaction in the same way Raymond Williams did for writings on society in *Culture and Society*? Not in the same way. Williams created for himself a 'tradition' of fictional and poetic writing and cultural criticism which was opposed to capitalism and industrialism – and which led inevitably to none other than Raymond Williams, novelist, critic and opponent of capitalism.[21] To follow this path would be merely to replicate one of the more damaging aspects of the ideology of cultural production: the hyper-individualised ideology of the romantic creative artist (a tendency which is indeed present in a great deal of music and writing about music). On the other hand, if, following aspects of Williams's work, we seek to find patterns of engagement, 'structures of feeling', in his terms, which can still be located in the power relations of musical culture in the present, we must start from the same place. *Culture and Society* commences precisely with that moment of the birth of the notion of 'the romantic artist' as privileged commentator rather than social servant. Williams points out that the same moment, the late eighteenth/early nineteenth century, also sees growing industrialisation and the commodification of literature.

Importantly, this historical moment is also the place at which Marshall Berman starts, in his classic eccentrism *All that is Solid Melts into Air*; as the preface to this book acknowledges, I owe something of a debt here to Berman's eclectic reading of Marx and history. Berman argues that what he calls 'modernity', the historical epoch entered into at the start of the Industrial Revolution, is always already *post*modernity as it is currently theorised: he explores the bewilderment, the pain of decentred experience, the crisis of identity of modern life. Looking at constant development and reconstruction, he analyses their impact on people's lives and senses of identity. He places the commencement of this heroic self-decentring, via Goethe's *Faust*, to that moment of Romanticism with which, as Raymond Williams argues, we see the birth of the Romantic Artist, and in whose image musicians from Beethoven to the Aphex Twin have been constructed (and have constructed themselves) ever since.

Berman misses a trick, however, and it is at this point that we must address the peculiarities of the British: 'all that is solid melts into air', no doubt, but in this part of the world at least some of the representational solidities which melt are fictions created through the process of modernising itself. The maelstrom of modernity doesn't just melt into nothing, leaving no sense of the past: it makes 'traditions', and, as chapter 1 will argue, it has done this in Britain since the massive urbanisation of the eighteenth century which was part of the Industrial Revolution. One such 'tradition', called forth for the first time during industrialisation, is the very idea of a trans-generational musical canon. 'Classical music' starts here, in the land without music.

The point must be underlined. Modernity's obverse is tradition; they are not sequential, but contemporary, inseparable, bound and twisted together, spiralling through history in a double helix of common development. We experience, indeed we often define, the 'modern' through an increasing ache for the 'past' we have ourselves constructed. The invention and reinvention of tradition have been constant companions of the urge within nineteenth and twentieth century states to modernise: to industrialise, to electrify, to build and rebuild. As all that is solid in our metropolitan environments melts into air, and in the nuclear age as we all live under the threat that we will melt along with everything else, we turn to a set of representations which can give us, however fleetingly, a feeling of connection with time and space. The Victorian (or older) house, the landscape art of a Constable, the fiction of a Jane Austen, and eighteenth- and nineteenth-century opera and concert music – these are a few of the favourite things of the British professional classes who perforce inhabit modernity but by choice also inhabit 'tradition'. It is considered by some a paradox that post-industrial Britain is also Heritage Britain, a land of castles and cathedrals, country houses and agricultural theme parks, of art exhibitions – and of the music festival. Music is often claimed to be among the most important of the national treasures: it is very much part of the solidities of Heritage Britain. And yet music, above all else, melts into air ...

Any account of music within twentieth-century British culture must confront this set of paradoxes, and this book will do so by examining the continuing re-creation of a set of traditions of musical production (composition, performance, reception and associated sales and marketing activities). This is, then, a narrative, tracing cultural change through time. But the trace is not a single line: although for the sake of the argument terms such as 'traditional', 'Modernist' and 'postmodernist' will be used, no account of musical 'progress' is offered, nor is there an explicit or implied hierarchy of genres or performers; indeed, the emphasis will be on the impossibility of assembling a single narrative from the multiplicity of events which constitute music within British culture. Exemplary in this regard, and one of the focal points of this book, is the moment of 'Thatcherism' – the ideological and political changes of the 1980s, including an important remaking of tradition – and the many contradictory impacts this has had on the place of music in Britain. But the starting-point for our consideration remains the textual construction of both music and musicians. What do writings about music tell us of music in Britain?

### The life of a hero?

Ben Watson's book *Frank Zappa: the Negative Dialectics of Poodle Play* provides a window on to the troubled relationship between text and music in Britain.[22]A materialist, convinced of the power of music to engage, to shock, to make people think as well as feel, Watson's Zappa occurs as the crossing-point of a great many tendencies within English cultural criticism, tendencies which are part of Watson's life story. The post-Leavisite (Watson is a Cambridge English graduate and a poet), paying attention to the question of value, delights in Zappa's compositional and instrumental virtuosity, his grasp of the potential within music and musicians, and is convinced that the act of listening to such music can of itself make better people and a better world. The radical political critic (Watson is also a lifelong member of the Socialist Workers' Party), committed to the positive value of Adorno's Freudian Marxism and of situationist art, examines Zappa's music-theatre, his subversion of boundaries, and finds them good. Recounting and accounting for the mix of the improvisatory with the carefully constructed; the parodic mix of genres from bubblegum pop through free-form jazz to Modernist classical; the univocal linearities and angular polyphonies of Zappa's most immediately recognisable 'personal' style; the albums of guitar solos taken from their composed contexts; the albums of orchestral music conducted by the avant-garde composer Pierre Boulez; and the obscenity and other problems associated with the lyrics; Watson concludes not only that the best moments in this mix are of polymorphously perverse pleasure, but that Zappa's project is potentially emancipatory. Ben Watson quite deliberately makes the music of Frank Zappa the small businessman, the opponent of government, into a post-punk, situationist, socialist music: a reading which amused Zappa somewhat when the two met just before the latter's death, and Watson read chunks of his manuscript to the dying musician.

Watson attempts to encompass Zappa's life and work within the contextual analysis of music – as business, as an aspect of life redolent with questions of capital, class and power, gender, sexuality, ethnicity and identity. It is a music with a lived history, with clear connections both with political developments such as the rise of the Christian fundamentalist right in the USA (which led Zappa to oppose censorship, fiercely and publicly), and also with technology and technological development (much of Zappa's late work was composed at the Synclavier, a digital sampling and sequencing device; to the annoyance of some of his fans, he continually remixed, reworked and sometimes re-recorded old material using the new technologies). Watson can honestly account for, and in most cases celebrate, his subject's activities in all these related areas, I think.

The British press, and the specialist music press, were not so convinced. The defensiveness of the rock press was predictable; rock journalists are usually male graduates (in English Literature as often as not)[23] who have a deeply masculine suspicion of anything academic which might try to tread on 'their' patch. For *Vox*, *Q*,[24] and *The Record Collector*, which, while granting the book a 'surprising' level of stimulating insight, said it was boring and 'at times formless', the Watson/Zappa meeting damned the whole project of a theorised engagement with music.[25]. Even in the New Music anorakzine *The Wire*, for which Watson has himself penned many a diatribe, the meeting is trotted out as a defining moment of failure.[26] Author and subject did not agree; therefore the problem was Watson's misunderstanding or misuse of Zappa. Some attention to Watson's presentation of the concept of negative dialectics would have shown this to be a fairly weak argument (in Watson's terms, at least). They got weaker. For Simon Frith, writing in the *New York Village Voice*, the 'problem' was Frank Zappa – by which he meant himself. After passing reference to the book's contents, Frith complained that 'standards' now meant 1960s rock, and that many of the musicians associated with that era have the cheek to be at it still. Most writers, like the rest of us, try to recapture their childhoods, which is one reason why bands such as the Rolling Stones remain successful. Frith, on the other hand, wants his youth back by proxy. 'Age ... matters. It does feel more convincing, more right, to have young men playing what was, after all, young men's music. And I guess that sums up, really, why I haven't found Frank Zappa very interesting since, oh, 1971?'.[27]

There were some more positive assessments – in the *New Statesman*,[28] *Mojo*[29] and *Red Pepper*.[30] But although the last is ostentatiously sympathetic towards aspects of Watson's project, reviewer Mark Sinker insists that *Poodle Play* will not reach the desired audience, even of Zappaphiles, let alone those outside the close confines of obsessive fandom. (The book immediately went into paperback, and has been reprinted several times in a second edition.) The broadsheet press was also negative,[31] the *London Review of Books*[32] more positive. The most bizarre contribution to this little subgenre was Steve Sweeney-Turner's in *The Musical Times*.[33] While this review engaged furiously with Watson's negative reading of aspects of McClary's work, it had nothing to say about Frank Zappa, his life or music, and therefore nothing to say about Watson's book. Sweeney-Turner gave no indication of having heard *200 Motels*, *Studio Tan*, *Jazz from Hell*, or anything else by Zappa. (None of these reviews, and I think I have located them all, was written by a woman – the gender politics of music criticism are more sharply exposed in this fact than in any amount of haggling over Watson's reading of McClary.)

It should be granted that the limits of space in review columns provide particular problems for anyone attempting to analyse a 600-page tome which is clearly its author's *Lebenswerk*. However. Apart from my own review of the book, which tried both to provide a brief conspectus of the argument and to engage with it,[34] only

Sinker in *Red Pepper* and Matt Ffytch, in a witty and insightful piece for the *Modern Review*,[35] managed to state Watson's position without condescension and/or travesty. No other review engaged with Zappa's music, or raised counter-arguments about the nature of Zappa's art, or challenged Watson's interpretation with reference to music he did not discuss in detail. In other words, either they all believed Ben Watson, or they didn't know or care either way. What was important to them was to reinscribe the boundaries of music and music criticism, and through denigrating the Other of *Poodle Play*, praise both rock criticism and classical music criticism as currently constituted. Subtexts of the reviews include the demonisation of the obsessive fan and/or the academic or critic who dares to argue with his or her contemporaries, and in many cases (e.g. Frith, and Ben Thompson in the *Independent on Sunday*)[36] the figure of Zappa himself. The reviews of this book were used to reconstruct the authority of the critics.

There is an interlocking set of boundaries here. Those hedgerows again; many people have no wish even to see into the next field, but are happy with rock, or jazz, or classical music, as separate areas of endeavour. They will, therefore, refuse the real point of the book (and of Zappa's work). *Poodle Play* is not a conventional biography, but an argument for the theoretically informed study of musical practices. The figure of Zappa is consistently displaced through the poststructuralist position that the author is not the final authority in textual analysis. In refusing to see or take this point, of course, reviewers insist on the maintenance of their own authority as critics.

What do these refusals tell us about the state of music or cultural criticism in Britain? Firstly that this is the land without an adequately theorised sense of the musical. It is a land in which obsessive musicality or fandom is suspect, but in which the amateurism of critics who can't create, play or read music but can throw together bellettrist reviews is celebrated, among themselves.[37] The gentlemanly values of criticism and connoisseurship are reinforced, as are the categories they have helped to construct: classical, Modernist, jazz, rock and pop. None of this meant anything to Frank Zappa, except in so far as he could get his teeth into it. But then Zappa didn't like critics; and he wasn't British ...

## The death of a hero?

'Das Land ohne Musik'. Perhaps in some ways that German insult was right after all; it isn't so far from conductor Sir Thomas Beecham's jibe, 'The British don't like music, but they absolutely love the sound it makes.' Music continues to have a deeply ambivalent place in British culture, as it struggles with class, value, heritage and Modernity, and we don't have to look at the reception of a radical figure like Frank Zappa to see it.

The Austrian conductor Herbert von Karajan died in July 1989.[38] Obituary assessment of the notable life is riven with the 'national characteristics' of fairness and respect for the recently departed, which are are usually presented with an apparent objectivity whose purpose is, precisely, the construction of the values of the obituarist. There are occasions, however, when the passing of a notable produces genuine tension in response. The mask of fairness slips to reveal less celebrated national characteristics – such as class, artistic and/or intellectual snobbery, and the fear of difference which constitutes the 'national' at so many levels of British culture. In Karajan's case, both inclusion and exclusion tell us much about the construction of music through criticism.

Karajan's death was newsworthy to all the broadsheet papers. The depth of coverage was comparable with that accorded another musician, the songwriter Irving Berlin, who died a month later – yet there was an important difference. Berlin's achievement was celebrated; Karajan's was, rather, questioned. Even in the obituary pages, Karajan was clearly a controversial figure.

This is due in part to Karajan's past. In the 1930s he was a member of the Nazi Party, which had aided his career at the expense of an older conductor, Wilhelm Furtwängler. And to some music critics, Karajan's music-making was implicitly Nazi, the well-rehearsed orchestral discipline carrying traces of authoritarianism. For David Cairns, writing in the *Sunday Times*, this 'darker side' of Karajan's achievement, a 'totalitarian spirit we sensed in the music-making', was always present.[39] Cairns called upon some disturbing metaphors: 'an overwhelming musical impression of combined smoothness and brutality … magnificent but barbaric'; 'the coda of Brahms's first symphony was the aural equivalent of someone being kicked to death'. Elsewhere, however, Cairns could only hear the smoothness and denied the power: 'Faced with the moral and spiritual energy, the subversive energy of Beethoven's music, Karajan could offer only blandness, materialist values, mere presentation ... the result, for all its splendour, was oddly lifeless; the beauty of sound was merely skin-deep: it left the heart of the music untouched'.[40]

But was this brutal blandness merely a product of the conductor's will? The blandness/barbarity contradiction *could* be explained by Karajan's insistence on working only with the best musicians and with adequate rehearsal. There are two distinct reasons for this smoothness in music from Bach to Bartok: all the musicians involved are virtuosi, and they are trying to reproduce in recording or concert what they have learned in rehearsal. The contrast with musical practice in London, where performances of standard repertoire works often follow a single rehearsal, and where the named ensemble can consist of deputising session musicians, could not be greater.[41] Sight-reading, however competent, and whatever the authority of the conductor, rarely achieves either a smooth blend or a convincing dynamic attack: neither blandness nor barbarity are routinely attainable in London performances and recordings, which is why Karajan abandoned the Philharmonia Orchestra in the early 1950s, and why the most talented English conductor of recent times, Sir Simon Rattle, has worked in Birmingham rather than London.[42] While all the obituarists drew attention to the relationship between Karajan and his orchestras, none made the comparison with standard London practice.

Writing these comments after the Arts Council had failed, under the farcical circumstances described above, to change the London orchestral scene, strengthens the point; but many music critics do not wish to connect the sounds they hear with any notion of how they are produced (in any other sense than the basic one of blowing, scraping, hitting and the excitation of pieces of tissue). Obituaries all noted Karajan's long relationship with the recording industry. Yet only in passing was it remarked that he was the first conductor, the only one of his generation, to be literate in music technology. Karajan's four recordings of complete cycles of the Beethoven symphonies each had a technological impetus. The first, recorded with the Philharmonia Orchestra in London for EMI in the late 1940s–early 1950s, was made just as the 12" vinyl LP, revolving at 33.33 r.p.m., was replacing the 78 r.p.m. disc as the common recording format. The early 1960s Deutsche Grammophon (DG) issues, played by the Berlin Philharmonic Orchestra, celebrated that company's embracing of stereophonic recording. The mid-1970s Berlin Philharmonic DG set was recorded in the acoustic of the Berlin Philharmonie concert-hall, using DG's studio specially constructed in the building, and employing multi-channel mixing techniques imported from rock music. The final set, made in the early 1980s, again made with the Berlin Philharmonic for DG, used the new digital recording technologies and was the first complete Beethoven set to appear on CD. Each recording was made in the light of a recent technological advance; each was made *in this light* with the enthusiastic partnership of the conductor. Perhaps this technological awareness contributed to Karajan's success as a recording artist; sales, at his death, of 115 million albums for DG alone (he also recorded regularly for EMI and Decca) can only be matched by the megastars of pop. This success brought the conductor great wealth, much of which he reinvested in his own companies, recording music and video projects under his direction. At the time of his death the first batch of Karajan-conducted CDVs (Compact Disc Videos, a technology Karajan had encouraged and invested in) were being prepared for release by Polygram; the comparative failure of this medium may be due to his death at that critical juncture.[43]

Of the obituary tributes, only a Channel Four television documentary emphasised Karajan's interest in media technologies. This film's representations of an opera production, a concert and the conductor's lifestyle (at the wheel of a Porsche 959 among other things) concluded by showing the high-tech virtuoso at work in a video editing suite, preparing his own opera productions for CDV. Here surely lies the key to Karajan's dominance in 'classical music'; he may not have been as great a conductor as Carlos Kleiber or Georg Solti, say, but he was committed to the technologies he used and to their economic and power relationships.

Here was a star who mixed socially with the wealthy, rather than with fellow-musicians; who drove fast cars and piloted his own aircraft; who ran businesses, encouraging the development of music production and recording technologies; and whose work appealed to large numbers of people outside the musically literate elite. Karajan didn't fit into the mythology of the performing musician which had been adopted since the end of the Second World War by the British middle class. No twentieth-century musician conforms less closely to the current version of the romantic myth of the artist starving in a garret, the lonely genius devoted to his art, relying on the patronage of the state and its self-appointed artistic advisers, the music critics.

Part of the problem, for believers in innate differences between true creativity and mere showmanship, is the very popularity of the performer. A stronger contrast could be made, between those who would like to keep classical music 'highbrow', to cloak the making of music with symbols of mystery and endow its creators and performers with the notion of genius, and to restrict its appeal and consumption by the public at large, and a performer who wished to popularise 'classical' music, to share its glories rather than restrict access to them. In the age of mechanical reproduction, the elitism of the first position is hard to maintain. Yet it is maintained, more successfully in Britain than elsewhere in Europe. Chief among the guardians of this elitism are critics who stress hierarchy, genius, the mystery of creation, rather than technique, athleticism, the power and sensuousness of performance. In Britain at least it is not only Karajan's 'failure' to interpret Beethoven according to the critics' lights which lessened his achievement, it was also the admitted excellence of his performance of works by composers not considered to be the equals of Beethoven. Thus Martin Kettle in the *Guardian*: 'In second-rate music he was untouchable. Think of his Respighi, Puccini, Honegger and [Richard] Strauss. It is ultimately far more convincing than his Mozart, Beethoven, Mahler or Debussy.'[44]

These conventional value judgements could, and perhaps should, be contested individually – for my money Puccini and Richard Strauss are as first rate as any member of Kettle's second group, and the power and lyricism of Honegger's efforts strike my ear more directly than the faded chintz of Debussy's formal experiments, however important they were to the mid-century avant-garde.[45] But the more important point is that we see here, as in the Cairns article, an arbitrarily ordered system of difference constructed around a single historical moment (the aftermath of the French Revolution throughout Europe and the Industrial Revolution in Britain) and predicated on a single life lived during that time (Beethoven's). This system of difference continues to support the absurd structure of cultural production in Britain, with its massive subsidies for museum-repertoire concerts and opera. Beethoven, the archetype of the bourgeois–Romantic man of genius, is the ultimate signifier of this symbolic order. The life story is a convenient monument to the values of self-made individualism: relatively unsuccessful in his own time, Beethoven struggled to assert his self-belief against the existing hierarchies of a society in the throes of the transition from post-feudal absolutism to the free market; he produced his great works despite increasing deafness. Both Strauss and Puccini, on the other hand, admitted that they wrote music for money, and enjoyed their wealth. A rather more genuine bourgeois position, one might think, especially at the moment of Karajan's death, the end of the eighties, the brief moment of entrepreneurial hegemony associated with Thatcherism/Reaganism.

We are dealing here, however, with a bifurcated bourgeoisie. The ideology of Romantic music belongs to the professional middle class; it is, in Pierre Bourdieu's useful distinction, cultural capital rather than finance capital, and the professional middle class tend to be wealthy in the status endowed by cultural capital, rather than financially rich. Their dealings with the making of money have always been tangential. Doctors, lawyers, academics and musicians alike profess the mysteries of their trades, and thus maintain the mythology of their privileged independence – talking of costs or salaries, rather than fees or wages. With the stress on Beethoven (and other hyper-individualised producers in the German tradition such as Brahms and Bruckner) the mystery can be preserved: music can remain ethereal, outside the sordid realities of the creation of wealth and the exchange of money. Karajan the contractual expert, the Porsche-driver whose lifestyle emphasised success within capitalism rather than artistic endeavour, the conductor who insisted on smooth, powerful renditions of Bach and Beethoven – and also the millionaire Strauss, thereby making his music sound uncomfortably 'great' – must therefore be a barbarian, someone who stood for a reduction of the artistic to the commercial, which commentators found distasteful.

Karajan's shady past as a member of the Nazi Party was convenient to this demonised reading, which in some places (not in the obituaries which appeared immediately after his death) took on the full panoply of comic-strip Germanophobia, and occasionally led to direct comparisons between the conductor and Adolf Hitler.[46] The supposed connections between popularity, populism, capitalism and authoritarianism are made repeatedly in musical analyses from the left and the right, about both classical and popular forms.

I should emphasise that this is not merely a suspicion of the foreign, or the German, but of certain kinds of musicality – especially of popular success. In 1930, the Professor of Music at Cambridge, Edward J. Dent, wrote that Elgar's music was vulgar and sentimental, and thus popular – the very charges laid at Karajan's door sixty years later.[47] This elitism is a prism through which we can begin to examine much of the way in which music has been discursively constructed in Britain over the last two centuries. It suggests a starting-point: analysis of the components of this discourse of semi-detached privilege which lies behind much of the valuation of music in Britain. To which end I return to that moment (from which Raymond Williams started his long march through culture and society) when the market-place began to assume roles formerly taken by patrons of the arts.

### Notes

1  One report recommending concentration of subsidy was presented to the Council in 1970: C. Ehrlich, *The Musical Profession in Britain since the Eighteenth Century*, Oxford, Oxford University Press, 1985, p. 227. See also J. Denison, 'Reflections on an Orchestral Theme for London', in J. Pick, ed., *The State and the Arts*, Eastbourne, John Offord 1980, pp. 99–107.

2  For an appreciation of the legal and commercial aspects of the business see S. Frith, *Music and Copyright*, Edinburgh, Edinburgh University Press, 1993. The PRS has since been forced into a co-operative agreement with another collection company, MCPS (The Music Copyright Protection Society). Both have been the subject of inquiries by the Monopolies and Mergers Commission.

3  See, for example, S. Frith, 'Anglo-America and its Discontents', *Cultural Studies*, vol. 5, no. 3, October 1991, pp. 263–9; and *Music for Pleasure*, Cambridge, Polity Press, 1988, p. 1; L. Grossberg, 'Is Anybody Listening? Does Anybody Care? On the State of Rock', in A. Ross and T. Rose, eds, *Microphone Fiends: Youth Music and Youth Culture*, Routledge, 1994, pp. 41–58.

4  One book from this conjuncture is Ross and Rose, eds, *Microphone Fiends*; this has much on rap and a chapter by Sara Thornton on the British dance music scene.

5  See, for example, B. Appleyard, 'Blame it all on the Beatles', the *Independent*, 2 January 1996.

6  Industry underinvestment in black music is discussed in S. Frith, 'Popular Music and the Local State', in S. Frith, L. Grossberg, J. Shepherd

and G. Turner, eds, *Rock and Popular Music: Politics, Policies, Institutions*, Routledge, 1993, pp. 14–23.

7 For a sardonic appreciation of the limits of the CD-ROM medium, see B. Eno, *A Year with Swollen Appendices*, Faber, 1996, pp. 308–9.

8 These texts are worth examining. Two studies are P. Théberge, 'Musicians' Magazines in the 1980s: the Creation of a Community and a Consumer Market', *Cultural Studies*, vol. 5, no. 3, October 1991, 270–93; and J. Toynbee, 'Policing Bohemia, Pinning Up Grunge: the Music Press and Generic Change in British Pop and Rock', *Popular Music*, vol. 12, no. 3, 1993, pp. 289–300.

9 See R. Middleton, *Studying Popular Music*, Milton Keynes, Open University Press, 1990; R. Walser, *Running with the Devil*, Hanover, New England, Wesleyan University Press, 1993; R. Hatch and D. Millward, *From Blues to Rock: an Analytical History*, Manchester, Manchester University Press, 1987; A.F. Moore, *Rock, the Primary Text*, Buckingham, Open University Press, 1993; T. Rose, *Black Noise*, Hanover, New England, Wesleyan University Press, 1994.

10 S. Reynolds, *Blissed Out*, Serpents Tail, 1990; J. Savage, *England's Dreaming*, Faber, 1991; G. Marcus, *Lipstick Traces*, Secker and Warburg, 1985; *Common Knowledge* is produced in New York for Oxford University Press.

11 R. Leppert and S. McLary, eds, *Music and Society: the Politics of Composition, Performance and Reception*, Cambridge, Cambridge University Press, 1987.

12 S. McClary, *Feminine Endings*, Minnesota, University of Minneapolis Press, 1991.

13 M. Citron, *Gender and The Musical Canon*, Cambridge, Cambridge University Press, 1993; J. Gill, *Queer Noises*, Cassell, 1995.

14 A useful brief guide to the complexities and debates of the genre is J. Kerman, *Musicology*, Fontana, 1985; more recent, if perplexing both in its inclusions and exclusions, is J. Paynter, T. Howell, R. Orton and P. Seymour, eds, *Companion to Contemporary Musical Thought*, 2 vols, Routledge, 1992. To get inside the practice of musicology, consult, among others *The Journal of Musicology*; *Contemporary Music Review*; *The Musical Quarterly*; *Music Analyses*; and *Tempo*.

15 See Middleton, *Studying Popular Music*, pp. 145–9.

16 For example, A. Durant, *Conditions of Music*, Macmillan, 1984; Middleton, *Studying Popular Music*; J.J. Beadle, *Will Pop Eat Itself?*, Faber, 1993.

17 J. Attali, *Noise*, trans. B. Massumi, Manchester, Manchester University Press, 1985.

18 Discussed in A. Blake, 'Listen To Britain: Music, Advertising and Postmodern Culture', in M. Nava, A. Blake, I. MacRury and B. Richards,

eds, *Buy This Book: Advertising and Consumption since the 1950s*, Routledge, 1996.

19   C. Flinn, *Strains of Utopia*, Princeton University Press, 1992; C. Gorb-mann, *Unheard Melodies: Narrative Film Music*, Bloomington, Indiana University Press, 1987; M. Chion, trans. C. Gorbmann, *Audio-Vision: Sounds on Screen*, New York, Columbia University Press, 1994 – the last is a particularly disappointing text which again promises more than it delivers.

20   An exception is A. Goodwin, *Dancing in the Distraction Factory: Music Television and Popular Culture*, Routledge, 1993, which is a good audio-visual analysis.

21   M. Tortora, 'Raymond Williams and Romantic Poetry', unpublished M.Phil. thesis, University of East London, 1996.

22. B. Watson, *Frank Zappa: the Negative Dialectics of Poodle Play*, Quar-tet, 1994.

23   See, for example, J. Aizlewood, ed., *Love is the Drug: Living as a Pop Fan*, Harmondsworth, Penguin, 1994. Three of the book's seventeen contributors, all professional writers/journalists, admit to having stud-ied English at university. None read music.

24   S. Dalton, *Vox*, August 1994; R. Beattie, *Q*, June 1994.

25   *Record Collector*, no. 178, June 1994.

26   D. Rimmer, in *The Wire*, no. 124, June 1994, p. 48.

27   S. Frith, *New York Village Voice*, 6 September 1994.

28   C.S. Murray, *New Statesman and Society*, 24 June 1994.

29   A. Gill, *Mojo*, August 1994.

30   M. Sinker, 'Mutters of Convention', *Red Pepper*, August 1994.

31   M. Wroe, 'The Politics of Poodle Rock', *The Observer*, 22 May 1994; M. Edwards, 'Out to Lunch', *The Sunday Times*, 19 June 1994.

32   I. Sinclair, 'Vermin Correspondence', *London Review of Books*, 20 October 1994, pp. 41–2.

33   S. Sweeney-Turner in *The Musical Times*, November 1994, pp. 716–17.

34   A. Blake, 'The Canine Mutineer', *The Times Literary Supplement*, 19 August 1994, p. 19.

35   M. Ffytch, 'The Far Side', *The Modern Review*, August/September 1994.

36   B. Thompson, 'Idol Speculations', *The Independent on Sunday*, 17 July 1994.

37   See, again, Aizlewood, ed., *Love is the Drug*, throughout.

38   This section is adapted from A. Blake, 'The Death of a Hero?', *Maga-zine of Cultural Studies*, no. 1, March 1990, pp. 32–5. This article pro-duced a spirited reply by G. Diggines in *Magazine of Cultural Studies*, no. 2, Autumn 1990, p. 45.

39   D. Cairns, 'The Iron Hand that Failed to Find the Beat of Humanity', *The Sunday Times*, 23 July 1989.

40   *Ibid.* Compare R. Morrison, 'The Podium's Playboy Pro', *The Times*, 17 July 1989; and the obituary by B. Northcott, the *Independent*, 17 July 1989.

41   For views on the orchestral malaise, see H. Cole, *The Changing Face of Music*, Victor Gollancz, 1978, p. 30; R. Simpson, *The Proms and Natural Justice*, Toccata, 1981, pp. 25–28; H. Carpenter, *Benjamin Britten*, Faber, 1992, pp. 60, 85; P. Martin, *Sounds and Society*, Manchester, Manchester University Press, 1995, p. 213.

42   For the Philharmonia in the 1950s see E. Schwarzkopf, *On and Off the Record: a Memoir of Walter Legge*, Faber, 1982.

43   This is suggested by Norman Lebrecht in his *The Maestro Myth*, Simon and Schuster, 1991, p. 122.

44   M. Kettle, 'A Maestro for the Millions', the *Guardian*, 17 July 1989.

45   Debussy is important to the avant-garde in many forms of music. See, for example, D. Toop, *Ocean of Sound*, Serpent's Tail, 1995; Debussy is afforded fourteen index entries in J. Paynter, T. Howell, R. Orton and P. Seymour's *Routledge Companion to Contemporary Musical Thought* (1992); this is fourteen more than one well-established living (i.e. contemporary) composer, Robin Holloway, who has written interestingly on Debussy (*Debussy and Wagner*, Oxford, Oxford University Press 1978) as well as using some of his techniques. Honegger is mentioned once.

46   J. Culshaw, *Putting the Record Straight*, Secker and Warburg; also Lebrecht, *The Maestro Myth*, some of whose ideas are developed further in his *When the Music Stops: Managers, Maestros and the Corporate Murder of Classical Music*, Simon and Shuster, 1996.

47   L. Foreman, ed., *From Parry to Britten: British Music in Letters 1900–1945*, B.T. Batsford, 1987, pp. 147–8.

# 1

# A British 'classical music'?

'Classical music' is a contested term. To many musicians and critics, the word 'classical' refers only to music written between *c.* 1770 and 1820, and only to a small proportion of that music; the most popular composers associated therewith are Haydn, Mozart and early Beethoven. But the word 'classical' has become routinely used as I shall use it here, as shorthand for written European and North American music from the foundation of the monasteries onwards, which has been associated since the eighteenth century with a tradition of writing and concert performance – in spaces whose prime purpose was performing and listening.

'Classical music', in this broader sense, is a conceptual product which, in Britain, has been formed since the eighteenth century, and at three moments in particular: the Industrial Revolution; the turn of the nineteenth and twentieth centuries, often called the 'English musical Renaissance'; and the post-1945 reconstruction in education, broadcasting and state policy for the arts. These moments will be sketched in turn as I enquire as to the emergence of a specifically 'British' classical music from within this created and re-created tradition.

## A bourgeois revolution?

Firstly, then, we have the emergence of the concert tradition, during the first industrial revolution. This economic process, historians are currently agreed, was the outcome of a gradual process of capital accumulation, based on the comparative stability of the regime. From the mid-seventeenth century, a series of victories against French and Dutch trading rivals, which gave Britain the command of the Atlantic economy, secured English as the most important language in the northern half of the American continent, and guaranteed the continuance of British expansion elsewhere in the world, both in formal empire (as in India) and in informal economic dominance (as, in the later nineteenth century, in Argentina). All this, including the slave trade and the work of slaves on the plantations of the Caribbean, fed capital back to Britain, and especially to the large ports such as Glasgow, Liverpool, Bristol and London. While great personal wealth was one outcome of this process, some of the money was available as, precisely, capital, to invest in the new technologies of the revolution: the steam engines, the railways, the new iron-making processes, the mills and spinning machines, and the town halls, churches and performance venues of the new urban centres.

For men and women of the middle class, all this meant wealth, a rising standard of living, and a life structured around increasingly clear divisions between public and private lives and between work and leisure. The new cultures of consumption produced new music; however, one culture did not simply replace another: these new products always evolved through negotiation with established values of taste and behaviour. Throughout the eighteenth century, the rapidity of modernisation was paralleled by an increasing sense of the importance, the value, of established knowledges. There was an increasing urge to classify and compartmentalise, to order the world through category and hierarchy, and to establish standards of correctness in all fields of knowledge. This is the time of Doctor Johnson's *Dictionary*, for example – part of a movement to classify the English language which arguably stultified its development thereafter – as it is of the botanical classifications of the Swedish scientist Linnaeus and the similar work of the English botanist and poet Erasmus Darwin.[1] Among all the arts, the establishment of certainty, both in lineage and in taste, was sought in the face of the increasing pace of change, of the growing maelstrom of incipient modernity:[2] Erasmus Darwin was as eager to welcome the machinery of the Industrial Revolution as he was to describe and order the natural world.

This modernising epoch established, for the first time, the notion of a 'tradition' of music with its own repeatable and absolute values. Before this point almost all music was 'contemporary'; however complex, scholarly and carefully constructed, music was written and performed for specific occasions and seldom revived, as with most music for film and television today. Haydn's 104 symphonies make the point. For Haydn, the symphony was an occasional piece: once it had been written, rehearsed and performed, another would be written for the next important occasion, and so on. By contrast, a generation later Beethoven fetishised the symphony not only as a piece displaying absolute and repeatable value, but as requiring so much individual effort from the composer that feats such as Haydn's, while not *physically* impossible, were seen as *psychically* outside the category of serious music. Beethoven's nine symphonies remained the norm of achievement for subsequent composers, with Schubert, Mendelssohn, Schumann, Brahms, Bruckner, Dvorak, Mahler, Sibelius, Nielsen, Bax, Vaughan Williams and many others constrained by it to the extent that none passed the number nine: Bruckner, for example, died before completing his ninth, and Mahler while working on his tenth.

While Beethoven's life and work undoubtedly mark a crucial turning-point in the general European sense of musical value, much of the conceptual apparatus of the classical music tradition was already in play in British musical life by the end of the eighteenth century. The historian William Weber has recently studied the emergent idea of classical music in eighteenth-century England, in the urban cultures of modernisation.[3] Here the political and cultural system based around the established families and their control of sinecures, the system often known as Old Corruption, was increasingly inflected by a mildly socially mobile grouping based around the exchange of information in the clubs and coffee-houses of the metropolis – what Terry Eagleton refers to as 'the liberal bourgeois public sphere'.[4] Grouped around the publications the *Spectator*, edited by Addison, and Steele's *Tatler*, and around the authoritative bourgeois figure of Doctor Johnson (but including aristocrats as well as middle-class men), this new social formation discussed the worlds of politics and trade, making cultural capital function as a sign of social worth in a society whose many active members transcended the limited world of the aristocracy – there were so many that they could only 'know' each other through pattern-recognition involving shared codes of knowledge and behaviour.

This version of polite society, the world of the clubs and coffee-houses, of an increasingly textualised, encyclopaedic political culture, was matched by a growing consumerism in the move towards a market economy; though here as elsewhere cultural capital aided the development of demand for goods and services: the exchanged signs included the 'classical' values of products such as Wedgwood jasperware and creamware, which were modelled on the products retrieved from the archaeological excavations at Pompeii and Herculaneum in southern Italy. Typically in this instance the new techniques of archaeology were marshalled to produce not merely knowledge of an ancient society, but of the correct taste for the contemporary world. Any kind of political allegiance could be symbolised by consumer goods, but the symbols drew in the main on classical models.[5]

So the market was, however subject to the vagaries of fashion, also very much status-based; it operated in a society still dominated by a monarchy and aristocracy, but based increasingly around another authority – of the texts and artefacts of the classical world. There was an attempt to dignify the music of the past with a similar gravity and authority. This could not be done with the music of the classical era itself (the music of ancient Greece or Rome), because hardly any of it survives: written descriptions can only suggest the basic compositional modes, and paintings show the instruments used to play them. Instead, the formation of a musical tradition was referred to the music of previous eras which was available in notated form; the music of the Anglican Church from its Elizabethan refoundation onwards, and especially the music of the Restoration composer Purcell; and the music of the early eighteenth century, notably that of Georg Handel and Arcangelo Corelli.

There were close connections between the new social formations of the coffee-house, the magazine and news-sheet, and the establishing of a taste for old music. But it was not an absolute homology. As Weber suggests, the promotion of the old began as the product of a reaction *against* the new, the fashionable and the commercial: a movement which has more in common with Burke's reaction to the early excesses of the French Revolution than a welcome for the harbingers of the free market.[6] The instigators of the taste for 'Ancient Music', as they called it, were reacting against the notion of music as one luxurious commodity among others; they reacted by forming an indigenous tradition. Many were churchmen or other Oxbridge High Tories, also trying to defend the values of hereditary nobility against the relative social mobility of the new club culture. The Academy of Ancient Music was founded, in 1726, for the performance of old (Anglican) church music; while churchmen, civil servants, lawyers and doctors were welcomed as members, businessmen were excluded from its ranks. This exclusiveness soon faded, however, as the Academy was joined by a growing festival movement in the provinces, including the Three Choirs festival (amalgamating the choirs of Gloucester, Hereford and Worcester Cathedrals for the performance of large-scale devotional works). Sacred music from the sixteenth and seventeenth centuries was revived around the key figure of Henry Purcell.

During the eighteenth century these festivals broadened to include appropriate contemporary music and to include a far wider social mix in the audience. The music of the contemporary composers Corelli and Handel became living classics, and after their deaths remained in the repertoire of these festivals and performing clubs. Corelli's music was esteemed partly because it was comparatively easy to play (it remains important to school and youth orchestras for this reason), while Handel's best-known sacred work, the *Messiah*, was also important to the amateur performers of the growing choral tradition. The performance of the *Messiah* became an icon (as, again, it remains to this day); already by 1785 it was the highlight of an annual festival at Norwich which was far from the socially exclusive regime of the Academy of Ancient Music. Businessmen joined with local aristocrats and gentry and Anglicans mixed with Nonconformists in supporting the event, which was one of dozens of such performances held regularly throughout the country, many involving massive numbers:[7] there were 525 performers at the Westminster Abbey celebration of the centenary of the composer's birth in 1784. This occasion, Weber claims, was an important political event, 'celebrating the end of the American war, the reunion of Whig and Tory in a new order'.[8] A ceremony organised around the music of a dead, Italian-educated, German male had become a cultural icon drawing together the opposing forces of British high politics in cross-party celebration of the new, post-colonial British nation. (New work had also played its part in this aestheticisation of Britishness: J.C. Bach, who worked in London from 1762 until his death twenty years later, had success in 1767 with *Carattaco*, an opera on a very British (and anti-Roman) theme which later inspired Elgar – and which prompted one reviewer to remark that J.C. Bach was 'a second Handel'.)[9]

This is not to say that music played an unproblematic part in any

British political settlement. The class, gendered and ethnic politics of the emergent tradition are more complex than Weber's conclusion would suggest. For Simon McVeigh, concert life was primarily about the re-establishing of a small elite.[10] But as Richard Leppert has noted, the very idea of musical performance was alien to many aristocrats.[11] Performance remained a gentlemanly skill on the Continent, where Frederick the Great of Prussia was a competent composer and performer on the flute. In Britain, however, for all the patronage of ancient music by a few High Tories, such aristocratic virtuosity became increasingly rare, and during the nineteenth century it vanished altogether.

One reason for the disappearance of the public amateur instrumentalist (singing remained an expected skill even for male aristocrats) may be the changing role of the musician, a change implied by the increasing authority of the composer and, more importantly, of the written musical text, within this growing canon. The orchestra, with its larger numbers, its time-beating conductor and its necessary discipline, robbed the gentlemanly performer of the ability to display his taste through the application of improvisatory and decorative techniques – gentlemen amateurs in an orchestra in Edinburgh in 1791 were implored to 'attend to the Forte and Piano passages and to play their parts plain as Marked in the Musick without any Flourishes'.[12] Deprived of the opportunity to show off, the gentleman's interest diminished. Indeed, Lord Chesterfield wrote to his son, 'Nothing degrades a gentleman more than performing upon any instrument whatever.'[13] The practice of music was often identified with the foreign: Continental teachers and performers, who formed the bulk of professional musicians in London, Edinburgh and Dublin, were the backbone of the new orchestras and the smaller groups of paid musicians.

Another reason for the disappearance of the musical amateur may be the social mix described by Eagleton, which involved an admix of bourgeois respectability into aristocratic culture, and which had by the 1840s curbed public drunkenness, gambling and duelling.[14] Below the aristocracy, suspicion of music as a profession matched the suspicion of acting; both those of the middle class who attempted to achieve gentlemanly status and those who were content to remain within the mainstream of bourgeois respectability contributed to the suspicion accorded to music and musicians within respectable British manhood, a suspicion still present in the first edition of the *Dictionary of National Biography*, compiled at the end of the nineteenth century and published between 1885 and 1900, in which there are very few musicians (among the more spectacular omissions, rectified along with eighteen others in the 1993 *Dictionary of National Biography Missing Persons* volume, were the eighteenth-century London musicians J.C. Bach and Muzio Clementi).[15]

This was not a simple ban on performance or bodily display: the gentleman was still allowed to perform in public, if only in more ostentatiously vigorous pursuits; in much sport, for example, amateurs and professionals competed side by side throughout the nineteenth century, and the mix of 'gentlemen' and 'players' continued to mark English cricket until the 1960s. It became 'ungentlemanly' to be a good musician, or even a competent one, while it was considered praiseworthy to be a good batsman. This was not because of any enormous technical or temperamental gulf separating the full-time professional from the gifted amateur. No doubt there were great professional performers like Liszt and Paganini, whose technique could not have been encompassed without the dedication of professionalism; there were also many very ordinary professional musicians and a fair number of incompetent ones, as a glance at the memoirs of any nineteenth-century composer, conductor or singer will indicate. It could equally be said that playing cricket involves such a high level of skill and determination that playing at the highest level would compromise gentlemanly status – and indeed many amateur cricketers of the late nineteenth century's 'golden age' of cricket were 'amateur' in name only.[16] What happens here is a class-based gendering of performance which associates sport with the public sphere and masculinity, and musicianship with artisanship and/or the private sphere, and with 'effeminacy', if not simply with femininity. The transferring of this perceived effeminacy on to the male Continental 'Other', and their accepted part in the very definition of musicianship, was such that French, Italian and German musicians found it easy to obtain work by virtue of their foreignness, and that British musicians often adopted Italian, French or German names. The perception of music was clearly that it was outwith the norms of acceptable bourgeois masculinity; there was continuing suspicion of the 'effeminacy' of French and Italian music teachers and dancing-masters, even when they had unequivocally indicated one important aspect of their masculinity by seducing their female pupils.[17]

For women, the range of musical skills expected of the 'lady' remained constant. As, in the aristocracy and middle classes, music-making moved into the private sphere, it became naturalised and feminised as a domestic activity. Female pianists and guitarists were legion; women were expected to play, at least before marriage. When they reached a level of attainment which could lead to public performance, they could both threaten the professional male and threaten the ladylike status of the woman. One talented female musician, Ann Ford, was actually abducted by her father to prevent her performing in public – and then rescued by an enthusiastic aristocratic patron.[18] Both sexes were expected to sing – and this helped to maintain the importance of the amateur choir, one form of music-making involving women which transcended the private sphere.

But this was not only a gender issue. Bourgeois distaste for the entertainment professions remained strong. The Wesleys, Charles and Samuel, were discouraged by their family from performing and composing music – and Samuel later regretted that the parental pressure had not been effective in preventing him from entering this 'trivial and degrading business' (similar pressures were later exerted by the businessmen fathers of the composers Delius and Bax and the conductor Thomas Beecham).[19]

The attainment of professional status by public entertainers was especially problematic where the audience wished to differentiate itself socially from the performer; to treat players as servants, hired for their pleasure, much as the aristocracy had always done. In London (as also in Paris and Vienna) the large middle-class public, unable as individuals to afford permanent musical servants but able to employ freelance music teachers and the price of subscriptions, led to the rise of the public concert. A few composers and virtuoso performers (including conductors) apart, this was low-status and poorly paid work before the twentieth century – indeed, it was a job whose practitioners eagerly sought the relative privilege of professional status, without ever attaining it. Again, most full-time musicians in London were foreigners; there was no state-sponsored training for musicians before the founding of the Royal Academy of Music in 1823.[20] The practising musician attained craft status at best; it is anachronistic to speak of the 'profession' of music before the twentieth century. This status underlined the defensive masculinity of the craft – as in other skilled unionism, women were often excluded by male groups which tried to control entry as a defence mechanism against the undercutting of wages and conditions. The continuing legacy of the English musician as a despised, alienated journeyman, starts here: it has had unfortunate effects in the way English musicians perceive their task and the ways in which they have themselves been perceived, ever since, as chapter 5 will argue.[21]

All these phenomena were consolidated early in the nineteenth century when, throughout Europe, interest in the work of eighteenth-century composers was widened to include the then little-known J.S. Bach. This revival, and the continuing interest in the work of Mozart, Haydn and especially Beethoven after their deaths, began to create a 'great tradition' of canonic works and associated compositional and performance techniques, including the increasing fetishisation of the composer's score as a sacred and fully authoritative text. One consequence of this was the gradual disappearance of any acceptable form of improvisation in orchestral or even chamber music (though individual musicians such as Liszt and Chopin were known as great improvisers, and there is evidence of orchestral players' continuing ability to improvise, whether or not they were encouraged to do so).[22] Mendelssohn and Weber, two of the Continental instigators both of orchestral discipline and of the creation of tradition, were often performers in London (both were among the earliest stick-waving conductors; Mendelssohn both revived the music of Bach and kept the oratorio form used by Bach and popularised by Handel alive with his *Elijah*), and the works of both were canonised in their turn on their early deaths. At this point, in fact (in the early nineteenth century) the tradition became Germanicised, finally losing the connection with Italy which had been important in the presence of Corelli and the Italian-trained Handel.[23]

A new tradition of concert-going was created along with this newly historicised repertoire. Where in the early nineteenth century this was almost entirely the preserve of the middle class, by the 1850s it was available to many outside that class, and was indeed being made available to the working class as an aspect of the 'rational recreation' proselytised by so many middle-class proponents, at cheap concerts at the Crystal Palace in Sydenham, for example. The success of the event for which the Crystal Palace had first been constructed, the Great Exhibition of 1851, had convinced many middle-class people that working-class people could take their culture seriously; the growth of amateur choirs and the brass band movement confirmed this later in the century.[24]

These connected traditions were always, as they remain, part of a modernising urban capitalism. The anti-commercial concerns of the Academy for Ancient Music were as unavailing against the desire for profit as were the similar concerns of underground pop in the 1960s or punk in the 1970s. In the concert system of musical production and consumption, capital was exchanged on two levels: the cultural and the economic. Entrepreneurs, paying musicians on a freelance basis, sold tickets for events which gave the audience purchasing the tickets (including many of new wealth and status) some guaranteed cultural capital in exchange for their money. The rise of the free-lance composer was paralleled by the rise of the middle-class audience, creating new public concert events in cities like London, Paris and Vienna.[25]

Through buying tickets, middle-class people could signal their own place – economic, cultural and emotional – in the evolving tradition of music-making. Economically, they could collectively own performers and performances, collectively play the role of patron of the arts (and the position of being patron/ising to the collectively owned musical servants, the composers and performers) which was impossible to them as individuals, and thereby inhabit a specifically middle-class collective culture. Concerts were, as to a certain extent they remain, important in the formation of middle-class consciousness.

There is also, and as importantly, a *psychic* economy of desire at work here. Emotionally, as Richard Sennett has suggested, despite the general view of performers as not respectable, *identification* with particular, heroic performers like the pianist–composers Chopin and Liszt and the violinist–composer Paganini was vitally important to an urban middle class trapped in codes of behaviour which denied them any public expressivity as individuals. The grey suits and stylised 'evening dress' uniforms of the men, and the increasingly restrictive and voluminous garments of the women, are clear signs of their absence of individuality, including any public display of their sexuality. Reaction at concerts by these 'demonic' performers was as hysterical as at any rock concert.[26] Though the general point holds throughout Europe, this identification was particularly important in the cities of Britain, to a Victorian middle class groping its way by the 1850s out of the gloomy fogs of Victorian 'respectability'.[27] Both Liszt and Paganini, playing deliberately on the fears of the bourgeois audience by associating themselves with the Devil as a source of inspiration, and whose playing seemed 'superhuman' to their contemporaries, provided massive emotional outlets, their publicly ecstatic performances commonly causing tears, fainting fits and other signs of profound identification and loss of emotional inhibition. The concert performer as star is a development of this moment – and a very important one: the star performer is at present more important in the psychic and political economy of classical music than the (often invisible) composer.

Sennett's argument should be qualified. Important as the great performers were in transcending the limits of orthodox subjectivity, they were rare in nineteenth-century Europe. The tradition of amateur performance, however, was massively, and regularly, present. The oratorio flourished throughout British society, both as a respectable Christian substitute for the public emotionalism of opera (which in many circles was impossibly risqué), and as a place where the amateur could perform great music.[28] In the choirs which flourished in Victorian Britain, members of this group could join in the performances of oratorios of Handel and later composers, and they themselves could play, collectively, an ecstatic public role as musicians, without compromising their respectable status with the taints either of secularism or of musical professionalism. (It was, of course, important that their musical ecstasy was sacred, rather than profane or demonic.)

### Mind the gap

Despite all this – despite the British lead in the establishing of a tradition of musical works, despite the continuing importance of music to the middle class, as signalled by the rise of professional orchestras in the cities and the continuing growth of the amateur choral tradition – and, perhaps most puzzlingly, despite the growing importance of national identity through music which was signalled throughout Europe by the work of, for example, Mussorgsky in Russia, Wagner in Germany and Verdi in Italy – no music written by Britons was accorded a place in this 'great tradition' of European composed music until late in the nineteenth century. It is impossible to explain this gap satisfactorily. Gentlemanly suspicion of musical

discipline and effeminacy and middle-class dislike of the entertainment professions no doubt played their part in suppressing what
native compositional talent there was. To many Europeans, because
of this absence of native composition, Britain remained 'das Land
ohne Musik'.

Even when at the end of the nineteenth century a number of
British composers did emerge, their reputations, and their musical
styles, remained largely parochial, semi-detached from the developments taking place in Continental Europe and the USA. This is partly
because their final emergence was in the shadow of the Continental
mastery of the trade and its various genres – many talented British
musicians practised existing styles rather than pushing them further.
While in the first twenty years of the twentieth century Ives and
Cowell in the USA and Mahler, Busoni, Debussy, Schoenberg, Bartok and Stravinsky in Europe were proposing their very different
visions of the future of music, many British composers were still
using or developing the musical language of the 1880s, the moment
of the final re-emergence of British music after 200 years of virtual
silence. Those who were not copying Brahms and the rest directly
were not avant-gardists like Schoenberg or Ives, but were developing
a music which was, quite deliberately, within a specific, if recently
invented, national tradition. It is to this paradox that I now turn.

## The invention of a musical Renaissance

The late nineteenth-century creation or re-creation of 'Englishness'
and other national traditions has been discussed at length, and the
contribution of music to this remaking has been acknowledged: in
books discussing the issue music makes more than a token appearance in relation to manufactured national traditions.[29] Throughout
Europe new forms of cultural practice were emerging, based in
some cases on practices of the past, in others on pure inventions
which merely claimed the lineage of the past. From complete languages to rituals such as coronation ceremonies, national cultures
remade themselves by remaking their most important symbols. All
these new traditions were ascribed to the past or to the transcendence of temporality – to 'time immemorial' or some such phrase,
beloved of commentators on monarchic ceremonial. The re-
emergence of British composed music is one such reinvented
tradition. Several strands of musical life were established at this

point, and each called on the rhetoric of tradition in rather different ways.

These differences have often been elided under the term 'the English musical Renaissance'.[30] At that moment of busiest tradition-
inventing – the 1880s – there was an identified 'national need' for
Great Composers, and to answer it we find first Arthur Sullivan,
then Charles Stanford and Hubert Parry leading the way, setting up
schools of composition in the newly established music colleges,
which for the first time turned out a steady stream of professional
musicians under the (limited) sponsorship of the state. These founding figures were themselves rather different. Sullivan, arguably the
most talented composer of the three, remains damned by his association with Gilbert in the successful Savoy light operas (and perhaps also by his homosexuality).[31] Stanford was the most eclectic,
the least dominated by the German tradition – much of his music is
(mildly) inflected by the music of his Protestant Irish upbringing: as
well as a series of Irish rhapsodies, hymns and folk tunes from this
tradition appear in his 'Irish' symphony, one of his most popular
works during his lifetime. For Parry, on the other hand, the German
tradition was so overwhelming that his primary inclination was to
reproduce it rather than challenge or add to it, and he certainly
believed that others should be taught how to reproduce it: much of
his music is ersatz Brahms. Both Stanford and Parry played an active
part in the maintenance of the amateur choral tradition, writing
short pieces and oratorios.

## Elgar – a voice for the people?

Perhaps because of this obeisance to the dominant German musical
tradition, the stream of talent from the colleges did not instantly
establish the new musical road to Englishness or Britishness. It is
one of the composers of the next generation who did not attend
music college, the Catholic Englishman Edward Elgar, who became
most closely identified with the new tradition. He also fits the common narrative of the self-made man. Elgar served a long appren-
ticeship as a composer, living in the heart of England at Worcester,
writing for choral societies such as the one at Hanley in the Potteries whose 1903 London performance of *The Dream of Gerontius*
helped to cement his reputation.[32] By his fortieth birthday he had
forged a personal musical language. As a symbolic system, this lan-

guage is most clearly exemplified in the use of the ceremonial march, which was an important part of the remaking of public ceremonial during the late Victorian moment of high imperialism; marches appeared in his symphonies as well as in Elgar's best-known work, the first 'Pomp and Circumstance' march, written in 1899. In its guise as the song 'Land of Hope and Glory' (with words added, to Elgar's dismay, by A.C. Benson) this march is still performed at the concluding moment of the national musical celebration, the last night of the Proms concert season, run by the BBC (the Proms are discussed here in chapter 4). Elgar's work clearly owes much to the German tradition in which Parry in particular was steeped; while attempts have been made to delineate the specific 'Englishness' of Elgar's melodic lines and/or his orchestration or harmonic devices, it was against German models that he was immediately judged and lauded by one of his German contemporaries, Richard Strauss, whose praise (along with that of the German conductor Hans Richter) served to seal his reputation in pre-war Europe. In many ways Elgar's musical Englishness is most clearly signalled by use of the oratorio form beloved of the English bourgeoisie; this places him not just within the amateur choral tradition, but at one of its apexes. Works like *The Dream of Gerontius*, for all its Catholic theology (it is a setting of a poem by Cardinal Newman), remain popular in choral society performance. *Gerontius*, *The Kingdom*, *The Apostles* and other Christian works were not the only essays Elgar made for pro–am choral performance, however; an earlier work, *Caractacus*, explores not 'Englishness' but Britishness, through one of its many contradictory aspects: the heritage of Celtic and Roman Britain.

In 1898 Elgar was commissioned by the city of Leeds to provide a choral work for a festival. He collaborated with H.A. Acworth, a librettist with whom he had already worked on the cantata *King Olaf*. *Caractacus*, a cantata for chorus, soloists and orchestra, tells the story of the defeat of Caractacus, the last leader to unite British tribes against the forces of Rome, in a battle on the Malvern hills. Enlivened by Druid ritual and love scenes between a young Druid priest and the leader's daughter, it is semi-operatic, and could be staged, in the same way as other quasi-dramatic works such as Berlioz's *Damnation of Faust* or Stravinsky's *Oedipus Rex* have been staged.

Writing in the preface to the orchestral score, Acworth insisted on the historical and geographical veracity of the project:

> The general lines of history – or failing history, of tradition – have
> been followed. The British camp on the Malvern Hills is locally attrib-
> uted to Caractacus. It is doubtless a British work, and is of such extent
> as infers occupation by very large numbers. The scene of Caractacus's
> last disastrous battle is much disputed; but it was almost certainly on
> the line of the Severn (Habern) and may probably have been at Caer
> Caradoc, in Shropshire. The unusual circumstance of mistletoe grow-
> ing on the oak may still be observed in the woods below the Here-
> fordshire Beacon. Caractacus's appearance before Claudius in Rome,
> his bold defence, and the pardon of himself and his daughter are his-
> torical.[33]

Elgar's music too makes some attempt at these specificities. In order
to portray the environment, the composer walked in the Malvern
Hills, finding and renting a woodland cottage called Birchwood
Lodge, in which he composed the music. Writing to his friend Jaeger
(the Anglo-German music publisher whom he was to portray as
'Nimrod' in his next major work, the 'Enigma Variations'), Elgar
reflected on his attempts to compose an environmentally-specific
music: 'This is what I hear all day – the trees are singing my music
– or have I sung theirs? I suppose I have.'[34] Elgar could not use historically specific music, of pre-Roman Britain; but there is much reference to older British musical styles, from the madrigal-ish final
quartet between the Emperor Claudius and his captives (Scene 6,
number 44), through the sea-shanty like chorus 'We were gathered
by the river' (Scene 4, number 13), to the folk-ballad simplicity
associated with Eigen, Caractacus' daughter, most of whose music
is in a flowing 12/8 time rather than the 4/4 or 3/4 which dominates
elsewhere in the score.

After a final scene at the Roman Triumph in which the captured
Caractacus wins his life by asking for the Romans to teach his people higher moral values, the cantata ends with a show-stopping chorus, a paean to the coming decline of Rome and the ascent of Britain
to a greater empire than the Roman. This Kiplingesque purple passage (with a very direct echo of Kipling's 1897 poem 'Recessional')
incorporates the paradox of the White Man's Burden. Britain (having, by implication, inherited the mantle of civilising imperialism
from Rome) will force the world to learn about, and then to practise, 'freedom'; after which the world will be truly grateful:

Britons, alert! And fear not,
But gird your loins for fight,
And ever your dominion
From age to age shall grow
O'er peoples undiscover'd
In lands we cannot know.
And where the flag of Britain
Its triple crosses rears,
No slave shall be for subject
No trophy wet with tears.
But folk shall bless the banner
And bless the crosses twin'd
That bear the gift of freedom
On ev'ry blowing wind.
Nor shall her might diminish
While firm she holds the faith
Of equal laws to all men
And holds it to the death.
For all the world shall learn it
Though long the task shall be,
The text of Britain's teaching,
The message of the free.
And when at last they find it,
The nations all shall stand
And hymn the praise of Britain
Like brothers, hand in hand.[35]

The music for this final chorus, like the similar passage extolling the
virtues of 'holy German art' at the end of Wagner's *Die Meis-
tersinger*, is appropriately simple and hymn-like, ending in the blaz-
ing E flat major often associated with power and nature in German
music (for example in Beethoven's *Eroica* symphony, Schumann's
*Rhenish* symphony and the opening of *Das Rheingold*, the first of
Wagner's Ring opera sequence). But though much of the score is in
the German-dominated tradition of European music proselytised by
Parry – the shadow of Wagner in particular never quite fades – there
are consistent attempts to provide a pattern of native music: the
folk- or ballad-influenced tunes and contrapuntal madrigal-style settings both acknowledge and foreshadow the major sources of musical 'Englishness', sources which were drawn on extensively in the
following forty years: folk music and the music of the Tudor era.

So *Caractacus* is an important forebear of the exploration of musical Englishness. But *Caractacus* is also about Celtic Britishness. It was not alone, though many characterisations of the Celtic heritage were used to construct difference, the regional specificity of musics in Britain: the feminisation of music within British culture and the feminisation of the Celts in the work of Matthew Arnold and others had already by this time begun to produce that strongest of invented traditions, the 'natural' musicality of the Celts – with by-products such as the Welsh male-voice choir. The folk music of Wales, Scotland and Ireland was a powerful source of inspiration (and long had been; both Haydn and Beethoven produced arrangements of Scottish folk-songs, and Haydn also arranged Welsh songs); the Celtic myths and legends which had been revived in the second half of the nineteenth century provided a fecund source of inspiration for poets, storytellers and musicians alike. One composer, Arnold Bax, not only used Irish folk-song as a source for his own music, but created an Irish literary identity, calling himself Dermot O'Byrne, writing poetry in Gaelic and becoming a member of Yeats's circle in Dublin. *Caractacus* was not alone, therefore. Indeed, it is an important forerunner, for over the next forty years a number of attempts were made to provide, for the British, not a sign of regional/national difference but a communalising narrative based on their heritage of folk-tales and romance, in precisely the ways in which writers since Geoffrey of Monmouth had used the (Celtic) Arthurian legends: Bax (*Tintagel*; *The Garden of Fand*) and John Ireland (*Forgotten Rite* and *Mai-Dun*) wrote tone-poems based on Celtic legend, while a generation later George Lloyd rose to fame with the Cornish–Celtic opera *Iernin* (1935).

For some of the pro-Celts, trying once again to construct a national musical identity in the overwhelming presence of German models, the attempt had to be an equivalent of Wagner's achievement in the *Ring* cycle. Between 1912 and 1929 Joseph Holbrooke wrote a Wagnerian trilogy of operas based on Welsh legends from the *Mabinogion*. Similarly, Rutland Boughton attempted to match Wagner by setting up a provincial festival based on a cycle of myth-based operas, as Wagner had done in the nondescript Bavarian town of Bayreuth. So he wrote the operas, basing them on the Arthurian legends, and founded a festival in the small Somerset town of Glastonbury, itself replete with Arthurian and mystical reference.[36] The festival was quite successful for a while; and one opera by Boughton, *The Immortal Hour* – setting a play by 'Fiona MacLeod', the pseudonym of the Scottish writer William Sharp – had a long run in London in the early 1920s. But the mixture of Celticism, nationalism and *fin-de-siècle* (it is tempting to say 'New-Age') mysticism did not in the end grab the public's wholehearted attention, partly due to one strand of the ideological mixture: Boughton was a Morrisite socialist. His socialism was, in other words, based on a version of pre-industrial Britain worthy of the vision of organic society which can be found in William Morris's utopian text *News From Nowhere* (1891). Such pre-industrial utopias were not necessarily of the left; a similar notion of an organic society was later promulgated by the liberal literary critic F.R. Leavis; Boughton's interest in the culture of 'the folk' was strong enough for his work at Glastonbury to attain the patronage of a prominent aristocratic fascist, the Marchioness of Londonderry.

Like Holbrooke, another socialist who wrote Celtic opera, and socialist composer and writer Christian Darnton, Boughton found that praise for the music was matched by hostility to the ideology; not from the general public who flocked to see *The Immortal Hour*, but from the political establishment, many music critics and the most important new patron of the arts, the BBC. By the end of the 1920s the BBC had emerged as a crucial force in the production of contemporary music, and the BBC had a clearly discriminatory policy from the start: after a brief flirtation with European Modernism, the patronage turned to British mainstream music without specific political messages. The politics of Darnton, Holbrooke and Boughton were rejected, their music was not broadcast, and they achieved obscurity.[37]

Elgar's lasting power, by contrast, came because he did not go for this politicising of music. The arguments he had – and there were many – were with musicians and about matters of training, or on the question of absolute as against programme music. And Elgar was clearly upwardly socially mobile, a hard-working local composer who achieved first national and then international fame, using his musical success and his marriage into the local gentry to play the country gentleman (and therefore cease to practise as a professional composer) as soon as decently possible – a narrative of the place of music within English life which still has force, incorporating pastoral melody and a fair amount of Elgar's music into a *Country Life* conservatism. For the BBC, at least, Elgar's mixture of German structural models and English/British themes was acceptable, and its continuing patronage (including the attempt to procure a third symphony from the tired old man who was more interested in going to the races) has been the most important single factor in maintaining Elgar's position as the crucial voice of the turn of the century.[38]

### The folk revival – the voice of the people?

Elgar's music, then, attempts to define an English musical identity which is aware of the British heritage, while also working out of the recognisable, and for many musicians definitive, German models. At the same time, however, a music which would claim for itself a far deeper authentic 'Englishness' was in the process of manufacture. English 'folk-songs' were collected by dedicated transcribers, convinced that they were preserving the last remnants of an oral tradition soon to vanish altogether from an England whose dialects and local cultures had been effaced by new forms of communication (railways and roads) and the new uniformity of grammar and pronunciation consequent on the mass state education which followed the 1870 Education Act. Yet – and this is a crucial point for the notion of 'Englishness' involved – the 'folk-music' collected by Cecil Sharp and his followers was not that of the folk in the industrial towns (by far the majority of the population), whatever their dialects or musical cultures, but of the rural areas, especially the South-West.[39] This was the music of an idealised English village, the ideal form of English life still to this day implicitly addressed through the folk-song and dance movements and idealised by publications such as the monthly magazine *Country Life*. As Georgina Boyes makes clear in her study of the folk revival movement, *The Imagined Village*, this was not an uncontested phenomenon; it was riven by class and gender politics, as rival collectors Cecil Sharp and Mary Neal promoted different visions of the use of folk-song and dance. Sharp, who soon controlled the 'folk revival' at the expense of the more liberal Neal, was as patronising, and as eager to classify and ossify flexible practices, as any other Victorian anthropologist. He argued that folk-song and dance had been supplanted by commercial cultural products such as the music-hall; authentic folk culture only survived in the memories of old people. He and his (mainly middle-class) collectors and performers had a historic mission to preserve the culture of 'the folk', and to return it to them: the site of this fantasy is the Imagined Village of Boyes's title.

All this reads like the emphasis placed by F.R. Leavis, editor of the journal *Scrutiny*, on the lost 'organic culture' of pre-industrial England, and equally like the idea of 'the folk' prevalent in Nazi Germany in the 1930s. The Scrutineers were supportive of the English Musical Renaissance: their chief music critic, Wilfrid Mellers, argued against the appointment of Bax as Master of the King's Music in 1936 partly because he habitually used Irish, not English, folk-music (though his favoured candidate, Vaughan Williams, was Welsh in origin). But Mellers was aware of the fascistic undertones of much of the folk revival; these became overtones in the activities of Rolf Gardiner's groups The Travelling Morrice and English Mistery, as with some of Boughton's support at Glastonbury. Likewise the left, imagined through an influential text like Blatchford's *Merrie England*, were as happy to dance Morris as the right of Gardiner's groups.[40] In both extreme right and left, a version of merry England as idealised song-and-dance village was available, though the left could also work with a model of urban and industrial folksong – something which was, and remains, impossible for the right.

Many of those who collected folk-song were themselves composers, and folk-song quickly became a major source of the new British music. Ralph Vaughan Williams studied briefly with Ravel in Paris, and although this influence is clear, it is as a musician of folk-inflected Englishness that he is usually constructed. In Wilfrid Mellers's study, *Vaughan Williams and the Vision of Albion*, the clear harmonies and melodies based on the hymns of the Anglican Church, and the folk-influenced modal, pentatonic and heptatonic melodies and harmonies, are seen as sources of a peculiarly English musical strength; certainly, whether strength or weakness, this removes his music further from the influence of the German tradition than Elgar managed (or wished to, for all his walks in the Malvern hills or his suspicion of the dominance of Brahms).

Another common source, for Vaughan Williams as for other composers of the turn of the century, takes us back to the taste, if not to the politics, of the Academy for Ancient Music. This was the composed music (for church and leisure) of the Tudor period, the 'golden age' revived by historians working in late Victorian Britain, and also re-created by F.R. Leavis and his followers – including Mellers, then a young Cambridge English graduate and composer whom we have just met both as *de facto* music critic for the Leavisite periodical *Scrutiny* and as commentator on Vaughan Williams, and who became the first professor of music in the innovative department at the new University of York in the 1960s.[41] The music of the Elizabethans in particular appealed to these historicists.[42] This was music created at a time of apparent binaries: the struggle between England and the Continent, and of Protestantism versus Catholicism; thus, to the later commentators and performers, it stood for a set of English values which became increasingly important in the twentieth century as the breadth and potential internationalism of the Empire became by force of circumstance the 'island race' standing alone against European fascism. Vaughan Williams's 'Fantasia on a theme of Thomas Tallis' (first performed at the Three Choirs Festival in Gloucester cathedral in 1910) reworks the idea of Englishness in two ways, firstly in its use of the Elizabethan composer's work, and secondly in the very adoption of the form: working its admiration of the national heritage not through the dialectical process of the sonata model dominated by the German symphonic tradition, but the more improvisatory, less ordered, fantasia.[43]

So we have a musical Englishness which used both the fetishised version of popular music under the 'folk' label, and the music of English consolidation and expansion; and we have the use of similar sources for the differentiation of the peoples and musics of the Celtic areas of Britain. Through all these sources, the ideology of romantic anti-capitalism was clearly reinscribed, in a repetition of the paradoxical creation of a 'past' within the process of modernisation which had seen the establishing of the classical music canon in the eighteenth century and after. To put the case more starkly, this neo-rurality, reworking the heritage of villages, country houses, the rural and the pre-industrial, was a music whose presence demanded the facilities of the industrial and commercial city. The music colleges and their Fordist production of graduate performers and composers are a far cry indeed from the informally apprenticed church bands and cathedral choirs of the early nineteenth century. Furthermore, the very presence of a growing tradition of symphonic composition and performance required the presence of large bodies of performers and audiences – the very conditions from which the modern musical profession had emerged. A music which proclaimed the values of the rural was, as it remains, necessarily urban.

The paradox contains, but obscures, an implicit denial of the economics of musical production. As the introduction indicated, this has itself become a vital tradition of English musical life. Studies of Elgar, for example, discuss the resonances of the music with those Malvern hills; or those of George Butterworth, his musical version of the Shropshire of Housman's poem 'A Shropshire Lad'. This commentary, however insightful, divorces meaning from the conditions of production, including education and training, funding and the role of the performing musician.

This is not to deny the importance or the vitality of the musical Renaissance. Within this continuing paradox, a vital school of composition was developed from the music colleges. There is a vast list of early twentieth-century composers using folk- and/or Tudor music, including, among many others, Cyril Scott, Rutland Boughton, Peter Warlock, Percy Grainger, John Ireland, Granville Bantock and George Butterworth. One of the most successful of all twentieth-century English symphonists, Arnold Bax, was mentioned above in the discussion of the Celtic revival: he used Irish folk-music to help his construction of an Irish identity, something he did so successfully that this man from a quintessentially bourgeois English family has often been referred to as Irish.[44] For Bax, this was an identification with a sense of national, Irish and anti-imperial tradition; for Boughton and Holbrooke, an identification of this national tradition with the sense of 'folk' as music 'of the people' made it apt for the message of socialism.

The purposes of these composers, then, may be completely different, along a range from the antiquarian to the politically activist. Yet the common coherence around notions of tradition, whether from the various folk lineages or the music of the Tudor period, or both, gives the experience of the music for the listener and performer a coherence which conceals the acute ideological differences of their creators. Whatever the difficulties of lumping them together, therefore, for the analytical purposes of this book, all this folk-influenced music will be called 'traditional'. They will be differentiated thus from two other musics created in relation to sets of influences: the modern (small-'m'), which was involved with contemporary popular music, and especially American sources; and the Modernist (capital-'M'), which was dominated by the very different notion of tradition as an evolutionary process whose outcome was the atonal or otherwise experimental contemporary music of Europe.

All were part of a developing and living music, not a series of available models taken from the shelf and re-presented. These three forms existed in relation to one another, in an uneasy relationship, even sometimes in the work of individual composers. Even as it came under increasing pressure from the institutional success of Continental Modernism, the traditional style was developed after the Second World War by Michael Tippett and by Benjamin Britten and his associates at Aldeburgh in Suffolk. Neither of these composers fits easily or uncomplicatedly into the generic model proposed above. Each wrote folk-influenced or Tudor-influenced music; in both the influence of certain aspects of European and American Modernism is also apparent, while Britten's music was sometimes inflected by, and Tippett has always been deeply influenced by, African-derived American popular music. Both have been constructed as quintessentially English composers.[45]

They therefore answer the continuing need for internationally successful but identifiably national composers, which was felt in the nineteenth century and which led to the canonisation of Elgar and then Vaughan Williams. On Britten's death in 1977 he was seen as a great British composer, his international success an important symbol of the fact that Britain had indeed played a part in this particular aspect of heritage culture, the European musical tradition. The beginning of this international success, with the acclaim for his opera *Peter Grimes* (1946) came at a very important moment for British culture. As the Labour government, elected at the end of the Second World War in a climate of optimistic hope in renewal, was trying with little success to reconstruct a shattered economy, there was a flourishing of national culture, with enormous pride and interest in sporting and artistic events – including the beginnings of the Edinburgh festival. At one high point, the 1951 Festival of Britain, the newly nationalised Coal Board ran a competition for new folk-songs, and received over 100 entries.[46] *Peter Grimes*, Britten's uncompromising portrait of a man suffering the consequences of his own passion, performed against the judgement of most of the orchestra and chorus,[47] translated him to the status of national composer. Like one of its successors, *Albert Herring* (1947), its Suffolk fishing-village location did not mean a parochial appeal but locked into the folkish nationalism discussed above. The financial success of the project led not only to more operatic commissions, including *Gloriana* (1953) for the coronation of Queen Elizabeth II, but perhaps more importantly to the founding of the festival in Aldeburgh, the town where Britten lived with his partner, the singer Peter Pears. The Aldeburgh festival is one of the first of many small-town provincial festivals which attempt to resolve the central paradox of this particular version of musical Englishness: its portrayal of the rural through the performing forces, concert mechanisms and public of the city. But the resolution is more apparent than real. Ticket prices are high enough to exclude local families, but low enough to entice professional city-dwellers out for the day (or the week); Aldeburgh and places like it become during their festivals centres of a vastly increased, often international, hinterland, while the performers are seldom local and usually metropolitan (for example, Mstislav Rostropovich, for whom Britten wrote several works for the cello, has been a frequent presence). The paradox of the festival in relation to culture, community and place, is explored further in chapter 4.

Again, however, the particular construction of the musical tradition symbolised by Aldeburgh is of creative activity somehow divorced from socio-economic processes – including those of domestic life: this implicitly masculine model of the lonely creator divorced from 'normal' society is perhaps one of the reasons for the importance of gay men in twentieth-century English music; a construction only recently and tentatively explored in music criticism and academic musicology.[48] Aldeburgh itself, a small town on the Suffolk coast, reinforces this sense of divorce from the everyday transactions of life, including the commercial: it is easy enough even now to symbolise this area as separate, because Suffolk is the only county anywhere near London which has not yet been torn apart by motorways. Long may it remain so. Indeed, Britten was insistent that his music was spatially located within this particular landscape, writing in 1964: 'I belong at home – there – in Aldeburgh. I have tried to bring music *to* it in the shape of our local Festival; and all the music I write comes *from* it.'[49] But Britten was no rustic journeyman, for all his Suffolk background. He was a professional composer – by and large, his music was commissioned or it didn't get written. Much of his success was due to the support he received before the Second World War from the BBC, and from the 1950s on from the music publishers Feber and from the Decca record company, two London-based commercial organisations which marketed his work. But there is no place for these economic facts in this version of the theory of national genius.

An English musical 'tradition', then, had been both constructed and confirmed during the twentieth century; and for all the presences within English composed music of American-influenced modernity and European Modernism, this tradition remains an influential way of constructing England and Englishness. Precisely in its appeal to 'tradition' it is a crucial way through which many middle-class people have experienced modernity: the cultural confusion engendered by continuing transformations – of, for example, the steam and internal combustion engines, the chemical industries and microelectronics, with their massive impacts on lives and work experience – are offset by the creation of a past (and to a certain extent, a present) peopled with heroic figures and great works, marshalled as expressing something of deep significance to the imagined continuities of English landscape, country life and patriotism.

These constructions continue; a more recent attempt in this direction shows both the continuing power of the legacy and its limitations.[50] In the summer of 1994 Decca's heavily promoted compilation *The Essential Music of England*[51] spent some time in the Classic FM top 10. At first sight this double CD was like a lot of other Classic FM chart material (CDs which consist of extracts from works, chosen to imply a common mood, rather than complete compositions – other summer 1994 hits included snippet compilations such as *Classic Moods: Passion* and *Classics from the Ads*). But this was more generous both in length and content: the two full-length CDs include several complete works along with the extracts.

The CDs are themed. The second, 'The Pastoral England', reflecting the country cottage on the cover, romps through folk arrangements by Percy Grainger, folk-related orchestral music by Butterworth and Delius, Peter Warlock's exquisite mock-Tudor *Capriol Suite* and Vaughan Williams's *Lark Ascending*, with its violin solo whirling so high that in the end it seems to disappear through the tweeters of the listener's loudspeakers. While the cottagey pastoral is a cliché which (whether in literary, celluloid or musical form) hides the remnants of feudal privilege, subsidised agribusinesses poisoning the land with fertilisers and pesticides, and far too much golf, it still exerts a powerful attraction from the smog-threatened towns and cities in which most people live and work. Because of the power of its alternative vision, this is very much a living tradition, still an important complement to the experience of modernity.

The positive attractions of this vision are, however, sharply con-
tradicted by the other 'essential' CD, themed as 'The spirit of England'. The 'spirit' is patriotism. There are hymns, including Parry's
setting of William Blake's poem 'Jerusalem'; excerpts from a few
orchestral favourites, Gustav Holst's *Planets Suite*, Elgar's *Enigma
Variations* and Britten's *Young Person's Guide to the Orchestra*; and
a complete performance of Elgar's *Cockaigne* overture. The predictable patriotism of ceremonial marches by Elgar and Walton are
compounded by film music (Eric Coates's title theme from *The Dam
Busters*, Henry Alford's title theme to *Bridge over the River Kwai*
and Walton's Agincourt battle sequence from Sir Laurence Olivier's
wartime version of Shakespeare's *Henry V*, complete with the
speech 'Once More Unto the Breach ...'). The final track, introduced by Churchill's 'fight them on the beaches' speech, is Vera
Lynn on the White Cliffs of Dover: for all the folksy music and film
sound-tracks, this is the only bit of immediate popular music on the
album. This stirring stuff commemorates, say the sleeve notes, the
high points of empire and the Second World War. The *Henry V*
extract is glossed thus: 'The year was 1944, and heroism was in the
air, as Britain was about to achieve total victory in the most arduous
war in its history.'

This fantasy (for all Britain's resistance in 1940, the war was
fought and won by an allied group dominated militarily by the USA
and the USSR) would be harmless enough by itself, perhaps. It isn't.
We could go on: 'The story of England is one of regimental honour,
daring exploits on the field of battle and great sacrifice. Thanks to
these things there is such a thing as the English way of life.' Thus
wrote Richard Johnson in the summer 1994 edition of the quarterly
magazine *This England*, a publication perhaps best characterised as a
*Country Life* for the extreme Eurosceptic tendency within English
conservatism. In this issue the D-Day landings were commemorated,
and the belief that the Second World War was won by the British,
with the help of God (in Her usual guise on these occasions as an
English country gentleman), was repeated, with the additional
liturgy, repeated in articles and letters, that this victory will have been
worthless if Britain loses its sovereignty to a Europe demonised as
bureaucratic and socialist. This England is the land of country cottages of the Decca front-cover; it is the land of genteel whiteness fig-
ured early in 1993 in Prime Minister John Major's vision of a
perpetual England of shadows on county cricket grounds, warm beer

and old maids cycling to communion. The journal helps to maintain the regression by running a nice little line in musical souvenirs – not, however, the pastoral or ceremonial marches of Decca's high-culture archive, but nostalgic recordings of dance bands and singers of the 1940s. Many of whom were not Little-English but American, or tried to sound as if they were. Those with recordings on offer include the very American Ink Spots, the only black faces in the magazine.

Musical cultures have a splendid habit of disrupting cultural isolationism in this way. Concert and folk-music are not the only aspects of twentieth-century British music. Official history and popular memory are not the same thing, and the re-creation of popular memory in the name of official history is always fraught with contradictions of this kind. In the end, any version of twentieth-century musical Englishness or Britishness which leaves out the dialogue with American popular music will fail to encompass the place of music in the past. However, the constant reinvention of musical tradition, through sources such as Decca's compilation, continues to offer a positive mode of identity, one celebrated at national and local levels by a bewildering number of music festivals, including that at Aldeburgh.[52]

## British modern/ist music

The other trends within British classical music should now be noted. Firstly, in the inter-war years, there were composers who did use aspects of the international and especially the American popular music scene, notably jazz and related African–American musics. Jazz and ragtime had been incorporated or at least commented on by the music of European composers since the turn of the century. Debussy's piano piece the *Golliwog's Cakewalk* and Stravinsky's *Ragtime* and his dramatic recitation piece *The Soldier's Tale* are well-known early examples of a development which became usual in the years after the First World War as both traditional and Modernist movements ran out of steam.

The First World War is an underexplored, but vitally important, watershed in the narrative of musical development in the twentieth century.[53] For many musicians (and much of the listening public), the evolutionary narrative of European music stopped here, shattered by the experience of trench warfare. Thereafter Elgar, Sibelius and the American Charles Ives virtually stopped composing, Richard Strauss completed his turn from experimentation to richly harmonised nostalgia, Bartok and Stravinsky turned from folkish neo-primitivism and became fascinated by the music of the Baroque and Schoenberg systematised his free-flowing atonal music into the calculated banalities of serialism. Many other European composers turned even further away from the idea of developing or reworking existing European modes of composition and looked instead to the popular music of the Americas in order to revivify what was seen as a dying art, in a continent as psychically disturbed by the excesses of mass trench-warfare murder as it later was by the mass murders of the dictators.

The influence of American music was already present, of course. African–American choirs and vaudeville shows had toured Europe from the middle of the nineteenth century. Negro spirituals and the music of the Native Americans had influenced Dvorak in the 1880s, and both were also forces in the genesis of one of the most popular oratorios in early and mid-twentieth-century England, the black Englishman Samuel Coleridge-Taylor's setting of Longfellow's story of Native America, *Hiawatha's Wedding Feast* (1898). This turn to the new world was commonplace after the war, as it inspired British composers as well as French and Germans. Constant Lambert, whose influential book *Music Ho!*[54] theorised what he saw as the decline of Western music and foresaw the triumph of jazz as the music of the future, turned to American forms for inspiration in his works such as *The Rio Grande* for piano, chorus and orcheatra (1927), the 1929 Piano Sonata and the Concerto for Piano and Nine Players of 1931.[55] Sir William Walton, likewise, used jazz rhythms and instruments as an integral part of his musical language, most notoriously in *Façade* (1922), his piece for reciters and musicians, setting the poetry of the Sitwells; the rhythms of jazz and dance music are never far away in his concerto for viola (1929) and even the oratorio *Belshazzar's Feast* (1931), with its chirpy alto saxophone solos. Similarly, Sir Michael Tippett's oratorio *A Child of Our Time* (1941) used negro spirituals as an equivalent for the chorale in the Bach cantatas, in conveying its pacifist message in time of war. Tippett's music continues to show the clear influence of the blues, jazz and other African–American musics, as his autobiography's title, *Those Twentieth-Century Blues*, indicates.[56] His 1972 third symphony's final movement, for example, juxtaposes blues-influenced songs with a very bluesy solo flugelhorn,[57] while with his opera *The Ice Break* (1976) he attempts to purvey a universalist message through an attempted mesh with the 'rock opera' form.[58]

This cultural hybrid, building on the evolution of 'rock' as the music of a generation for whom the sophisticated harmony but punchless rhythms of classic Broadway musicals were unattractive, emerged in the 1960s with shows like *Hair*, reached its nadir with Leonard Bernstein's *Mass* (1971) and was popularised in England by Andrew Lloyd Webber in shows like *Jesus Christ Superstar* (1970). Again, in *The Ice Break*, Tippett attempted to use African–American forms. Both Tippett and Walton turned to black American music from within the musical languages and forms of the nationalist tradition: the blues and jazz are companions of the choral tradition, the oratorio form and folk and Tudor-influenced melodies and harmonies. There was, then, a populist modernism to complement (rather than replace) the traditional – a populist modernism which had resonances in the work of European composers like Kurt Weill, Paul Hindemith and Ernst Krenek, and Americans like George Gershwin and Aaron Copland, in all of whom a mix of contemporary vernacular voices became part of the composing style. If, then, for the sake of argument, we call the music of Vaughan Williams and the rest 'traditional', that of Walton and Lambert we can call small 'm' 'modern'.

### A British modernist music?

But not, it must be stressed, capital 'M' Modernist. This epithet has to be reserved for a genre which at least on the surface, rejected all dialogue with the vernacular. The second variation on the traditional form was the gradual emergence in England of musical composition in this pan-European style of 'high Modernism', and in order to approach it we must delineate the third moment in the making of classical music in Britain which was noted at the beginning of the chapter: the age of broadcasting.

European Modernism was pioneered in Austria by Arnold Schoenberg, whose mature 'serial' music denied the structural use of narrative tonality, the organising principle of all European music since the eighteenth century. Tonality was based around an artificial division of pitches, arranged to suit the currently accepted configuration of the piano keyboard, tuned in regular intervals known as 'equal temperament': it is an equivalent of the system of perspective in European visual art. Serial music keeps these equal pitch differences, but ignores their accepted relationships, substituting instead a set of mathematical processes. European musical Modernism parallels the rejection of perspective and other realist notions in modernist art, and the similar rejection of realist techniques in modernist writing. Again, there is a military watershed in this breakdown in musical form. Before the Second World War there was very little Modernism in British music: thereafter, this style gradually achieved a kind of hegemony, through the new patronage system of state subsidy, higher education and broadcasting. Music in Britain was back in many ways to the problem faced by Stanford and Parry in the second half of the nineteenth century: given the existence of an ideal of composition overwhelmingly dominated by Continental Europeans, how should music and musicians in England respond? On the whole, they responded as perhaps no other segment of the post-war Establishment did, by becoming wedded to that European model at the expense of both the traditional and the Americanised-modern. The education system, the BBC and the Arts Council combined to valorise this version of the European music tradition, a narrative of 'progress' based upon consequent development through the works of succeeding generations of German and Austrian composers (Bach, Beethoven, Brahms, Schoenberg, Webern, Stockhausen).

The coherence of this Great Tradition of musical composition proved fatally attractive to the meritocrats reordering British society after the Second World War in the spirit of the post-war Labour government, or the Conservative equivalent, the consensual 'one-nation Toryism'. Both political programmes involved a mixed economy aiming to sustain full employment with a large public sector funded through taxation, and included mass education and provision for the arts in this public sector. They were building on a notion of educational value in the reproduction of the national culture which had been developed in the inter-war years both by Leavis and his followers and by the BBC under its first Director-General, Lord Reith.

The BBC, set up in 1922 as a limited company and incorporated by Royal charter (with a monopoly over broadcasting in Britain) in 1927, was always acutely concerned with an educational role. This was, in the arts of music, literature and drama, precisely to lead the public taste, to provide access to work which had been denied the majority of the people and to lead them, through exposure to this work, to richer and more valuable lives: an ideal of social 'progress' which readily adopted the idea of 'progress' in musical history. For Lord Reith, this was the whole point: 'It must not be used for enter-tainment purposes alone.'[59] The music writer Percy Scholes, writing in the *Radio Times*, claimed optimistically in 1923 that thanks to national exposure to BBC broadcasts, 'In five years' time the general musical public of these islands will be treble or quadruple its present size.'[60] While the BBC always broadcast more 'light music' than clas-sical, including regular broadcasts of dance bands from hotels, clas-sical music was consistently seen as an important part of this mission 'to improve'. The Proms concert series, then heading for oblivion, was rescued by the BBC in 1927, and remains among its flagship programming; Covent Garden opera was BBC-subsidised from 1930, to the disgust of the *Daily Express*, which bewailed 'subsidis-ing a form of art which is not characteristic of the British people'.[61] And there was a continuous commitment to musical Modernism. The 1929 BBC handbook proudly proclaimed that space had been left in the broadcasting schedule for chamber music 'of an advanced and difficult order'.[62]

In fact concerts of less advanced orchestral music were more rou-tine (10–15 per cent of the annual output, as against 3–4 per cent of chamber music, in the late 1920s), and in the inter-war years con-certs of European and British music were an important part of the schedule. There was a perceived duty to find and promote the best of British music, which led to systematic discrimination in a medium whose exposure could already by the 1930s make or break careers. The discrimination was justified as a pure meritocracy: the organi-sation decided early on to promote the young Benjamin Britten, for example.[63] Its exclusions, however, seem to indicate that there were other factors at work than any abstract notion of the aesthetic 'suc-cess' or otherwise of compositions as judged by a neutral reading panel. The BBC chose not to push Havergal Brian, a composer with a reputation established in the early years of the century, who was a working-class autodidact from the Potteries, rather than part of the comfortable Oxbridge–Royal College of Music nexus (he was also a temperamental alcoholic, but so was the more middle-class John Ireland, whom the BBC supported);[64] then again, John Foulds was also under-represented, because he had the temerity to write light as well as serious music; as was Christian Darnton, partly because of his socialism. When the piano concerto by communist Alan Bush was performed in 1938, there was an internal debate over the desirability of printing the words sung by the chorus in the final movement; eventually this hymn to the forward march of the people was printed in the BBC's weekly magazine *Radio Times*. After the performance, the conductor Adrian Boult cut short the applause with a political gesture of his own, launching the orchestra straight into the national anthem.[65]

There was a broadening of the concept of mission during the Second World War, as the need for entertainment rather than instruction produced programming ideas such as 'music while you work', a chain of light melodies broadcast without interruption – an equivalent to the government-supported ENSA (Entertainments National Service Association), which organised light entertainment performances for troops and factory-workers. One aspect of the post-war BBC which built on this type of programming was the Light Programme, a radio channel devoted exclusively to light music and comedy (it became Radio Two in 1966). But the mission to improve remained strong, with the drama, poetry and music channel, the Third Programme given a protected, subsidised place in the Corporation's output. As with both public education and the work of the Arts Council, within the outreach to democracy of the consensual vision there was an implicit cultural 'screening', dividing people according to taste and expectation, which was based securely on education-derived class/status. For all the language of democracy, this model quickly achieved the kind of elitist vision for which such Arnoldian versions of education have often been blamed.

F.R. Leavis's contribution to this value system, as regards music at any rate, is tangential, if important. Leavis was a petit-bourgeois fish out of water in the relaxed and gentlemanly atmosphere of inter-war Cambridge; he sought to avenge his deeply felt humiliation of class inadequacy by substituting a strict meritocracy in the field in which he had some kind of expertise, English literature. He argued, like Reith, and as Matthew Arnold had argued before him, that access to the insights contained in the best literary works would, if deeply felt, improve the lives of those reading them. Furthermore, he established (to his own satisfaction, at least) that there had once existed in England a golden age of life and letters, a pre-commercial arcadia in which language and people developed organically. Unsurprisingly he located this arcadia at the same point as many musicians had done since the eighteenth century: in Elizabethan England, precisely when a newly constructed Protestant national culture was in opposition to the dangers of Catholic Spain. The journal run by Leavis and his friends, *Scrutiny*, promoted this idea with intelligence and enthusiasm. It was thus, roughly speaking, on the side of the traditionalist composers – as we have seen in the comments of its principal music writer, composer (and Cambridge English graduate) Wilfrid Mellers. The idea of the organic past was, like much else, damaged by the Second World War, even as the search to regain it became more desperate. The chip on Leavis's shoulder deepened, he became increasingly elitist, and *Scrutiny* itself, with its potential address beyond the ivory tower, seemed anachronistic. It was dropped in 1953. But the notion of an elite, learning refined sensibilities through contact with the best of all possible works, was deepened as the vision became less democratic, and increasingly this vision dominated music education and broadcasting, as it dominated the study of English Literature.[66]

It also dominated the formation and first few decades of the Arts Council of Great Britain, the organisation set up to channel state subsidies for the arts – though the elitism was presented, at first, with a populist face. The Arts Council was one of the post-war initiatives towards a better world which had, like the Beveridge report on the welfare state and the Butler Education Act of 1944, emerged towards the end of the war, from a Committee for the Encouragement of Music and the Arts (CEMA) set up for a similar purpose under the direction of the economist John Maynard Keynes. ENSA, the committee set up to promote light entertainment, was disbanded at the end of the war. CEMA, however, was institutionalised. Keynes was convinced that the educational role of the BBC had proved successful, and that the war had underlined a general public hunger for high art which could and should, under the auspices of this committee, be made as widely available as possible.[67] To this end the general committee of the Arts Council, meeting in London, was soon supplemented by Councils for Scotland and Wales and by local Councils in the English regions, which gave enthusiastic support to the development of programmes for touring musicians.[68] The continuity between Keynes's notion of the role of the arts in society and that of both the Reithian BBC and the vision of

Leavis can be located in one of Keynes's talks, broadcast by the BBC in July 1945:

> The purpose of the Arts Council of Great Britain is to create an environment, to breed a spirit, to cultivate an opinion, to offer a stimulus to such purpose that the artist and the public can each sustain and live on the other in that union which has occasionally existed in the past at the great ages of a communal civilised life.[69]

It is worth underlining the implied difference between 'artist' and 'public' as Keynes saw them: almost from the start, the Arts Council divided those it was trying to bring together (culminating in the subsidy, in 1969, of a piece of performance art by the American Newton Harrison, which consisted of the electrocution of a number of catfish – a show which went on despite massive public hostility).[70] Keynes's talk was delivered when the Council was on the cusp of this dilemma. The CEMA had been set up, with the help of a grant of £25,000 from the American Pilgrim Trust, at a time when the preservation of a national culture was seen as a priority, and its destruction was predicted by the adage 'the bomber will always get through'. Art galleries were dismantled and their paintings and sculptures hidden in remote caves; the recording of rural folk-song entered a final golden age; orchestras left London and rehearsed and performed where, it was felt, the bomber would not wish to get through. CEMA's musical brief had been twofold: to promote and make available, throughout the country, music performed by professionals, *and* to promote and subsidise music-making by amateurs. The Council's attitude to the balance between the metropolis and the regions has continued to shift in emphasis (one report, the 1984 *Glory of the Garden*, proposed a massive devolution to the regions; though this has not happened altogether, in 1993 the Arts Council of Great Britain was renamed the Arts Council of England, and more autonomy was given to the Councils for Scotland and Wales).[71] The amateur, however, has been displaced. Keynes and Glyndebourne Opera founder John Christie combined to undermine the amateur principle. Their stress was on 'excellence', by which they meant things they liked performed by full-time professional performers. Keynes, again: 'We look forward to a time when the theatre and the concert-hall and the gallery will be a living element in everyone's upbringing, and regular attendance at the theatre and concerts a part of organised education.' Though Keynes ended this talk with the stirring evocations: 'Let every part of Merry England be merry in its own way. Death to Hollywood!',[73] the implied division is clear: there will be an educated audience, ready and willing to sit at the feet of professional performers, who will be paid taxpayers' money to do what they and their administrators think best.

The Arts Council has entrenched this vision in its first half-century by, for example, establishing and subsidising professional opera companies in London and Leeds, Wales and Scotland – though Welsh National Opera for its first decade (in the 1950s) operated for a limited annual season, and with an amateur chorus. These are the first such companies to operate in Britain, and they and the big theatre and ballet companies take the majority of the available subsidy. Nevertheless, the Council has maintained and promoted a massive variety of other work, though its attitude to music outside the classical tradition has always been ambivalent. The hierarchy of forms has changed somewhat, with a predictable input of avant-gardism in the 1960s, though it is indicative that Andrew Sinclair's recent official history of the Council contains no index entry for jazz (and indeed hardly any mention of jazz or any other non-classical music in its 400 pages).

The Arts Council and its regional counterparts have for the most part been producerist organisations, maintaining supply with comparatively little concern over demand. Only in the 1980s did the emphasis on education, clearly part of Keynes's agenda, emerge as a priority, as concern over falling audiences reminded the administrators of the need to create an informed public. It was increasingly difficult to apply for grants, let alone win them, without suporting education programmes. In music the example was set by the work of Gillian Moore with the London Sinfonietta, an orchestra which, because it was dedicated to the Modernist tradition and to the avant-garde, was in especial need of saving grace. The Sinfonietta's musicians were to be found working in primary and secondary schools, on short courses and even in prisons, working with contemporary composers and trying to explain their work and working methods.

## Learning to play

So this vision of a Merry England served by the arts was shared by

Reith and his successors at many levels of the BBC, as well as by Leavis and Keynes. It called for a shared culture, but one based on a continuing, and entrenched, division of labour between the artist and the (enlightened) public. Both were to be provided through the education system. The pyramidal structure of music education was based, in this post-1945 settlement, on the teaching of music performance and appreciation to all at junior level. Performance skills were rudimentary: pupils were introduced to simple instruments like the recorder or basic percussion instruments, and were led in mass singing (increasingly, schools also offered specialist instrumental tuition through the skills of 'peripatetic' teachers, retained by local education authorities to visit a number of schools on a weekly basis). Many schools also taught 'country dancing', an important component of the twentieth-century 'folk' revival. In senior schools, however, the skills and techniques of classical music appreciation, performance and composition were taught at a far higher level, but only to those who were judged to display outstanding talent and who would enter state exams in the subject. Popular music was ignored virtually altogether until the 1980s. At the tertiary level, musicians with acceptable school qualifications were taught to perform, or occasionally to compose, in state-funded colleges and universities (1945 saw the first Music Tripos at Cambridge, offering music as a routine part of the B.A. programme as opposed to the Mus.B. or Mus.D.; its equivalent in Oxford was introduced in 1950).[74]

If judged by their elders to be successful, the products of this expensive elitist education graduated to work in a twilight world of state-funded support for concerts of standard repertoire, the mainstay works of the European tradition, and performances and commissions for new compositions (commissions from the new patrons, the central and local Arts Councils, and the BBC itself). The less 'successful', including those less committed to either Modernist or traditional styles, could find more financially rewarding work either as composers or as session musicians in film, radio and television. The unsuccessful, those who had studied music but had been weeded out either at school or college, were constructed as sensitive appreciators of music, much as students of English literature in Leavis's model were constructed as sensitive readers rather than as writers. Many of these became teachers in their turn. Most of their pupils, from whatever class background, were completely untouched by this process, from secondary school onwards: for all Keynes's vision of a downwardly mobile cultural production and appreciation, both the appreciation and especially the performance of classical music remained hedged by semi-permeable boundaries of class, ability and taste. The appreciation, performance and composition of music, indeed the very meaning of the word 'music', thus tended to be very different for the majority of the population than for the minority of trained musicians and appreciators.[75]

However, as this chapter's analytical framework of traditional, modern and Modernist styles indicates, within that minority itself there were serious subdivisions. In particular, between the university-educated composer and the A-level 'appreciator' there arose, from the 1960s on, increasingly bitter differences of emphasis. The general concert-going public was and still is wedded to the heroic, individualist notion of music implicit in the tradition of emotionally engaged virtuoso performance. It was, therefore, at best uninterested in, more often often hostile to, the technically able but (apparently) emotionally arid manipulations of the composers who were given prominence throughout Europe after 1945, Karlheinz Stockhausen, Pierre Boulez and Iannis Xenakis among others. The valorisation of this music by the elite of composers, educators and funders was productive of a crisis within concert music, increasingly apparent from the 1960s on, which has yet to be resolved – though in my final chapter some of the recent potential solutions to this very real problem will be addressed.

It remains surprising, perhaps, that this crisis arose, that at a time of comparative consensus (the 1950s to 1970s), the music of a very few was increasingly imposed on an unwilling many. One reason may be the apparent political cleanliness of this music. For forty years, since the retreat of Schoenberg and his followers into the avowed elitism of a private society for the performance of each others' works (since public performances were often met by riotous disapproval) the products of this avant-garde had remained on the fringes of European music. This meant that, unlike most of the music of the European tradition, they were unsullied with the taints of nationalism and especially Nazism (both Nazi and Communist regimes had in fact proscribed Modernism as against the interests of the people). This may be one reason why the works of the Modernists were embraced by an influential minority as a new, pure, musical language after the Second World War: here, sometimes quite explicitly (as with Krzystof Penderecki's 1960 *Threnody for the Victims of Hiroshima*), was a music which could both transcend and express the horrors and guilt of a world coming to terms with the holocaust and the use of the atomic bomb. Vaughan Williams, for instance, though he continued to write until his death in 1958, and for all his eloquent contribution to this understandable post-war nihilism in the epilogue to his sixth symphony (1948) was considered by the younger generation of composers to be a painfully anachronistic figure. It is one of the pleasanter paradoxes of twentieth-century music in Britain that performance royalty earnings since his death have gone, through the Vaughan Williams Trust, to the performances of new music whose composers would, especially in the 1960s, have had very little time for Vaughan Williams's own music.

Although the European Modernist movement was late arriving in Britain,[76] musical Modernism did eventually become entrenched, and once established, it was hard to shift. The Cheltenham festival, for example, which between the wars had routinely premiered British music of the traditional type, changed at the end of the 1950s into a showcase for Modernism, to the consternation of critics, who claimed after a performance of Peter Maxwell Davies's *St Michael Sonata* that they couldn't tell which notes were right.[77]

The entrenchment of Modernism took place throughout the upper echelons of social organisation. The 1960s expansion of the universities following the Robbins Report on higher education (for music, notably the new universities of Sussex and York and the older university of Leeds) established the teaching of Modernist composition as the curricular norm; and by the late 1960s the apostles of Modernism (for example, the composer Elizabeth Lutyens and BBC Radio Three controller of music William Glock) were in high places in British musical life.[78] Largely university-educated, possessed of the self-confidence of the 'expert', often indeed with contempt for the audience whose tastes they could bypass by means of subsidy from the Arts Council and elsewhere, most of the new composers and administrators were suspicious or frankly contemptuous of the folk-song derived musical nationalism of the previous generation, and many thought of jazz and pop musics in an Adornoesque way as poisonous American mass culture, when they thought of them at all.[79] They were committed instead to the writing of music via the operations of pure mathematics ('total serialism') or chance ('aleatoric music'), and to the development of electronic musics which would liberate them from the traditional musical instruments, as well as the usual rhythms and harmonies, of the music of the West. Glock enthusiastically championed the Modernists, appointing Pierre Boulez to the post of chief conductor of the BBC Symphony Orchestra in 1970 with a brief to perform as much of the New Music as possible. The public remained unconvinced, and often actively hostile. Apart from the BBC Symphony Orchestra, 'New Music' became the preserve of small, specialist performing ensembles (such as the London Sinfonietta), and equally small, specialist audiences. It continued to attract the support of the Arts Council and BBC, whose Radio Three network under Glock and his successors broadcast a great deal of Modernist contemporary music, arguably at the expense of the national music of the 'tradition', certainly to the apoplectic rage of an increasingly vocal group of 'appreciators'.

The publication in 1991 of Glock's autobiography raised the public profile of the 'traditionalist' lobby group. Although he was not the first programme planner more interested in European avant-garde than traditional music (Edward Clarke, chief music programmer from 1930–36, was similar in outlook),[80] he came to power in 1959 after a decade of profound conservatism in music broadcasting presided over by the BBC Symphony Orchestra's chief conductor, Sir Malcolm Sargent – a musician conservative in taste and limited in ability.[81] Glock cheerfully admitted that he had ignored the traditional composers ('It was this middle of the road policy I was determined to undermine'),[82] putting forward the Reithian view that he had given the audience not what they liked but 'what they would like tomorrow'.[83] While debate over these revelations was fresh, the then director of the Proms, Sir John Drummond, repeated this position of contempt for the Radio Three audience in a widely reported after-dinner speech, insulting both the musical taste of his listeners and their ability to write in clear English.[84] The traditionalists, led by conservative anti-Establishment (and anti-Europe) historian Corelli Barnet, argued for the continuity of music with the past, invoking the decisive role of tradition to dismiss Drummond's embrace of the new.

The Barnet conservatives demanded the dismemberment of Radio Three in recompense for Glock and Drummond's confirmation of their prejudices. One government action at the time, arguably a response to this debate, was to sanction the creation of a new national radio station to broadcast 'light' classical music (mainly of *c.* 1700–1850) in assumed opposition to the elitist BBC network. Classic FM duly began to operate in September 1992, and quickly found an audience big enough to please its advertisers, overtaking Radio Three within six months and by early 1994 regularly reaching 4.5 million listeners weekly against Radio Three's 2.75 million. Radio Three's response was to stress its diversity and eclecticism and to rework the channel's output from mid-1992 in what its Controller avowed was a more 'down-market' direction, upsetting many regular listeners by running commuter-hour chat shows, and by making the composer of musicals Stephen Sondheim 'composer of the week' to signal this change; subsequent composers of the week have included Duke Ellington and Jerome Kern.[85] Interestingly, both are American – as Stradling and Hughes have argued, British light music has been consistently marginalised by the postwar musical establishment; jazz, however, has been slightly better treated – it is not inconceivable that British jazz composers such as Mike Westbrook or Mike Gibbs could gain the accolade accorded to Ellington, but unlikely that the British light music composer Ketelby, for example, will follow the American songwriter Kern as composer of the week (though Radio Three did, surprisingly, broadcast a brief tribute to the eclectic musician Vivian Stanshall, founder-member of the Bonzo Dog DooDah Band and best known for his voice-overs on Mike Oldfield's *Tubular Bells*, on the morning after his death in March 1995).

Classic FM's ratings triumph has largely been based on the broadcasting of snippets of compositions: in other words, its DJs introduce single movements rather then whole symphonies or concertos, with a reliance on the more famous composers and a marked absence of the Modernist. The station does play twentieth-century music, some of it 'serious'; indeed Classic FM's greatest coup has merely served to underline the fact that the BBC's programming of Modernism to the exclusion of other genres of twentieth-century composed music has been myopic self-indulgence, contemptuous of its audience. In the summer of 1992 the station began to broadcast movements from a symphony by the then little-known Pole Henryk Gorecki, the 'Symphony of Sorrowful Songs'. This tonal meditation on the Holocaust for soprano voice and orchestra, an hour or more of repetitive, minimalist, utter misery, entered first the station's own classical charts and then the pop charts, and stayed there for three months. In mid-1994 the pop charts saw perhaps their most remarkable entry ever from non-pop, *Canto Gregoriano*, a double CD reissue of Gregorian chant recorded in a monastery in Spain in the 1960s (which again had been widely played by Classic FM), while the Classic FM chart contained *Officium*, a disc on which the early music vocal group the Hilliard Ensemble is accompanied by the improvisations of Norwegian saxophonist Jan Garbarek.[86] The success of Classic FM has proved unsurprisingly that people like the hummable bits of Mozart, but as these examples show, it has proved far more than that; the implications of this shift will be addressed in the concluding chapter.

In the venom of their attacks on Radio Three, on the BBC's Proms concert seasons, and in general against the public subsidy of music they had no wish to hear, the conservative appreciators shared one obsession at least with the former Prime Minister, Margaret Thatcher. They wanted 'the market' to replace the interventionist elitism of monopoly broadcasting and state education, subsidy and control. Certainly Thatcherism's stresses on privatisation and on an imaginary national entrepreneurial spirit (an elision of the commercial with the cultural which was deeply imbedded within the creation of the 'heritage culture' of the 1980s) helped to open the space within which the new musical conservatism could campaign against Modernist music, and for a specifically English classical music, as they saw it (a gap which the routinely Eurocentric Classic FM has not filled). In their attacks the musical conservatives could both call on the 'tradition' as an aspect of Englishness which should be continually available over the airwaves, and point to its recent successes.

The Chandos record company, for instance, was astonished as well as pleased in the early 1980s at the high sales figures for its recordings of symphonies by Sir Arnold Bax, whose music had been virtually ignored by the Glock BBC (and still is, in comparison with the established German symphonists). Sales in the new, highly profitable CD format were particularly impressive, and the Chandos label has since embarked on large-scale projects to record the works of other underexposed English composers, such as Edmund Rubbra. The free market, it seems, had undermined some of the Reithian assumptions – to caricature them, that public education in the 'best' would eventually lead to people merrily humming Stockhausen's greatest hits as they dusted the furniture, or whistling along to Cage's studies for prepared piano as they manoeuvred the Mondeo along the cone-strewn desert of the M25. They did not; but many people came to know and love the music of Bax, even if they could hardly ever hear it on radio or in the concert-hall (and even if they were little Englanders unaware that Bax had been a fervent Irish nationalist, who as well as routinely using Irish folk-music as source material had written both music and poetry to celebrate the Easter Rising of 1916, and whose musical remains are in a memorial library in University College, Cork).

By itself the success of the Chandos catalogue hardly falls within the purview of Thatcherism, at least in its populist sense. For all the exceptions, such as Classic FM's Gorecki, the symphony remains an elitist form. More than this, however, Chandos is a specialist hi-fi label. 'Hi-fi' in Britain is a gendered category; it is and always has been a hobby aimed at middle-class men with sufficient wealth and leisure to search for and purchase equipment delivering the perfect sound. Perfection is usually in this instance considered to be the simulacrum of the voice and/or instruments making the recording (rather than the ability to remix, filter, distort or otherwise process the sound to one's own satisfaction, as with the reggae 'sound system', say). So hi-fi here stands for high fidelity, or 'high faithfulness' to the recorded sound.

The 'authentic' hi-fi amplifier, for example, often has no tone controls or other distortion devices, let alone the graphic equalisers and artificial reverberation programs which litter many expensive Japanese amplifiers. So hi-fi is not just 'stereo equipment'; it is not, usually, a Japanese mass consumer product, but British-, European- or American-designed and hand-built equipment (with prices to match) which falls under the purist's definition. Its setting up and use is addressed principally through magazine reviews which employ the masculine lexicon of technological terms, involving a reified concept of 'performance' in terms of the measurement of frequency range, power output and sound dispersal. However, only in the most directly professional of contexts (for example, *Studio Sound* magazine) does this approach to sound stand alone; in the hi-fi 'audiophile' magazines it is always allied to the reviewer's personal response to the resulting sound: the utilitarian positivism of measurements is qualified by the discourse of pleasure. The Chandos Bax recordings, with their wide dynamic range, were good at

demonstrating hi-fi equipment from both these points of view, as
the discursive constructions of hi-fi man, magazines like *The
Gramophone* and *HiFi News And Record Review*, implied: *The
Gramophone* gave the first of these recordings, of the fourth symphony, an award for sound quality.[87]

Even more commercially impressive during the 1980s was the
revival of interest in opera. Again, CD and video sales rose sharply,
but there was also increasing demand for live performance. From
about 1985, demand for tickets at the Royal Opera House began to
exceed supply for even the most ordinary performances: these tickets were very expensive. Just down the road, English National
Opera was at the peak of its success, with a series of witty, parodic
and, routinely, very camp productions drawing full houses; Opera
North, Scottish Opera and Welsh National Opera had successes to
match. In 1989 promoter Harvey Goldsmith mounted a production
of Bizet's *Carmen* at the vast Earl's Court indoor arena. It made
money, and further stadium promotions of Verdi's *Aida* and Puccini's *Turandot* were planned (to be fair, both made losses, and the
experiment has not been repeated since 1991). Then the BBC chose
as its signature tune for the 1990 football World Cup (held in Italy),
the aria 'Nessun Dorma' from *Turandot*, sung by the Italian tenor
Luciano Pavarotti. A concurrent single release of this rendition
reached no. 2 in the British pop charts; a concert by the three leading tenors Pavarotti, Placido Domingo and José Carreras, broadcast
world-wide live from Rome during the World Cup, realised enormous sales in follow-up recordings, and was repeated in the 1994
World Cup, with another 'Three Tenors' concert held in the USA on
the eve of the tournament's final match. To return to the paradox
opened at the start of the chapter in discussion of the Industrial Revolution: music from within the European tradition was fuelling the
commercial modernity of the global leisure industry.

The 1980s saw a renewed drive to achieve just this, as all the
major record companies with classical recording interests began to
market their products more aggressively and to seek markets
broader than the middle-aged, male, AB hi-fi enthusiast – chain
stores such as Boots, Woolworth and W.H. Smith all set up their
own labels to capitalise on this moment of widening address. This
movement away from the dignity of the middle-aged, implicitly
professional–masculine audience incorporated image-making for
performers, conductors and even composers. Young female per-

formers like the singers Ute Lemper and Cecilia Bartoli and the cellist Ofra Harnoy were photographed as sexualised models; the young(ish) male violinist Nigel Kennedy was remade as a punk(ish) populist, complete with spiked hair and a Cockneyfied accent seen and heard to good effect on one or two television advertisements; his chosen promotions included appearances at football matches. Kennedy's recordings of Vivaldi, Mendelssohn and Brahms concertos entered the pop album charts, despite the snobbish contempt of John Drummond and hostile critics' reviews in the hi-fi magazines and broadsheet papers. An orchestra of young players, the London Chamber Orchestra, even tried to capitalise on Kennedy's success by promoting a series of concerts of classical music, playing routine eighteenth- to twentieth-century repertoire, but using the lights and amplification of the rock concert, promising that the result would be 'seriously loud'. (It wasn't.) There was even, in early 1995, ambivalence about the status of the young violinist Vanessa-Mae, whose first pop single was a Bach arrangement (by career light musician Mike Batt), advertised by photographs of the performer emerging from blue water draped in a translucent wet dress: was she a pop star or a classical musician – and if the latter, was she any good? (The debate continued to surround her during early 1997 as she set off on a 'Classical Tour'.) The Great Musical Tradition, so deliberately uncommercial in the hands of the BBC, the Arts Council and the Aldeburgh myth, was itself being used iconoclastically, against its elitist appropriation and for mass sales, in a way which Walter Benjamin would no doubt have noticed with satisfaction.[88] While sales of classical CDs and opera tickets nosedived during the 1990s recession, aggressive marketing and the success of Classic FM have remained. This has meant, among other things, the establishing of a classical music chart, usually dominated by mood-music collections such as *Classics for Lovers*, *Classics from the Films*, *Turbo Classics* (for driving) and so on, rather than complete works.[89] There is no going back to the boundaries either of teleologicised Modernism or pre-Modernist bourgeois concert music, whether 'essentially English' or European.

There is another reason why neither of these solutions is operable: one of the reasons, indeed, for the success of Classic FM, a pop station whose DJs play classical snippets. Thanks in large measure to the economic and institutional success of British popular music and the continuing transformations operated in the field of popular music since the 1960s, classical music has been joined in the affections of the middle-class public on which it was centred in the mid-twentieth century by a widening variety of musical forms. Because of this, the boundaries of taste so painstakingly built since the 1930s by the forces of education, broadcasting and arts subsidy can no longer stand. This narrative must now be interrupted, as the narrative of British musical development itself was interrupted, by consideration of the greatest international success story of twentieth-century British music.

## Notes

1   See J. Barrell, *English Literature in History 1730–80: an Equal Wide Survey*, Manchester, Manchester University Press, 1983.
2   The emphasis is that of Marshall Berman; see his *All that is Solid Melts into Air*, Verso, 1983.
3   W. Weber, *The Rise of Musical Classics in Eighteenth-Century England: a Study in Canon, Ritual and Ideology*, Oxford, Oxford University Press, 1992.
4   T. Eagleton, *The Function of Criticism*, Verso, 1984, p.10.
5   For aspects of the argument over taste and commodification see N. McKendrick, J. Brewer and J. Plumb, *The Birth of a Consumer Society: the Commercialization of Eighteenth-Century England*; and L. Colley, *Britons: Forging the Nation 1707–1837*, Yale University Press, 1992; especially the fourth chapter discussing the Wilkes campaigns.
6   E. Burke, *Reflections on the Revolution in France* [1792], Harmondsworth, Penguin, 1988.
7   Weber, *The Rise of Musical Classics,* pp. 126–40.
8   *Ibid.*, p. 224.
9   E.T. Harris, 'Handel's Ghost: the Composer's Posthumous Reputation in the Eighteenth Century', in J. Paynter, T. Howell, R. Orton and P. Seymour, eds, *Routledge Companion to Contemporary Musical Thought*, Routledge, 1992, vol. 1, p. 218.
10  S. McVeigh, *Concert Life in London from Mozart to Haydn*, Cambridge, Cambridge University Press, 1993.
11  R. Leppert, *Music and Image: Domesticity, Ideology and Socio-Cultural Formation in Eighteenth-Century England*, Cambridge, Cambridge University Press, 1988.
12  *Ibid.*, p. 12.
13  *Ibid.*, p. 22.
14  See F.M.L. Thompson, *The Rise of Respectable Society*, Fontana, 1988.
15  C.S. Nicholls, ed., *The Dictionary of National Biography Missing Per-*

*sons*, Oxford, Oxford University Press, 1993.

16  See C.L.R. James, *Beyond a Boundary*, Stanley Paul, 1963; M. Down, *Archie: a Biography of A.C. MacLaren*, George Allen and Unwin, 1981; C.B. Fry, *Life Worth Living*, Pavilion Books, 1986.

17  Ehrlich, *The Musical Profession in Britain since the Eighteenth Century*, Oxford, Oxford University Press, 1995, pp. 8–9; Leppert, *Music and Image*, p. 62.

18  Weber, *The Rise of Musical Classics*, p. 41; see also Ehrlich, *The Musical Profession in Britain*, pp. 7, 14.

19  Weber, *The Rise of Musical Classics*, p. 7; M. Trend, *The Music Makers: Heirs and Rebels of the English Musical Renaissance*, Weidenfeld and Nicolson, 1985, p. 4.

20  Ehrlich, *The Musical Profession in Britain*, pp. 11–14.

21  A.V. Beedell, *The Decline of the English Musician 1788–1888*, Oxford, Oxford University Press, 1992.

22  E. Newman, *Wagner: a Biography*, Cambridge, Cambridge University Press, 1978, vol. 1, chapter 3. Eighteenth-century British musicians are known to have been improvisers; see R. Nettel, *A Social History of Traditional Song*, Adams & Dart, 1969, p. 105.

23  Compare the implicitly carping view of this Germanisation taken by R. Stradling and M. Hughes in their *The English Musical Renaissance 1860–1940: Construction and Deconstruction*, Routledge, 1993.

24  Ehrlich, *The Musical Profession in Britain*, p. 108.

25  For the city and the new concert publics see W. Weber, *Music and the Middle Class*, Croom Helm, 1975.

26  R. Sennett, *The Fall of Public Man*, Faber, 1986, pp. 200–5; compare R. Walser, *Running with the Devil: Power, Gender and Madness in Heavy Metal Music*, Hanover, New England, Wesleyan University Press, 1991, an exploration of the very similar construction of demonic performers in heavy metal.

27  See P. Bailey, *Leisure and Class in Victorian England*, Routledge Kegan Paul, 1978; H. Cunningham, *Leisure in the Industrial Revolution 1780–1880*, Croom Helm, 1980; H. Meller, *Leisure and the Changing City*, Routledge Kegan Paul, 1976; more concisely, D. Cannadine, 'The Theory and Practice of the Victorian Leisure Class', *The Historical Journal*, vol. 21, no. 2, 1978, pp. 445–67; Thompson, *The Rise of Respectable Society*, pp. 303–5; W. Mellers, *Vaughan Williams and the Vision of Albion*, Barrie and Jenkins, 1989, pp. 4–6.

28  McVeigh, *Concert Life*, p. 21.

29  See E. Hobsbawm and T. Ranger, eds, *The Invention of Tradition*, Cambridge, Cambridge University Press, 1982; R. Colls and P. Dodd, *Englishness: Politics and Culture 1880–1914*, Croom Helm, 1986; R. Porter, ed., *Myths of the English*, Cambridge, Polity Press, 1992.

30  There were two books of this title before the Stradling and Hughes volume referred to above: F. Howes, *The English Musical Renaissance*, Secker & Warburg, 1966; P. Pirie, *The English Musical Renaissance*, Gollancz, 1979.

31  See Stradling and Hughes, *The English Musical Renaissance 1860–1940*, pp.186–9.

32  R. Nettel, *Music in the Five Towns 1840–1914*, Oxford, Oxford University Press, 1944, pp. 87, 92.

33  Elgar and Acworth, *Caractacus*, full score, Novello, 1905, p. v.

34  M. Kennedy, programme notes to the recording of Elgar's *Caractacus*, Chandos CHAN 9156/7, Colchester, Chandos, 1993, p. 6.

35  H.A. Acworth, *Caractacus* booklet, pp. 22–4.

36  See M. Hurd, *Rutland Boughton and the Glastonbury Festivals*, Oxford, Oxford University Press, 1993.

37  *Ibid.*, pp. 193–4, 234.

38  The relationship continues. In October 1995 the *BBC Music Magazine* included a cover CD of extracts from two incomplete Elgar works – the opera *The Spanish Lady*, and that third symphony. Some reason for the special place of the Europeanised Elgar in a BBC dominated since the 1960s by Continental Modernism can be found in publisher and critic Donald Mitchell's essays on Elgar in his collected essays *Cradles of the New*, Faber, 1995.

39  See C. Sharp, *English Folk Song: Some Conclusions*, Taunton, Barnicott and Pearce, 1907; commentaries are provided in D. Harker, *Fakesong: the Manufacture of British 'Folksong' from 1700 to the Present Day*, Milton Keynes, Open University Press, 1990; and G. Boyes, *The Imagined Village: Culture, Ideology and the English Folk Revival*, Manchester, Manchester University Press, 1993.

40  A. Blake, *Reading Victorian Fiction*, Macmillan, 1989, pp. 140–4, attempts to synthesise an argument around this seeming paradox. Compare P. Anderson, 'Components of the National Culture', *New Left Review*, no. 23, January/February 1964; and M. Wiener, *English Culture and the Decline of the Industrial Spirit*, Cambridge, Cambridge University Press, 1982.

41  For *Scrutiny* and its influence see W. Mellers, *Vaughan Williams and the Vision of Albion*, Barrie and Jenkins, 1989, pp. 24–30; D. Laing, 'Scrutiny to Subcultures: Notes on Literary Criticism and Popular Music', *Popular Music*, vol. 13, no. 23, January/February 1994, pp. 209–22; in general the authoritative account remains F. Mulhern, *The Moment of Scrutiny*, New Left Books, 1979.

42  See the discussion in A. Durant, *Conditions of Music*, Macmillan, 1984, chapter 4.

43  Howes, *The English Musical Renaissance*, p. 319, discusses the 'phan-

tasy' genre used in the chamber music of Britten, Ireland, Bridge and Bush as a specifically English form.

44  A. Blake, 'T.H. White, Arnold Bax and the Alternative History of Britain', in D. Littlewood and P. Stockwood, eds, *Impossibility Fiction*, Amsterdam, Rodopi International, 1996, pp. 25–36.

45  See W. Mellers, *Music and Society*, 2nd edn, Dennis Dobson, 1950, on Tippett, p. 175, and on the more 'European' Britten, pp. 179–82. It should be noted that in mid-1996 a decision by the town council of Aldeburgh not to place a statue of Britten in the town square led to a show of hostility during which the current Master of the Queen's Music, the Australian Malcolm Williamson, claimed that Britten's music was ephemeral. See *The Independent*, 24 July 1996.

46  E. Lee, *Music of the People: a Study of Popular Music in Great Britain*, Barrie and Jenkins, 1970, p. 124.

47  H. Carpenter, *Benjamin Britten*, Faber, 1992, pp. 215, 219, 224.

48  Carpenter's *Benjamin Britten* is a serious biography; on Britten see also D. Mitchell, *Cradles of the New*, Faber, 1995, p. 311; and P. Brett, ed., *Benjamin Britten: Peter Grimes*, Cambridge, Cambridge University Press, 1983, pp. 180–96. More generally B. Hadleigh, *The Vinyl Closet: Gays in the Music World*, San Diego, Los Hombres Press, 1991 and J. Gill, *Queer Noises*, Cassell, 1995, are gossipy, though the latter makes interesting generic connections; more scholarly work is in C.K. Crechmair and A. Doty, eds, *Out in Culture*, Cassell, 1995 which has a section on popular music, while P. Buett, E. Wood and G.C. Thomas, eds, *Queering the Pitch: the New Gay and Lesbian Musicology*, Routledge 1994, addresses more orthodox musicological concerns. The domestic ideology has also marginalised women's compositional skills: see Leppert, *Music and Image* and D. Hyde, *New Found Voices: Women in Nineteenth-Century English Music*, Canterbury, Tritone Music Publishers, 1991.

49  Trend, *The Music Makers: Heirs and Rebels of the English Musical Renaissance*, Weidenfeld and Nicolson, 1985, p. 235.

50  This section is based on A. Blake, 'Village Green, Urban Jungle', *New Statesman and Society*, 12 August 1994.

51  Decca 443 936–2.

52  See my discussion in chapter 4 and B. Appleyard, *The Culture Club: Crisis in the Arts*, Faber, 1984, p. 97.

53  Pirie, *The English Musical Renaissance*, p. 76, makes a similar argument.

54  C. Lambert, *Music Ho! A Study of Music in Decline*, Faber and Faber, 1934.

55  For Lambert's life and work see A. Motion, *The Lamberts*, Faber, 1986.

56   M. Tippett, *Those Twentieth-Century Blues*, Hutchinson, 1991.

57   Mellers, in *Vaughan Williams*, p. 236, suggests that the flugelhorn in
     Vaughan Williams's ninth symphony of 1957 (supported by three sax-
     ophones) may be an echo of Miles Davis's then-new 'cool' style.

58   Tippett's earlier set of writings on music, *Moving Into Aquarius*, first
     published in 1959, was reprinted by Paladin in 1974 to mark this
     moment.

59   A. Briggs, *A History of Broadcasting in the United Kingdom*, Oxford,
     Oxford University Press, 1965, reprinted 1995, vol. 1, p. 306.

60   *Ibid.*, vol. 1, p. 13.

61   *Ibid.*, vol 2, p. 167. The *Daily Express* echoes the opinions of *The
     Quarterly Review* of 1823; see Beedell, *The Decline of the English
     Musician*, p. 113. Subsidy of opera remains the most controversial sup-
     port of music: compare the newspapers' reaction to the news in 1995
     that Covent Garden had been awarded £55 million from the National
     Lottery.

62   Briggs, *A History of Broadcasting*, vol. 2, p. 34.

63   Carpenter, *Benjamin Britten*, p. 48.

64   Compare the BBC's treatment of the eccentric but tonal composers
     Robert Simpson and Andrew Lloyd Webber senior.

65   L. Foreman, ed., *From Parry to Britten: British Music in Letters,
     1900–1945*, B.T. Batsford, 1987, p. 154. Alan Bush's opera *Wat Tyler*
     won a prize at the 1951 Festival of Britain – but no one in Britain
     staged it; see Trend, *The Music Makers*, p. 209. Bush's musical politics
     can be gauged from his article 'Soviet Music in War-Time', *Penguin
     Music Magazine*, vol. 1, no. 1, 1946, pp. 35–40.

66   The broadcaster Donald Mitchell quotes Leavis in a 1955 essay, 'A
     State of Emergency', reprinted in his *Cradles of the New*, Faber, 1995,
     pp. 3–13.

67   Keynes and his committee did not manufacture this hunger for music.
     Compare the attitude of populist desire for classical music displayed in
     the *Penguin Music Magazine*, which first appeared in 1946.

68   R.F. Harrod, *The Life of John Maynard Keynes* [1951], Har-
     mondsworth, Penguin, 1972, pp. 613–19.

69   *Ibid.*, p. 619.

70   A. Sinclair, *Arts and Cultures: the History of the Fifty Years of the Arts
     Council of Great Britain*, Sinclair-Stevenson, 1995, p. 160.

71   *The Glory of the Garden*, Arts Council of Great Britain, 1984.

72   Sinclair, *Arts and Cultures*, pp. 46–7.

73   *Ibid.*, p. 47.

74   Howes, *The English Musical Renaissance*, pp. 287–8.

75   There is no space here to deal with the modes of listening wich were
     ranged against the official model of 'appreciation'. See L. Green, *Music*

on *Deaf Ears: Music, Meaning and Ideology in Education*, Manchester, Manchester University Press, 1988; J. Shepherd, *Music as Social Text*, Cambridge, Polity Press, 1991; K. Swanwick, *Music, Mind and Education*, Routledge, 1988; A. Peacock and R. Weir, *The Composer in the Market-Place*, Faber, 1975.

76  Anderson, 'Components of the National Culture', is useful on the conservative nature of inter-war immigration; conservatism in literature is ably explored in A. Light, *Forever England: Femininity, Literature and Conservatism between the Wars*, Routledge, 1991.

77  Pirie, *The English Musical Renaissance*, p. 182.

78  For Lutyens's life and work see M. and S. Harries, *A Pilgrim Soul*, Faber, 1989. For Glock, see his *Notes in Advance*, Oxford, Oxford University Press, 1991.

79  The twenty composers interviewed by Paul Griffiths for his *New Sounds, New personalities: New Music of the 1980s*, Faber, 1985, mention popular music precisely once. For Adorno's views (discussed here in chapter 3), see, for example, 'On Popular Music', *Studies in Philosophy and Social Sciences*, vol. 9, 1941, pp. 17–48, and 'Perennial Fashion: Jazz', in his *Prisms*, New Left Books, 1967, pp. 119–32. Adorno's views are sympathetically interrogated in R. Middleton, *Studying Popular Music*, Milton Keynes, Open University Press, 1987, and P. Martin, *Sounds and Society: a Sociology of Music*, Manchester, Manchester University Press, 1995.

80  Briggs, *A History of Broadcasting*, vol. 2, p. 160.

81  *Ibid.*, vol. 4, p. 670.

82  Glock, *Notes in Advance*, p. 58.

83  *Ibid.*; see also pp. 26, 35, 45, 49, 59, 197.

84  See reports and letters in *The Independent* of the 10, 11, 12, 14, 15 and 16 June 1991.

85  Nicholas Kenyon, interviewed in the *Radio Times*, 4–10 July 1992. See also A. Blake, 'Summer's Lists', *New Statesman and Society*, 7 June 1994.

86  Jan Garbarek and the Hilliard Ensemble, *Officium*, ECM New Series CD 1525 445 369–2.

87  L. Foreman, *Bax: a Composer and His Times*, 2nd edn, Aldershot, Scolar Press, 1988, p. 376. The recording had sold 10,000 copies *before* the award.

88  Benjamin's work is discussed in chapter 3.

89  One such, *Karajan Adagio*, was followed by its label Deutsche Grammophon's attempt to cash in by releasing a disc of Mahler slow movements conducted by Claudio Abbado. The conductor refused to sanction what would have been a money-spinner, on the principle that people should listen to complete works, not what they liked.

2

# A story of British pop

The high moment of nationalist music-making and the establishing of the great classical music tradition with its implicitly anti-commercial ideology had already been subverted well before the 'entrepreneurial revolution' of the 1980s, not only by the institutional success of subsidised Modernist composition, but also by two other, related aspects of British musical life: by the enormous international commercial success of British pop music since the early 1960s and by the arrival in Britain since 1945 of musicians and musics from the former colonial and imperial territories. Both aspects involve moments of cultural miscegenation which have been massively productive for the development of music in Britain; both also involve continued negotiation with American culture, negotiation of the type which had produced the modernism of Lambert, Walton and others, and had also produced a large part of the English light music scene in the inter-war period.

**Popular music before the 1960s**

The primary purpose of this chapter is to discuss British pop and related musics since the 1960s. As with chapter 1, it will not be a straightforward narrative of successive musical styles and performers. But since it is an important part of the book's argument that while late twentieth-century popular musics were connected to previous musical cultures, the emergence of 1960s British pop constitutes a very important shift, I shall first sketch hinterland of these moments, in order to clarify subsequent continuities and discontinuities.

While aspects of the story of British popular music are relatively

well known, much of the history of light entertainment and mid-
dlebrow music is buried deep. To pursue the analogy, further work
on the archaeology of popular music is needed before the history
can be told. People will have to dig through a good many layers of
American forms to get to it. Most writing about popular music in
the twentieth century merely adds to the detritus. Tony Palmer's *All
You Need is Love* (1976), a book-companion to his television documentary series, opens with the phrase 'Popular music is a paradigm
of American culture';[1] the rest of the book follows this predeter-
mined path, with the occasional glance at British popular music traditions. At a more scholarly level, Edward Lee's *Music of the People*
(1970) reviews British popular music from the Anglo-Saxons
onwards; but as soon as the story reaches the twentieth century,
Lee's attention is diverted to American popular music. He
announces calmly at one point: 'I have not ... mentioned the quite
remarkable popularity of Billy Cotton, whose music ... was the very
antithesis of that of Frankie Lane or Elvis Presley ... the manifesta-
tion of the interests of an older generation'.[2] The reasons for this
ageist stance are left to the reader's imagination. Equally representative of the problems here is a more recent narrative, Donald
Clarke's *The Rise and Fall of Popular Music*.[3] This promises a thesis-
driven history of Anglo-American popular music in the twentieth
century (the 'fall' being a decline in songwriting standards). Instead,
a brief history of Anglo-American and Euro-American musical interaction up to *c.* 1900 is followed by an orthodox trace through the
history of American popular music and jazz, until the narrative
reaches the 1960s – when the international success of British pop
makes an America-centred history impossible, and we return to
interaction. British music and musicians are mentioned before this
point; but there is no narrative, let alone analysis, of popular music
in twentieth-century Britain before rock'n'roll – and hardly a mention of music from elsewhere in the world.

I suspect that an account which left Billy Cotton in the story
would change our view of popular music, that it would necessarily
offer a different perspective. The nearest we have to this can be
found, again through archaeological work, in the reference books
which, it seems, every publisher wishes to disgorge. The *Guinness
Book of British Hit Singles* and its companion volumes in the *Guinness Encyclopaedia of Popular Music* series, the Faber, Oxford and
Penguin Companions/Encyclopaedias of/to Popular Music and var-

ious anthologies of criticism published over the last decade all provide information useful for the archaeologist.[4] But perhaps the most important of these for the purpose of reconstructing the story of popular music is the shortest, the directory edited by the radio journalist Sheila Tracy, sometime trombonist in Ivy Benson's All-Girl Orchestra[5] and subsequently presenter of a BBC Radio Two series on big band music. Tracy's collection, *Who's Who in Popular Music*, published in 1984, consists of reports on questionnaire returns from a wide cross-section of light music, mainstream pop and jazz singers and instrumentalists, held together with the writer's anecdotes. A story of post-war popular music based on its material would depart radically from the pop-driven orthodoxy: Light Programme/Radio Two staples such as 'Music while you Work' and 'Sing Something Simple' are mentioned here as often as 'Top of the Pops'. Tracy argues her criteria for inclusion thus:

> The Concise Oxford Dictionary defines popular music as: 'songs, folk tunes, etc., not seeking to appeal to refined or classical taste'. Another way of saying music for the unrefined masses! But even we in the masses have our likes and dislikes. Some people are into pop, others into jazz, the majority, I would suspect, wander along whistling a happy tune somewhere between the two. That is what is known as MOR, middle of the road. I've tried to cater for all three of these categories. Not all the people in this book are stars, but all of them play an important role in the overall British music scene, in the recording and television studios, on radio and the musical stage.[6]

This is a very different popular music from the Dark Stuff of rock romanticism. While there is a very important story of, precisely, the musically independent youth culture of the 1960s and its continuing development and fragmentation, one of the main reasons for the romantic emphasis is the attempted homology between music, youth and subculture which has characterised so much of the sociology of popular music. This leaves out a great deal of music which was not ostentatiously youthful or 'radical'. In the absence of a detailed archaeology of knowledge, however, this account will dig as it may, then proceed towards that moment, celebrated in the orthodox accounts of pop, of British international success.

## Popular music before pop

As with the classical concert scene, the parameters within which popular music was created were altered by industrialism and urbanism. But these changes did not produce a simple division between a high bourgeois/aristocratic, and a low working-class culture. British popular music from the nineteenth century onwards operated within a very wide repertoire, an admixture of religious and classical music, opera and operetta, and song and dance musics from both folkish–oral and urban–commercial milieux. Amateur and semi-professional musicians played and sang in brass bands, orchestras and choirs. In all, the best of these groups competed at national level for prizes, and while the *repertoire* may have been mainstream classics by Mendelssohn or Verdi, the music contest as a *popular ritual* was as much a centre for competitive working-class masculinity as professional sport; the behaviour of participants and crowds alike was often rowdily assertive.[7] Public participation in these forms of music rose throughout the century, and was very widespread at its end – just as the new machinery for non-participatory reproduction (player-pianos and gramophones) appeared. However, despite the triumph of machine-made, disembodied sound, local participatory music-making remains widespread; amateur performances of Handel's *Messiah*, or the Gilbert and Sullivan operettas, are still routine occurrences throughout Britain, as are amateur folk evenings and gigs by semi-professional rock bands.[8]

Any version of the story of British popular music as an adjunct of American music necessarily sweeps much of this mixed repertoire, and the scale of democratic participation in performance, under the table. But even though this chapter concentrates on pop, the Anglo-American angle is not the only one. While British popular music has never been completely isolated – its connections with American forms beginning, of course, with the settlement of British people in the Americas from the sixteenth century, which exported hymns and psalms, and the interest being returned with the first visits to Britain of black entertainers in the middle of the nineteenth century, and continuing thereafter[9] – there are several indigenous forms which have influenced its subsequent development in parallel with the Anglo-American story. Music-hall is arguably the most important of these forms, partly because almost all popular music is (however reluctantly) perforce part of the music business, and music-hall always involved the relation between capital and melody which has been taken for granted in most pop. Since it involves a tradition of songwriting and performing which can be traced through bands like the Beatles, the Small Faces and the Kinks in the 1960s, the pantomimic camp of Roxy Music and David Bowie in the 1970s, the witty stories of Squeeze and lovable cockneys Chas'n'Dave in the early 1980s to their very aware inheritors like Pulp and Blur in the 1990s, the music-hall tradition remains important.[10]

Music-hall was one aspect of the popular culture of urban industrialism;[11] Britain was the first country to industrialise and urbanise. However, in some eyes it is not a pure popular culture, and it is certainly not in any simple way working-class culture, since music-halls *were* commercial, and some of the leading performers, and much of its audience, were middle-class (as are Blur).[12] Where the public house had always been a centre for public entertainment, and where that entertainment had often involved singing, including the interaction of the audience with the leading singer, this had not always been run along commercial lines – many folk-clubs today involve similar musical relationships and are similarly unconcerned with profit. No doubt the early generations of the industrial urban poor brought their songs, and their traditions of songwriting, with them from the villages and into the cities.[13] Yet already by the 1840s this informal musical culture was being complemented, if not entirely replaced, by a circuit of semi- or fully professional entertainers. Thereafter, first publicans and breweries built and furnished specific rooms in pubs, which quickly became known generically as music-halls; and by the end of the century they were being built as large stand-alone theatres – such as the 3,000-seater Colosseum in London, currently home to English National Opera. By this time the professional circuit was established, with comedians and magicians as well as singers and novelty instrumentalists. Many of the entertainers received star status within their communities, a few (such as Marie Lloyd and Charles Lauder, who were popular tourists in the USA, and of course Charlie Chaplin, who built a career there) elsewhere as well. By the turn of the century there were music-halls in most large towns and cities, and the shows had audiences across the class spectrum – a point dramatically confirmed by the presence since 1912 of the Royal Variety Command Performance, in which light entertainers perform before the monarch or other leading members of the royal family.[14]

Music-hall artists were important in the early history of the recording industry in Britain, while for all Reith's ambitions, radio always had a strong element of 'light entertainment'; indeed, music-hall entertainers such as Flanagan and Allen (who first performed on BBC radio in 1932)[15] and then Morecambe and Wise (whose television career spanned the 1960s and 1970s) stretched aspects of the format into the second half of the twentieth century. There are specific local continuities and developments here, for example in staged variety entertainment by and for East Londoners, from the beginnings in the 1840s through the mid-twentieth-century heyday of Flanagan and Allen, the 1950s moment of transition when pop acts often appeared as part of variety bills, to the 291 Club, an all-black variety show which was held at the Hackney Empire (and televised from there) in 1991. This theatre was built specifically for music-hall in 1901, and also hosts regular Old Time Music-Hall shows aimed at older people. Similarly, at the time of writing the borough of Redbridge and the London Boroughs Grants Committee support the work of Gilt and Gaslight, a company which provides music-hall-style entertainment for people in residential and day centres for the elderly, and which works all over East London. Even in its most traditional forms, music-hall is not dead.[16]

Partly through the related development of the American vaudeville theatre, connection can also be made between aspects of music-hall and the musical theatre of the 1920s and thereafter. Here too there is an indigenous form of 'musical comedy',[17] including shows by Vivian Ellis and Noel Coward. One of the best known of these, Coward's *Bittersweet* (1929), was a response to, in his words, 'the endless succession of slick American Vo-do-deo-do musical farces in which the speed was fast, the invention complicated, and the sentimental value negligible'[18] – such as Jerome Kern's 1928 success *Showboat*. This tone of anxious isolationism was common among British musicians wishing to promote their own goods in a market constantly threatened by American imports. Well into the 1950s the Songwriters' Guild of Great Britain was pressing the BBC to play a part in 'the creation of a specifically British culture in the realm of the song'.[19] There is an important analytical category here, but it is not easily isolatable. Coward's elegant songs and scores, whatever they owe to the music-hall or musical comedy traditions, can also be displayed under the 'specifically British' and very catch-all banner of 'light music'.

Light music's connection with the lineages of music-hall and musical comedy is clear. Equally clear is the connection with classical music, one of whose branches is labelled 'light classical' – this is arguably what was produced in nineteenth-century programmes by choirs and brass bands and in the 1990s is produced by the Classic FM radio station. (However, the light/serious border was unpoliced until the mid-twentieth century: there is a strong working-class amateur connection with the English Musical Renaissance, with composers such as Holst and Elgar writing for both bands and choirs).[20] At the end of the nineteenth century the informal Promenade Concerts began, in an attempt to keep concert-halls and orchestras in use during the summer – 'Promenade' shortened to 'Proms', the idea being that people could walk, talk and smoke around the venue, rather than sit and listen in silence, in the heat of the July evening: a nice idea which would be frowned on at present. In their early years the Proms were 'light classical', mixing movements from repertoire classics with arias from operas or operettas and ubiquitous novelty items, including an import from the brass-band contest, the cornet solo. Many of the musicians who played in, arranged and conducted, and wrote for the music-hall were products of the music colleges; many were also involved with other aspects of light music in its various guises. In part, then, as with the pre-BBC Proms, the definition of light music has to encompass music for active use, rather than for passive listening – and especially for dancing: from the tea-dance trio to the frozen 1950s sound of the Latin-American big bands which still at the time of writing perform for the televised contest *Come Dancing*.

A close definition of 'light music' may be impossible, but specific examples are available. Albert Ketelbey deserves particular mention, if only because his reputation has survived in the particularly annoying form of a 'cult following' which almost everybody seems to be part of. Ketelbey was born in Birmingham in 1875, studied at Trinity College of Music, London, and after a brief career as a (classical) piano soloist worked in music-hall and comedy theatre as a conductor, then composer and arranger. While in his thirties, he achieved great success with a string of melodic pieces written to fit on one side of a 10 inch 78 r.p.m. record – in other words, about four minutes long. Typical titles are 'In a Persian Market' (the Orientalist imagery being a constant theme), ''Appy 'Ampstead', and 'Bells across the Meadows'. The coincidence of his fluent writing

prime and the heyday of silent film allowed his music, either written for particular films or as music for general use in love scenes,
crowd scenes, chases and so on, to become part of the general musical background of his time, and he became very wealthy. In his early
forties, in fact, he decided that he had enough money to retire, and
retire he did, spectacularly and absolutely, to the Isle of Wight, from
which he rarely ventured until his death in 1959.

For all the lyrical inventiveness of his melodies, then, there is
nothing in Ketelbey's career of which the Romantic Artist can be
made. He wrote music for money, and when he had made enough,
he stopped. He was not the only one: Charles Coborn, a music-hall
songwriter, described himself as 'a tradesman supplying a public
want'.[21] Elgar's career could be described in this way (he too wrote
to commission, made enough money, then stopped), but it is crucial
to his reputation that it is not. An impersonal, functional attitude to
'work' is part of the definition 'light music' and light-music composer. It is usually seen negatively – one reason for its having been
hidden from history. Like middle-of-the-road commercial pop, light
music, whatever its contemporary impact, has been denigrated in a
culture which continues to value the romantic or demonic in both
performer and composer. This remains a problem for those committed to the preservation or furtherance of music which has been
categorised as 'light' – as Joseph Lanza has recently argued in his
iconoclastic defence of 'elevator music' (which tries to reverse this
tendency by comparing its everyday noise to the avant gardism of
the Italian Futurists).[22] Nevertheless, in Britain the notion of light
music *has* been preserved, and its health is currently assured.

This preservation, and much of the categorisation, started in the
Light Programme of the post-war BBC, building on the success of
the wartime broadcasts for the forces or for factory-workers, programmes such as *Music While You Work*. Radio exposure was
important in the maintenance of a light-music audience. Where
Keynes, trying to establish the Arts Council at the end of the war,
took it for granted that broadcasts and concerts given during the
war had increased popular exposure and response to classical music
(and the evidence is that more people did listen to classical concerts),[23] in fact the proportion of light music (and other light entertainment such as comedy) broadcast on radio had increased.[24] As I
pointed out in chapter 1, the most common positive identification
of British music with wartime is around figures like Vera Lynn, with

dance music and other American-influenced forms. There was, then, a thriving musical Light Britain. One exasperated German commentator wrote in 1942 that 'London goes on with its radio programmes as if nothing had happened ... reports from a cricket match, nice and clever people make their talks, there is more dance music than ever before.'[25]

While claims that the BBC's output was transformed in the direction of light entertainment during the war have been somewhat exaggerated, the proportion of light and dance music broadcast did increase, as it had done fairly consistently over the previous decade.[26] The usual Platonic fears of music as a seducer of the rectilinear masculinity deemed necessary for a warrior spirit in wartime were expressed in oft-stated official BBC dislike for American dance bands, described as 'anaemic and debilitated' (i.e. menstrual–effeminate) male crooners and 'insincere and over-sentimental' female singers.[27] However, the dislike was not reflected in programming, with series such as *Forces' Favourites* and *These You have Loved* providing a mixture of up-tempo dance and low-down sentiment.

This type of programming, embodied in the post-war Light Programme, was preserved virtually intact as Radio Two was created on the reformation of the medium in 1966 with the emergence of a separate pop station, Radio One. Radio Two has survived, and in the early 1990s was picking up audience figures while Radio One was losing listeners; meanwhile the second London-wide commercial music radio channel licence awarded in the early 1990s went to a light-music station, Melody Radio (while the first of them, launched in 1989 as Jazz FM, had in effect become a light-music station by 1991, playing more middle-of-the-road soul than anything else). Again, one aspect of the general retrospective vision of the 1960s which informed the pop world of the mid-1990s was a specific revival of the light-music cultures of the period, with renewed interest in the work of some of the composers (such as John Barry and Burt Bacharach) and the phenomenon Mike Flowers' Pops, retailing, with apparent sincerity, a pastiche of 1960s light music.

There is in this new interest, as in both of the light-music stations' programming, evidence of the continuities which marked the popular musical world of the 1960s themselves, and which became tenuous in the more segmented age- and culture-specific markets of the 1970s and beyond. Continuities, in other words, across a spectrum of musics from pop music on the one hand – especially that brand of pop identified by Sheila Tracy as middle-of-the-road, putatively aimed at lower-middle-class or working-class 'housewives' or 'secretaries' – women who are assumed to form the majority of the day-time audience (for example, the music of Barry Manilow or Barry White) – and larger forms such as Hollywood cinema and the American musical, on the other. (The controller of BBC Radio Two announced in July 1994 that it was her channel's role to preserve and proselytise the last form, and it has since begun to do so.)

For all the importance of indigenous tradition, then, Anglo-American interactions are important in all aspects of twentieth-century British music. However, there has always been differentiation and divergence, rather than the simple reproduction of American models, partly through the maintenance of tradition, partly through general cultural resistance and partly because of the specific protection afforded to British musicians by the Musicians' Union. Resistance in general often took the form of specifically racialised discourses: hot jazz in the 1920s, swing in the 1930s, and rock-'n'roll in the 1950s were all resisted from within and without the British musical establishment on the grounds that these were black or black-derived forms and that black music was dangerous; that it would infect the white 'race' with its open eroticism and its association with illegal narcotic drugs. There was a particular fear that eroticised and narcotised music would make white women open to the advances of black men, the common fear of 'miscegenation' around which many forms of racism have been organised.[28]

Resistance in particular was crystallised when in 1930 the dance-band section of the Musicians' Union was set up, specifically to police the membership of dance bands plying their trade in Britain and to exclude Americans. In connection with this, a series of 'needle-time' agreements were negotiated with the BBC, which restricted the amount of recorded material the organisation could broadcast (much of which was American in origin) and therefore guaranteed the BBC's continuing employment of British musicians. Licences were needed for any visiting American artist; they were not given casually. These protective measures were fully matched on the other side of the pond with a series of reciprocal arrangements, though until the Merseybeat boom of the 1960s the loss appeared to be to British audiences deprived of the chance to see American performers, rather than American audiences frustrated at the absence from their shores of acts like Ambrose and his Orchestra (exceptions such as the visit to America of the Ted Heath band in 1955 attracted national newspaper headlines).[29] The strategy worked splendidly, producing a tradition of British dance-band music which kept musicians in what many would see as anachronistic employment. The last BBC big band was disbanded only in 1993; the light-music BBC Concert Orchestra is still at the time of writing on Aunty's payroll, and performs annually at the Proms (usually a programme of twentieth-century, jazz-inflected, American and/or French music) as well as regularly on Radio Two. Before the 1970s, then, it was relatively difficult for any American artist to perform in Britain, which is one reason why Elvis Presley's only visit to British shores was to touch down at a remote Scottish airbase as a brief journey-breaker. British pop would not have happened without this isolation.

So from the 1930s on there was a large, protected group of English musicians playing what came to be known as 'variety', a blend of light classical, music-hall/musical comedy and American or American-influenced light music, dance music and the more orchestral (whiter) version of jazz, including by the 1940s rather tame versions of swing. The coincidence of this music, these musicians and the Second World War is noteworthy, especially because that event is the focus of much nostalgic heritage-culture pride among those who would see England Great Again (rather than Britain part of Europe). As pointed out in chapter 1, because of the proximity of this music and the war, the conservative, anti-European magazine *This England* promotes nostalgic recordings of American and Anglo-American dance bands with the same vigour it devotes to the promotion of cottage gardens, cricket on the village green, honey still for tea, floggings at prep school and other traditional English pastimes.

### Aspects of amateurism: folk roots and r'n'b

However important the activities of professional musicians, the amateur performance traditions are also important in the story of twentieth-century popular music, offering continuities through choirs and brass bands, the home-made instruments of skiffle in the 1950s, through punk in the 1970s and the various New Wave revivals thereafter, in all of which playing standards are considered to be less important than taking part. The apogee of this tendency was the Portsmouth Sinfonia, in which people who by agreement could not, or would not, play their instruments well (by otherwise agreed standards), met to perform works from the classical music repertoire as shambolically as possible. This was a one-off, of course; there are many amateur groups, working in whatever style, who refuse this convoy-system approach to musical participatory democracy, and whose performing standards are at least as high as those of professionals – the national youth orchestra, for example.

The importance of amateur participation in the world of folk-song and dance is one of the strongest of its continuities. But it is not quite the democratic form which some have claimed or would wish it to be. Folk was for Sharp and his associates a music which had to be preserved and given back to 'the people' when they had tired of the fripperies of music-hall or other commercial popular music. The collection, preservation and performance of songs and dances was dominated in the first third of the twentieth century by various rival middle-class cliques, most of them with highly questionable ideas about authenticity, and some of them politically unsavoury. Here there was a very important change in the post-war period: a 'revival' which was far more than a mere replication of the song-collecting efforts of the early twentieth century.

The early phase of the revival, discussed in chapter 1, had a formative effect on much of the classical music written in England. At the end of the nineteenth century one imperative was to find the roots of a national music to set against that of Germany, in a musical equivalent of the naval race which preceded the First World War. The middle-class collectors toured the villages, bribing and/or cajoling elderly people to perform their repertoire of vanishing songs. The lyrics were then made acceptable to a bourgeois audience through bowdlerisation. Through the twentieth century folk-songs and dances were continually the site of political activity, as fascist and socialist visions of 'the folk' were promoted.

After the Second World War the political imperative and source-material changed, principally through the dominance of organised communism. A.L. Lloyd and Ewen McColl, realising the potential in the folk-song for radical politics and protest, promoted the songs of the industrial working class (especially of the North of England and of Scotland and Wales) as folk-songs; to these were added, in some configurations, songs of the American radical elite (Pete Seeger in particular) and the folk-blues of the American deep South.

The enthusiasts for the last virtually created, certainly rechristened as 'authentic', a form that had ceased to have any provenance in America: visiting blues musicians from the USA were criticised if they used electric guitars, to their confusion.[30] At the time of writing, British television advertising was reworking these clichés of the rural American South and black music, chiefly in trying to sell various unpalatable lagers through a patina of 'authenticity'.[31]

These orthodoxies around 'authentic' source-material and instrumentation rapidly became an invented tradition, which still obtains in many folk-clubs. Thanks to the imperatives of the communists, this orthodoxy was quite deliberately created as a counter to capitalism, and its tenets include the participation of the audience as equals to the named guest performer, including 'floor singers' as solo performers: a denial of the star system's part in the mechanics of capitalism which has always been underlined with an emphasis on small venues, low fees and voluntary work by committees. The relatively autonomous local folk-club continues to be, of all continuous musical organisations, at the furthest remove from the drive for profit which dominates most aspects of the music business – though, as Neil MacKinnon has recently demonstrated, this does not mean an excessively proletarian membership. His findings indicate that the most enthusiastic members of the folk scene are middle-class professionals – with the important caveat that the majority are employed in the fading 'public-sector' professions such as teaching, social work and local government administration, rather than law or finance.[32]

But the influence of folk spread widely beyond the relatively small autonomous realms of the club circuit. In the early 1960s its politicisation, portability and participatory nature had given it input into CND and other protests against military power and other impositions of the state; the lineage continues with some versions of ecological protest, including travellers, New Age philosophies with some of their claimed roots in an imagined Celtic or other pagan past, and the anti-roads movement, all often being accompanied by non-technological music-making (though there are also important connections between New-Ageism/paganism and high-technology music, as chapter 3 will explore). The influence of folk melody became more widely available within more commercial music through various currents in rock music, from the relaxed folkishness of Pentangle, the more fundamentalist Albion Band and the eventually rocky Strawbs in the 1960s, to more politically tinged Celticism – for instance, Irish bands like Tir Na Nog in the 1960s, the London–Irish Pogues in the 1970s and after and in the 1990s the Welsh bilingual indie band Gorky's Zygotic Mynci, or Scottish bands like Runrig, Capercaillie and Coelbeg, who have used their 'national' musics, including reinventions and reworkings in dialogue with established Anglo-American or other forms, to promote the ideas of cultural and political independence for Ireland, Wales and Scotland.

One slightly more amorphous non-r'n'b source for British pop should be mentioned: the 'popular song'. Like light music, this is a difficult, catch-all label, and can in this instance encompass Victorian parlour-songs written for and performed by amateurs, the work of professional solo singers in musical theatres and songs written for the British or American crooners like Johnnie Ray in the 1950s. By the 1950s, in fact, whatever the aspirations of the Songwriters' Guild of Great Britain, the popular song was dominated by the very restricted range of topics and structures associated with the Tin Pan Alley model: the AABA format, 'moon in June' lyrics and the predominance of ballads or medium-paced over up-tempo songs. It was this range which was subverted – by the impact of the new American forms rock'n'roll, rockabilly and country'n'western, and by the do-it-yourself simplicities of skiffle. In the end, 'popular song' may only be useful as a way of thinking which disinters songs otherwise destined for a communal coffin marked 'pop music', and reminds us that before the early 1960s pop just didn't exist as a stand-alone phenomenon.

To exemplify the point, this compressed history ends with a brief glance at British popular music in about 1960, through some of the names appearing in the top twenty best-selling singles, the 'chart', of that year. It is worth pausing to reflect on the chart, which plays its part in the fetishising of the high/low culture divide which was so loose in the world of the brass band and choir, but was increasingly taken for granted in the twentieth-century music business.[33] In 1936 a chart of sheet music sales appeared in the *Gramophone*; a 'top fifteen' of record sales first appeared in the *New Musical Express* in 1952, and by 1956 this had been doubled to a listing of the 'top thirty'; an 'independently audited' top fifty became the norm in 1963.[34] By the early 1960s, then, the notion of a restricted list of best-selling records was dominant within both the music business and the media which symbiotically reported music. (While it has been extended since with charts for albums and other catch-alls like 'soul' or 'dance-music', and even, under Classic FM's direction, classical CDs, here 'the chart' will mean the general singles chart unless otherwise stated.)

Reading back through 1960s charts, several things are striking, compared with the relatively homogeneous youth-market domination of the chart in the 1990s. There is an admixture of material clearly aimed at 'teenagers' (for example, by Adam Faith and by both Cliff Richard and his backing band The Shadows), with material clearly targeted at older people (Perry Como's 'Delaware' or Ken Dodd's 'Love is like a Violin') and a large number of novelty/humour items such as Rolf Harris's 'Tie me Kangaroo Down, Sport', Lonnie Donegan's 'My Old Man's a Dustman' and most infamously Brian Hyland's 'Itsy-Bitsy Teeny-Weeny Yellow Polka-Dot Bikini'. The comedy elements can be traced back through the music-hall/vaudeville line; the older-audience material is medium-tempo or slow, Tin Pan Alley inflected by the indigenous popular song; the teenage material is more energetic and either American or at least influenced by, often a pastiche of, the new youth musics from the USA, whose most successful artists on this year's chart were not Elvis or Pat Boone but the Everly Brothers, who had four number ones. This Atlantic traffic was almost entirely one way; the British answers to rock'n'roll, such as Cliff Richard, were neither heavily marketed, nor particularly successful, in the United States. American popular music, limited as it was by format and marketing concerns, was already global, whereas British (both light and pop) was local. This power relationship was about to change.

### The 1960s and after

The story of British pop from the 1960s on is well enough known, partly because of its presentation as a national, but especially as an international success story. To summarise the situation before the Beatles. Built on the various lineages identified above, in the early 1950s there was a national light music industry based less on record sales than on radio performance and the sale of sheet music, privileging the composer rather than the performer. While there was a tradition of composition and performance dating from the music-hall and there was also an important tradition of music for dancing influenced by American big bands, much British light music was derivative of American 'Tin Pan Alley' models. But it was American at one remove. Artists and writers alike had benefited from the protectionism of the Musicians' Union ban on American performers.

This established system had clear advantages both for songwriters and, if in a more limited way, for British performers, and it survived the early years of rock'n'roll relatively unscathed. The political economy of music had acknowledged the youth market and catered for it, but it saw popular music as a wider field and tried to address many specific segments of that field; the kind of music which became 'pop' was not privileged in this set-up. The first generation of British 'teen idols', Tommy Steele, Cliff Richard and their contemporaries, sang other peoples' songs, and, with an eye to long careers, became general light music entertainers as soon as decently possible, with Steele's career on stage and in film very much a contemporary continuation of music-hall; in Cliff Richard's case, as a pop singer for the family, the results have included a knighthood in 1995.[35]

This comfortable and insular system was interrupted by the success of the Beatles and principally by the establishing of John Lennon and Paul McCartney as songwriters as well as performers. This marks a most important interruption both in the way in which the music business worked (i.e. in terms of the flow of capital), and in the relationship between British pop and the American model. It *created* what came to be known in Britain as 'pop' from rock'n'roll, Tin Pan Alley and the lineage of local traditions. Other bands which formed around songwriters (such as The Rolling Stones and the Mick Jagger–Keith Richards partnership; The Who and Pete Townsend; The Kinks and Ray Davies) became similarly successful. Because of this redirection of earnings, the writer/performer became more important in the political economy of music-making, and potentially at least, a more independent figure than the Tommy Steele-type teen idol. The whole basis of light music production was fractured (though not broken, as the 1980s success of pop svengalis Stock, Aitken and Waterman as writers and producers, and their stable of name and face performers, indicates). Thanks to the continuing international success of British pop – with vastly increased sales over those of the domestic 'stars' of the 1950s – musicians who wrote their own songs, and performed and recorded them with anything more than modest success, could now expect to become millionaires, to have long careers without necessarily changing their point of address from 'youth' to 'adult' (middle-of-the-road or light) music, to have some control over the shape of those careers – and to move away from dependency on managers, agents and record companies.[36] In most cases, they would also move away from their class backgrounds and local peer groups.

Such changes were neither instant nor universal, as managers and agents had no particular wish to devolve either power or wealth; the comparative independence of the artists, and their abilities to negotiate contractual relationships in their own right – and in their own favour – evolved through a series of legal disputes.[37] Record companies remained powerful, even if they were rewarding their contracted artists more highly: as the 1993–94 legal battles involving U2 and the PRS (Performing Rights Society) royalty collecting organisation, and George Michael and Sony Music, indicate, the relationships currently constituted between the artist, record label and financial accounting systems have brought their own problems, whatever the amount of cash given to the singer/songwriter by the company eager for his or her copyright.

This is, then, a continuing narrative, of a developing political economy; but it develops from this important interruption in the mode of musical production, whose commencement in the early 1960s caused a distinct shift in the *social* (as well as the economic) position of the popular music performer. Perhaps most importantly, if unquantifiably, the change, partly because of the change in capital flow in favour of the artist, altered both the status and the subjectivity of the pop musician. This was immediately obvious even in the early years of the British pop revolution. One of the most clichéd versions of the story of Britain in the early 1960s is that by common assumption it was becoming a 'classless society'.[38] The fluid mix of social groups in the London arts and media world of the early 1960s seemed to confirm the notion that youth and talent had transcended the remaining social barriers of class. Music was only one aspect of this general shift, if one of the most important: the international success of the Beatles, given an MBE by a vote-hungry British (Labour) government in 1965, came after years of apparent social fluidity and cultural change. The aristocratic photographer Lord Snowdon, soon to marry Princess Margaret, negotiated London's mean streets at the wheel of a Mini; cockney Michael Caine displayed his accent with pride, and displaced the middle-class actors of Ealing comedy, in such films as *Alfie* and *The Ipcress File*, while sometime milkman Sean Connery brought his Scottish brogue to the film role of James Bond. The modelling careers of Twiggy and Jean Shrimpton brought new accents as well as new shapes to the world of haute couture. All these, together, suggested that talent was more important than birth, and would be rewarded. Youth was portrayed as a homogeneous entity driving Britain forward. 'I hope I die before I get old', wrote Pete Townsend in the classic Who song 'My Generation'. Class as the motor of history was off the agenda, and youth took the wheel instead, with the willing agreement of a Labour government whose vision of modernisation had moved sharply away from the politics of the previous, 1945–50, Labour administration.

To repeat the crucial economic point: as that collective MBE demonstrates, music was important as its success was international. At a time of economic difficulty (with the car industry, for example, on the cusp of its terminal decline to foreign-owned, kit-assembly status) British music was exported world-wide for the first time, and record companies and music publishers, recording studios and session musicians based in London became leaders of the world music market for a decade. As the almost immediate praise given to Lennon–McCartney by critics and composers indicates, this changed the world's view of British music in general.[39] Only Elgar had achieved an international reputation in the time of the English musical Renaissance, and this reputation did not survive the First World War (though there were post-war cachets for Delius and Cyril Scott); Benjamin Britten had become an international success in the 1950s, and his success had been built on by a generation of younger classical composers; but classical music by this point had airline status – prestigious, necessary for national pride, and financially disastrous. The Beatles, on the other hand, had begun to make British music commercially successful.

Through this success and the accompanying changes in the status of the music industry and its musicians, the subjectivity of the pop star was changed. The possession of vast wealth, the MBEs for the Beatles, the awards for export sales, the press attention (for example, a *Times* leading article of 1 July 1967, 'Who breaks a Butterfly on a Wheel?' was followed by a sympathetic interview with Mick Jagger conducted by the young William Rees-Mogg, then editor of *The Times*, after Jagger had been convicted of personal drug use) certainly changed the social position of the pop star. Managers and agents remained, as they remain, powerful within the industry, and still form strong relationships with some musicians, but the relative independence given by massive earnings meant there was no need to lean on the svengali's arm, or to share his bed – disappointment over this change is one reason often given for the suicide of the Beatles' first manager, Brian Epstein.[40] But the new position afforded the artists, the new subjectivity which they experienced both collectively and individually, was one reason for the change which overtook British pop towards the end of the 1960s, when expectations of the kind of work pop musicians did changed, and under the influence of the development of 'rock', the politics and poetics of the American hippy movement and the indigenous emphasis on the rock musician as 'romantic artist', pop music for a few years attempted its own transcendence. The eventual failure of this attempt, which will be discussed in the next chapter, was partly because the subjectivity of the artists had become constructed within the very small world of the 1960s classless society, and divorced from those of the majority of the consumers of popular music.

It is partly because of this divorce that the sociology of youth is vital to our understanding of the shifts which occurred here. However important the subjectivities of individual musicians, the base for this transformed superstructure, the teenage and young people who bought the records made by the new wealthy, have to be an important focus of attention – as indeed they have been since the invention of the teenager as an analytical construct in the 1950s. The consumer of pop has consistently been theorised in very particular ways, and if this narrative is to take account of the relations between music, culture and society it must also take into consideration these theoretical and empirical accounts of young people, their tastes and behaviour: the context of the music. This will in turn help to explain the restricted versions of popular music which have been offered in most studies of music and youth, and most histories of pop.

## Theorising youth and music

While the impact of rock'n'roll in Britain, with its associated emergence of the teenager as at the same time folk devil, consumer cate-

gory and sociological subject, was derived from American models
and events,[41] sociological research immediately began to qualify the
American picture. Because of the almost overwhelming association
between music and youth in the narrative of popular music since the
1950s, here I examine the academic studies which have accompanied the growth of spectacular and musical youth cultures from the
1950s on, and comment on their production of restricted views of
youth and music.

British sociologists challenged the Americanised model of the
teenager. American teenagers were college kids, products of their
parents' prosperity. As consumers, they spent their parents' money,
drove their parents' cars, and so on. The young British people
labelled teenagers, groups like the mods for example, came from
working- or lower-middle-class families. They spent money they
had earned themselves, usually in dead-end jobs. Their ability to
spend in this way ended with marriage, which was usually in their
early twenties. These teenagers were neither affluent nor socially
mobile; the fluid social mix of London's artistic community, where
Mick Jagger and Lord Snowdon met on friendly terms (and probably still do), remained inside the boundaries of the 'Royal Borough'
of Kensington and Chelsea.

Working with young men, Paul Willis and Stan Cohen argued that
they were working-class both in origin and destiny, and that their
'deviance', either as school drop-outs or as petty criminals, reproduced them as the unskilled working class still necessary to society.[42]
There was no such thing as the classless teenager. Cohen went on to
claim that groups like mods and rockers were labelled, and sometimes punished, as 'deviant' by police and broadcast media, through
what he called 'moral panics'. They became internal Others, sites
for the focus of social anxiety about the present and future; through
these panics repressive policies and policing strategies were developed. This routine of youth demonisation and consequent legislation has continued to operate around music-related events such as
pop festivals, with rave music and its associated parties being
quickly demonised by the tabloid press in the late 1980s. Fiercely
repressive legislation was enacted in 1994 to control these events
(and to protect the notion of private property consequent on privatisation).

A pattern was established in this 1960s academic work: small
groups of young men who rejected perceived bourgeois values of

thrift, discipline and social conformity were studied; their 'resistance' was tabulated according to their deviance and the reactions of the legal apparatus and the media. However, the theoretical basis for the interpretation of their behaviour changed. During the 1970s the focus moved away from the explanation of criminality and towards the appreciation of culture – a move which eventuated in Cultural Studies as we know it today.

The founding texts of this movement were written at the moment of the impact of rock'n'roll in the late 1950s and early 1960s, with its accompanying ideologies of classlessness and Americanisation. All were against the notion that class was no longer important. E.P. Thompson's *The Making of the English Working Class* (1964) told a history of a class which had actively produced its own consciousness, its own culture, from the experience of industrialisation. Raymond Williams, in *Culture and Society* (1958), identified a continuous tradition of criticism in all forms of literature – criticism of that same dehumanising industrial society. Richard Hoggart's *The Uses of Literacy* (1957) argued against the Americanisation of British culture, offering instead a nostalgic celebration of the interwar Northern English working class (the culture of his childhood, a common trope in such assertions).

Each text emphasises agency, the creation of culture by the people within it; sees the arts, and the role of the intellectual, as critical, especially of capitalism and industrialisation; and stresses the importance of indigenous tradition – an emphasis which in Hoggart's hands seems embarrassingly xenophobic (and is a contemporary of the Communist Party-inspired re-creation of a specifically British 'folk' music, by Ewen MacColl and others). Paradoxically, though, Hoggart's Adornoesque hatred of the symbols of American 'mass culture' – the milk bar, the juke-box and rock'n'roll, and hard-boiled detective fiction – was matched by an insistence that these forms should be studied. Bringing these aspects of culture into academic discussion then made it possible for the negative critique to be refused.

The University of Birmingham Centre for Contemporary Cultural Studies, which Hoggart helped to set up, turned to theories of culture in trying to explain precisely how class worked. After a palace revolution in which the Anglocentric Hoggart was replaced by the Jamaican, Stuart Hall, the work of the Centre became more subtle and more positive under the influence of Continental European Marxist theory. During the 1970s work on cultural use and interpretation became increasingly influenced by European cultural and political theory; perhaps the most influential voice was that of the Sardinian communist Antonio Gramsci. The notion of 'hegemony' was developed from one of Gramsci's ideas, which interpreted class relations as a set of negotiations from positions of differentiated power and authority. While this allowed space to oppositional views, in the end one group's power was reproduced. Culture was seen as one of the principal sites of the negotiation of this power – and the cultures of the young, their fashion and body-style, music, sport, drug use and other cultural practices were interpreted as resisting dominant cultures and undercutting dominant or preferred readings. By interpreting the cultural products of mass society in their own ways, and by using available items of dress to form symbolic uniforms of their own, young people could 'resist through rituals'.[43]

The key text from this moment is *Subculture: the Meaning of Style* (1979), Dick Hebdige's catalogue of youth cultures from teds to punks. In Hebdige's view British subcultures are engaged in a long imaginary 'phantom dialogue' with Black American and Caribbean culture, a dialogue focused around dress and music, and embracing the marginality of those cultures against mainstream white culture. Hebdige's positive consideration of the role of ethnicity is worlds away from Hoggart's cosy terraced-cottage xenophobia, as was the society he explored.

More openly than *Resistance through Rituals*, *Subculture: the Meaning of Style* is concerned with culture as sign-system, through the application of 'semiotics', the conceptual product of French structuralism and poststructuralism. Hebdige's text parallels, in fact, the arrival of Continental theory; its very writing style is a phantom dialogue with the emergence of poststructuralist thought in British academia. *Subculture* moves from an orthodox social history, an account of teds in the 1950s which is socially grounded in class and ethnic relations, to an emphasis on bricolage in the punk of the 1970s, which (like Malcolm McLaren himself) Hebdige ascribes to a deliberate use of the politics of situationism (the antagonistic use of 'spectacle', inspired by the activities of a few disgruntled French art-school graduates). So his description of punk is formed from the matrix of academic debate about culture and meaning. In this semiotic reading the youth subculture becomes not so much a grouping defined through its relation to existing, 'real' socio-economic conditions, but a textual object, if one which makes its own meanings: part of a discourse of differences which is validated internally (if at all) and not subject to the absolute meaning bestowed by a clear relationship to an external referent.

Whatever the class of the participants, we're a long way from class as the motor of history, and even from history as progressive change: the bricolage of punk may have challenged received ideas of gender and/or sexuality, but it used ideas of resistance and revolutionary politics in exactly the same way as it did the swastika; all became part of the symbolic mess whose overriding slogan was 'no future'. It is hard, two decades later, to see what was worth celebrating in this moment, for all that young people were making meanings for themselves. Though people do: Greil Marcus and Jon Savage, for example, have both provided Hoggart-like journeys into their respective youths, dressing their nostalgia for the punk past with a mess of politics, while, as we have seen, Ben Watson has read the work of Frank Zappa, whose values were as far from those of punk as is humanly possible, through a personal politics informed by punk-as-situationism.[44]

For all the problems associated with this kind of interpretation of punk, clearly at the generational level it was a highly antagonistic phenomenon. Later work has sometimes used semiotic readings of culture and moved further in this direction, almost to the point of farce, in the attempt to present positively the cultural practices of the young. Paul Willis's *Common Culture*[45] stresses the making of meanings in and through everyday experience, in what Willis calls 'grounded aesthetics'. While the only young people discussed in this text are working-class, unemployed or otherwise underprivileged, class analysis (Marxist or otherwise) has disappeared in favour of a stress on the creativity of the young, rather than their oppression or lack of opportunity to express that creativity either in paid work or in other public activities. This argument about young peoples' construction of their own culture is attractive to young people themselves, some of whom are pleased to discover that whatever they did or do is laden with cultural significance, but it is disturbingly relaxed about the implications of its own catch-all relativism. To mention the worst example: a celebration of the everyday which accepts the pleasures of pub violence because young people commit it and in many instances like it, seems a very short step from the celebration of racist violence by young people on the extreme right, because (presumably) they like it.[46] Willis is so keen to place young peoples' activities on this pedestal of grounded aesthetics, that he cannot criticise, let alone attempt to deconstruct, aggressive masculinity.

This introduces one of the most important qualifications to British subcultural studies. Throughout the 1980s, feminist work by Angela McRobbie, Mica Nava and others addressed the absence of women, or indeed any notion of a politics of gender, from the 'youth' studies of the 1960s and 1970s.[47] 'Youth', as I mentioned above, tended to mean young men. The ways in which young girls as consumers of popular music express their collective power have raised the question of autonomous female subcultures, which have, arguably, existed since the 1960s and Beatlemania, though to some the St Trinianite image of hordes of pubescent teenagers bussing after their idols and discussing the minutiae of their hair-styles seems a long way from the antagonistic self-creation of mod or punk.[48] We now know far more than we did at the beginning of the 1980s about girls and young women as teenage consumers and dancers,[49] but we need to know more.

Feminism has also brought psychoanalysis into the frame of study. This has exposed masculinity, both as a social construct and as a problem. The deviants celebrated by Willis and Cohen in the 1970s were openly misogynist, homophobic and racist; the observers seemed to regard these attributes as just another aspect of their subjects' praiseworthy rejection of bourgeois values. Such an attitude is unacceptable, especially since the vision of the working class, or any fragment of it, as the inheritors of the post-revolutionary future, now seems like looking through the binoculars the wrong way. Indeed, this is the failure of a peculiarly masculine vision of heroism, in which groups of young men could positively remake the world through stylistic terrorism or mutual confrontation. The general failures of men as leaders and followers, their tendency to smash the world up while attempting 'heroically' to transform it for the better, have been placed on the agenda for analysis. Youth here is the father of the problem gender, and not something to celebrate. The debate initiated by Greil Marcus and others about the 'death of [Anglo-American] rock' is an aspect of this deconstruction; another is the psychoanalytic history of rock rebellion by Simon Reynolds and Joy Press.[50]

Three final points about the subculture-based study should be made. Firstly, subcultures, as studied until now, can be seen as small metropolitan groups with very little purchase outside their own backyards until the media globalise what has hitherto been intensely local.[51] Secondly (a related point), most youth culture is and always has been lived at the weekend or in the evenings, and not at a general daily level – this is the point of the 'mod' of the early 1960s: as a movement, partly based on the consumption and display of clothing, music, scooters and so on, it relied on people who were employed, and could only live the subculture part-time. The fulltimers are, by their nature, exceptional. Thirdly (again a related point), academics are too often excited by antagonism, reading it as 'resistance', and fail to examine or explain what they see as cultures of conformity. This means that many potential differences or ruptures within young peoples' cultures have been ignored.

So Hebdige in *Subculture* ignores not only weekend punks but a concurrent weekend alternative culture, the disco boom. It was *Saturday Night Fever* and the hits of ABBA, not *Never Mind the Bollocks, it's the Sex Pistols*, which dominated the British charts in 1978. And there *was* a disco subculture, even in Hebdige's terms. All-nighters imported from the (more exclusive and arguably more male-dominated) Northern Soul phenomenon, and their apotheosis, 'Soul weekenders' (in which entrepreneurs hired holiday camps such as Caister in Norfolk, and a few DJs and large groups of young people danced the weekend away) were a challenge to parental orthodoxy in their hedonism; they involved gay as well as heterosexual people, and were certainly not routinely homophobic in the way groups like skinheads were; they were most definitely part of the 'phantom dialogue', the urban engagement between black and white cultures around imported American music; they had a well-defined supporting cultural apparatus, including as well as the various parties and weekenders, record stores importing 'rare grooves' from America and illegal pirate radio stations, which were necessary (and popular) because the official broadcasting apparatus ignored their music, and which brought them into clear and continuous conflict with the state. So, while if you see them as leisure practices, the soul weekenders offered no resistance to the mainstream values of consumer capitalism, if you see them as conflicting centres of power and pleasure – involving illegal entrepreneurship around drugs, parties and broadcasting – and thereby as oppositional to the state and its official economy, they were at least as subversive as the punks.[52]

(Isaac Julien's 1990 film *Young Soul Rebels* tried to capture the spirit of this movement, its comparative openness to differences of sexuality and its connectedness with the antagonism of punk).[53]

One more recent development in academic work has asserted a new typology of youth culture. Steve Redhead's *The End-of-the-Century Party: Youth and Pop towards 2000*[54] critiqued (sub)cultural theory thus:

> What, in practice, we witnessed in the 1980s was the break-up not simply of former theoretical traditions (or master and meta-narratives) about the emancipatory potential of youth in the West, but the disintegration and restructuring of those formations (rock culture, youth culture) which were produced as their object. 'Authentic' subcultures were produced by subcultural theories, not the other way round. In fact, popular music and 'deviant' youth styles never fitted together as harmoniously as some subcultural theory proclaimed.[55]

This does not mean, however, that the end-of-the-century party will see the end of the relation between youth, music and deviance. The most tenuous link, in Redhead's eyes, is that between contemporary music-driven subcultures and politics – or rather, the politics of subcultural theorists. To differentiate these, he calls one strand of the music of the late 1980s 'post-political' pop; it is not, he argues, 'post-cultural' or trivial. Music plays its part in the making of new cultural formations.

The Manchester research group founded by Redhead has continued this kind of work. *Rave Off*, for example, is one of the first attempts at a theorised academic approach to the recent history of youth, dance, music and drugs. There are competing histories here of the derivation of the rave phenomenon: from Northern Soul, Chicago gay clubs, Ibiza's night-life and/or the ethnic and musical mix of the big cities in Continental Europe and Britain. There is more agreement over the importance of drugs to the experience, and of the effect these have, in conjunction with the musical and visual effects of the music. Raving, especially in conjunction with the drug Ecstasy, is a psychodynamic experience which privileges the unconscious and the collective at the expense of the individual and the rational. As Antonio Melechi points out, this gives particular problems to those commentators still trying to find directional, articulate political positions in all this: repression, revolt, even the traces of social structure like gender and class are often effaced by the experience itself.[56]

Outside this Manchester grouping academics and journalists have echoed these claims, and also used the work of a pair of 1970s French theoretical writers France enjoying a vogue in 1990s Britain, Gilles Deleuze and Felix Guattari, to sugggest that unconscious connections are made between people to form a 'desiring machine', a 'collective body without organs'.[57] Well, fine, when the chemicals have taken effect, the strobes are on and the sounds are swirling through the speakers, it is possible to characterise desire, identity and experience in these ways. But when the lights go up and the crowds come down, we/they return to a reality which is less hyper than lower, and in which class, gender, sexuality and power relations still exist. An E may be the quickest way out of Manchester, as opium was said to be in the 1820s, but it is not a permanent route; and in a political economy based on that gross parody of the free market, the illegal drugs business, there are so few guarantees of chemical purity and personal safety that there are grounds for a pessimistic reading of this culture, however nice a time is had by the participants at immediate and particular events.[58]

As Redhead has argued more recently, much cultural studies has been about an area also covered by the theory of jurisprudence: the study of 'deviance', and more broadly the study of legal constraints on behaviours which allow such a concept. Aware of 'the dangers of reading the "popular" as always either "conservative" or "rebellious"; or as a "site of resistance"; or as equal to, or synonymous with, the "people" ',[59] Redhead deals with work which has done all of the above. Looking at the law as it attempts to regulate public behaviour (through the police control of parties and crowds, licensing laws, etc.) and the concept of property, which in recent years has been allied ever more closely with our idea of the private as it has been conceived by the political right since 'privatisation' (copyright law and attempts to control and censor television, rock and rap lyrics, the internet and so on), Redhead argues that the law is now engaged in a thoroughgoing attempt to regulate popular culture; but, he claims optimistically, the attempt will fail as, in the age of instant information transfer, the authority of the law has fragmented.[60]

## Youth, culture and pop: towards divorce?

With these important insights and caveats in mind, we return to the narrative of the development of pop in the 1960s. For all the importance of developments in the political economy of the music business, especially the change in the position of the performer/writer, these should not obscure the complexities and differences within the music itself. Even without admixing the remaining presence of light musics (from Billy Cotton's band to the middle-aged erotics of 'Engelbert Humperdinck') there can be no simple narrative of British pop in the 1960s. The emergence of rock'n'roll in late 1950s Britain[61] was shadowed by the emergence of a night-club-based connoisseur's appreciation of both country blues and urban r'n'b, interests which complemented the folk movement which had helped to promote interest in the rural blues. Both country blues and r'n'b were important sources for the future development of British pop. Take the Beatles, for example. The Lennon–McCartney songwriting partnership emerged from a band which did not at first attempt to create original music, but played both rock'n'roll and r'n'b – copied American models, in other words. In Dave Harker's simplistic retelling of their story, there is a deliberate taming of the more raucous elements of r'n'b as the band becomes successful, with the tone of voice used by both Lennon and McCartney becoming softer and smoother.[62] One could equally say by contrast that the band moved away from a single, limited means of vocal realisation, based on the mimicking of r'n'b performers, as it quite literally began to find its own voice – and that in any case many of its quieter numbers, even those recorded in the mid-1960s, were already stage material in the band's pre-EMI career; the raucousness was still ready and waiting for numbers like 'Helter-Skelter' on the *White Album* (1968).

In the case of the similarly successful Jagger–Richards writing partnership, the Rolling Stones was a band which started life in south-east London, playing Chicago blues and r'n'b in an attempt to duplicate those specifically African-American forms rather than the more culturally hybrid rock'n'roll, and the Stones moved less far, less quickly from the rawness of vocal expression as Jagger and Richards embarked on their songwriting career – though they did move away from it; 'Lady Jane' (1966) has more to do with British folk ballad-writing than the American bar-room stomp. This sense of dialogue between African–American forms and British pop has, of course, continued. The work of singers Joe Cocker and Chris Farlowe in the late 1960s, and George Michael in the post-Wham! 1980s, has often been labelled white soul (Michael, perhaps after the prompting of his then record company, was even given a *Downbeat* award as best soul singer of 1989); and the Scottish bands Average White Band (in the 1970s) and Wet Wet Wet (in their early days in the late 1980s), for example, attempted with international success to re-create the soul musics of their times within the changing commercial imperatives of the British music industry.

And yet, while this particular British–American dialogue continues, and has remained important in the emergence of British hip-hop, house and techno musics among other forms, the continuing story of British pop cannot be characterised so simply. There are more voices in play than the American and the British: it is and has been since the 1950s less a dialogue than a *multilogue*, a mixture of musics intersecting in the various urban centres to produce, among other things, many new local forms of Caribbean-derived music, such as reggae and the 'new ska' of two-tone; Asian musics reworked through the use of technology and the influence of Western pop to produce bhangra and Indi-pop;[63] and indeed forms dominated by whites such as punk and the indie-rock still favoured by some on the university gig circuit, and from which much of mid-1990s 'Britpop' derives; all these are constantly subject to interactive evolution and reworking. British cities have been the site of these cultural developments for two related reasons.

### The urban soundscape

Firstly, the very success of the early 1960s pop groups made first Liverpool and then London into world musical centres. It was to 'swinging' London, mythologised as the place of classless social mobility where young talent could find its true reward, that Jimi Hendrix came in 1966, to escape from the stereotyped role of the black r'n'b guitarist which was all that had been afforded him in the United States, and to forge a new expressive language of guitar-playing. Hendrix developed this from r'n'b, the solo guitar voices of American urban blues players like B.B. King and Buddy Guy, and the more obsessive English blues guitarists like Peter Green and Eric Clapton. Working outside the cultural, ethnic, political and legal constraints which had made the blues and r'n'b in the USA, but inside the cultural constraints defining musical value in Britain, guitarists working in British blues bands like the Graham Bond Organisation, John Mayall's Bluesbreakers, the Alexis Korner band and the Yardbirds abstracted and reified the virtuosity and romanticised the position of the musician.[64] They saw themselves through the eyes of a culture dominated by the idea of the Romantic Artist as inspired, as a shamanistic commentator separate from the common herd, rather than, say, the dance-band leader as servant of popular entertainment. As with many jazz musicians who left the United States to work in France or Scandinavia, where they were treated with far more public respect than in their native land, Hendrix arrived in London, where he too could more easily become the inspired solo voice. And he did.

This solo voice was developed within a songwriting context which did not rely merely on blues harmonies or the controlled rhythmic repetition of r'n'b or soul, but also paid respect to white popular musics – as signalled by the use of white English musicians Noel Redding and Mitch Mitchell as fellow band members in the Jimi Hendrix Experience, and by the obvious debt to Bob Dylan as songwriter and lyricist, celebrated in Hendrix's version of Dylan's song 'All Along the Watchtower'. Hendrix's role as the pivotal musician in the emergence of 'rock music', the concert music developed from 1960s pop and other musics, has been emphasised (perhaps over-emphasised) in *Crosstown Traffic*, Charles Shaar Murray's study of the guitarist.[65] Here the importance of London as the site through which Hendrix was able to operate during this transformation should be stressed: without it, he would probably have remained another Buddy Guy.[66]

Singer Marsha Hunt followed the same path in order to realise her ambition:

> The American music scene was still severely segregated. They wanted me to be a soul singer, but I wasn't into bubble haircuts and short dresses, I wore leather and I had a large Afro. I said, I wanna sing rock. They said, black women don't sing rock. So I had to come to London to do it.[67]

The melting-pot of this relatively unsegregated city led to innovations in other directions. Jamaican saxophonist Joe Harriott was one of the first wave of Caribbean immigrants to Britain, arriving in 1951. Having played in accepted jazz styles, Harriott attempted in the mid-1960s to create a specifically post-colonial music featuring the violinist John Mayer, with Indian musicians and instruments as well as Caribbean and white musicians and styles: the result he called Indo-Jazz Fusions, releasing an eponymous album in 1967. If the 1960s were positive for British jazz, which underwent a revival in the latter part of the decade, they were equally so for Indian 'classical' music in Britain; it is perhaps the first genre to qualify for the ambivalent title 'World Music', after the exposure given to the sounds of sitar, tanpura and tabla on the Beatles' *Sergeant Pepper* album and batter drums and bamboo flutes on the Rolling Stones' reply to the Beatles' effort, *Their Satanic Majesties Request* (both, as with the Harriott *Indo-Jazz Fusions* album, released in 1967). The Indo–Jazz Fusion tours received some Arts Council support, though jazz musicians were paid lower fees than classical musicians – presumably the Arts Council identified jazz creativity with poverty, and was happy to keep its creators poor romanticised artists starving in garrets. Again, it was through London that this post-colonial interaction took place; it continues to do so, with the Caribbean/Asian group Shiva Nova, for example, reworking the rhythms of through-composed, jazz and South Asian musics in similar ways in the 1990s, while artists such as Nitin Sawney and Najma Akhtar move between North Indian forms and jazz, Sheila Chandra creates a hybrid musical spirituality, Talvin Singh makes music for the dance/club world, and young white band Kula Shaker propagate a neo-hippy Hinduism, complete with sitar and tabla atmos behind the guitars.

Another post-colonial transformation of a music from the West Indies occurred in the early 1970s. Calypso had achieved a certain niche popularity in the London of the 1950s, its socially engaged lyrics (as well as its infectious rhythms) appealing to comedians and satirists, but it had not left that niche. Ska attained a certain popularity in the early 1960s, with Millie's 'My Boy Lollipop' (1963) generating a few essays in a form which was then known in London as 'bluebeat'.[68] Ska's musical descendant reggae, on the other hand, was internationalised. It was from London that the white Jamaican entrepreneur Chris Blackwell's Island label launched reggae as a world-wide musical form, principally through the elevation of Bob Marley as a 'rock' superstar, and his band the Wailers as a stadium rock band.

Reggae was transformed through Blackwell's investment. It had been based on the economics of an impoverished island, in which cheap recordings were quickly made and played in public by DJs, with a small number of professional musicians working in the studios and hardly any live bands – due to the expense, indeed the unavailability, of musical equipment. Many different songs were performed to the same backing tracks. The stars were the DJs rather than the singers; much of the profit was retained by the studio owners. Blackwell imbued reggae with the more ostentatious values of the global music economy: for a while, thanks to Marley's success, expensive studio recordings and world tours by groups of musicians became the norm, while the album rather than the single became the most important form of production. Since Marley's success, reggae rhythms have become part of the orthodoxy of popular music all over the world. Reggae and the musics derived from it, meanwhile, have in some ways returned to their roots. More recent developments in reggae-based or derived music, from dance-hall to ragga and their own subsequent derivatives, are based on the MC or DJ-based 'versioning' performance mode which was the norm before Island Records' intervention. Meanwhile, another derivative based on studio techniques, dub (which was pioneered in Jamaica by King Tubby in the early 1970s and has been developed in Britain by, for example, Adrian Sherwood, working with bands such as African Headcharge), has been crucial in the development of high-technology dance musics.[69] One recent London-originated development which owes much to these derivatives, jungle/drum'n'bass, is discussed below.

### City, colony, moving people

The examples of Joe Harriott and Bob Marley point to the second reason for the importance of Britain as the site for the transformation of pop musics: the nature and extent of post-war, post-colonial immigration. Since 1945, millions of people from the Caribbean, from India, Pakistan and Africa, have arrived and settled permanently in London and Britain's other large cities. While there has been a black presence in Britain since at least the sixteenth century, and while there have always been musical cultures associated with black people in Britain,[70] the relative concentration of peoples in the last fifty years has produced specific responses, creating new markets for musical forms developed by and for specific ethnic groups and providing the site for the interaction of these with existing forms and the consequent re-production of musics. Reggae was reworked in Britain as a live form partly because there were substantial numbers of British people of West Indian origin prepared to buy the resulting concert tickets and albums. Yet while the international commercial success of reggae has not survived Marley's death, and while many versions of reggae continue to address quite specifically a British West Indian audience, important points of crossover remain, in part under the banner waved by Hebdige in his discussion of the phantom dialogue: the moment of punk in 1976 and the subsequent infusion of reggae in the Rock Against Racism movement of the late 1970s.

Since then, the success in Britain of the many house-derived or developed musics since 1988 has been due in no small part to the presence of a reggae aesthetic making bass and drums the most important part of the mix. A typical early house 'band' name, Bomb the Bass, and the typical acid-house track title 'Bass: How Low can You Go?' emphasise this aesthetic, which has been underlined in more recent house-derived dance music (especially jungle/drum'n'bass) by an increasing effort to program and record bass lines in the register C1–c, which is below the normal capabilities of the bass guitar. This is often done using old analogue synthesisers, such as the Roland TB303; the demand for obsolete equipment has led to the manufacture of clone machines capable of similar sounds, but with the added convenience of large patch memories and the ubiquitous and very necessary MIDI connections – clones such as the splendidly titled Deep Bass Nine made by Control Synthesis. The dub revival of 1993–94 (which was led, if not initiated by young, mainly white, dance-music technicians), and the commercialisation of the speedy dub/techno form which was first known as jungle (which was led by young black musicians and MCs, and involved more racially mixed audiences than was usual at white-dominated raves or black-dominated dance-halls), underlines the continuing importance of this Caribbean-influenced, bass-end aesthetic: a music which, even if called 'intelligent techno' or 'intelligent drum'n'bass', is perforce of the body as much as of the mind.[71]

## The ambivalence of broadcasting

But dance music is still not quite mainstream pop (if there is, or remembering those 1960 charts, if there ever was, such a thing). To the extent that reggae, ragga and jungle remain on the margins of British pop music, however, they do so because they have historically been treated as marginal by the national broadcasting service, the BBC. This organisation, prevented by its charter from advertising, and yet complicit with the commercial practices of the record industry (to the extent that potential chart material is still at the time of writing 'playlisted' by radio producers on a weekly basis), long enjoyed an official monopoly over the national radio broadcasting of pop music which only the last knee-jerk processes of Thatcherism have deconstructed via the setting-up of rival, privately owned national radio stations – though the first of these, Virgin, explicitly set out to fill a different 'niche' by broadcasting 'album rock' rather than chart pop.

The BBC's broadcasting of pop music on a dedicated network (Radio One) was established as late as 1966, and then only under severe pressure from commercial pirate radio stations and from their backers in the City of London, who wished to emulate American practice and make money from selling advertising through 24-hour pop broadcasting.[72]. Before this point pop on radio had been a relatively minor constituent of the Light Programme's output. Many people had, therefore, tuned in to Radio Luxembourg, whose programming was also based around light music, but with a higher admix of pop. The success of Luxembourg had led to the setting-up of 'pirate' radio stations such as Radio Caroline, broadcasting from ships anchored outside territorial waters.

The first appearance of Radio One was a messy compromise. It was at first confined to the AM waveband, with consequent poor sound quality – singles are still mixed as over-compressed 'radio edit' versions. The needle-time problem meant that it could not be an all-day record station; much of the daytime programming was in effect light music, designed to appeal to a creature rare even in the 1960s, and currently threatened with extinction: the 'housewife'. As with Radio Three, every reorganisation of the Radio One schedules and wavebands since then has been driven by outside pressure. A problem since the late 1960s has been the constant bifurcation of popular musics, each with their own dedicated audience of young people (and also since that point, ageing people whose tastes have remained static). The appearance in the late 1960s of 'progressive music' was greeted, eventually, with the setting-up of the first 'ghetto slot', firstly in the early evening and then from 10 p.m. to midnight, where by and large such music, and other music outwith the three-minute single format, has remained. Heavy metal, ambient house, ragga and other forms, however 'popular' in terms of sales, are not, by and large, played on daytime Radio One. Thus the demand for and success of inner-city pirates continues, and thus also the eventual legitimisation of sometime pirate station Kiss FM to play 24-hour dance music to Londoners, and Virgin to broadcast album rock nation-wide.[73]

Radio One has not, meanwhile, quite been the Channel that Time Forgot. Competition from new stations, as with the pirates in the 1960s, eventually prompted an overdue rethink and an attempt to capture a younger audience. The mid-1990s have seen a massive restructuring of the station, with, in the evenings and weekends at least, a more differentiated spread of programmes and the employment of younger, less unctuous and self-important DJs. While at first the sacking of familiar voices led to a massive drop in audience figures, the hiring of the entertaining breakfast-time chatterer Chris Evans plugged the leak until his attitude forced a separation, though by that time the new image had been consolidated through an emphasis on the under-24s. While there is a huge potential problem if Radio One continues to seek a young audience while the population ages, it is quite possible that the station will enter the new millennium in better, more diverse, shape than it has been for over a decade.[74]

The story of pop music on television is similar, but perhaps even more depressing. Until the advent of the MTV video music channel (available on cable and satellite only – in other words, by subscription) pop was confined to a few weekly programmes, despite the presence since 1957 of commercially successful competition for the BBC. ITV's mix of live music, dancing and rudimentary interviews, first 'perfected' in the early 1960s show *Ready, Steady, Go!*, has remained the norm for such efforts.[75] Channel Four's launch on an unsuspecting world, in 1984, included a revamped version of this format, *The Tube*. The chaotic inconsequentiality of Tubestyle programming did not preclude the presenters' and interviewers' rise to fame and/or infamy, for all the supposed focus on music (not for the first time has the messenger dominated the medium: *Ready, Steady, Go!* presenter Kathy McGowan remains an icon of the early 1960s moment of classless optimism). The point being that music is all too easily used on television as a background to other agendas.

The BBC's early 1960s mould-breaking riposte to this format included one of the most sublime of all television shows, *Juke Box Jury*, in which records were solemnly played to a panel of celebrities, tapping their pens or not, as they listened and the camera scanned their faces, and on whom was thereafter laid the burden of predicting whether a record would be a hit or a miss. (In the heritage-conscious late 1980s, this ludicrous format was revived, to no great effect). The BBC did, however, institute a show which became a national institution: *Top of the Pops*, a *Ready, Steady, Go!*-derived half-hour chart run-down with a mix of live performers, presenters, in the early days, featured dancing by both studio-audience amateurs and choreographed professionals, and in the video age, well, videos.

By the 1980s, pop video television had manifested itself through MTV and its derivatives, programming sequences of generic material provided for them by the record companies. This has had a spin-off back into terrestrial television, with more use of video and video-related material in pop and youth programming; but there is no direct BBC or ITV equivalent. The impression remains that neither the BBC nor the commercial channels can quite work out the place of popular music on television, the most important national institution. Evening prime-time guest appearances and late-night chat shows (*The Word*) or connoisseur slots (*The Old Grey Whistle Test*; *The Late Show*; *Later with Jools Holland*; *Unplugged*), imply that popular music is still for young people only, and that it would alienate the mainstream audience to carry, say, a Madonna gig as opposed to a football match involving Maradonna, on prime time.

One very important phenomenon cuts across this conservatism. Arguably the most creative and entertaining British programming on the medium, since the lamented days of *The Prisoner*, *The Avengers*, and the heyday of *Doctor Who*, has been advertising. Since the early 1980s (if not before) advertising has used popular music as a deliberate part of its ploy to draw in, not young people, but as wide a consumership as possible.[76] 'Classic' popular songs have been used to advertise cars (Berlin's 'Take my Breath Away', which featured in the film *Top Gun*), car tyres (The Velvet Underground's 'Venus in Furs'), jeans (a lovingly re-recorded pastiche of Marvin Gaye's version of 'I Heard it Through the Grapevine') and insurance services (Nat King Cole singing 'Let's Face the Music and Dance'). The implication is that enough people will be drawn together through the use of such music for the royalty costs to be worth while: this is not, then, advertising aimed at teenagers, but at a wider age-range, including many with real purchasing power.

Advertising's realisation of the place of popular music within British culture, its range of styles and appeals, must be contrasted with the conservatism of the rest of television and radio. Astonishingly, when the National Lottery was launched in 1994 and the BBC won the contract to broadcast the weekly draw, the music chosen to accompany this was game-show light music of the type which had launched down-market television in the 1950s: predictable, Billy-Cottonish big-band arrangements of predictable chord sequences. This is the musical Britishness identified by that 1942 German commentator: Light Britain Lives ...

However, most popular music is not that of the 1940s – the basic constituents of successful chart material have continually changed, despite Aunty's careful conservatism. Again the presence in the bigger cities of large populations with cultural imperatives other than those of the BBC has helped to effect this transformation – and important though the post-colonial is in this process, Caribbean and Asian immigrants are not the only groups who have helped such changes. The adoption by gay men's clubs of the Eurodisco of the 1970s and its subsequent developments (hi-nrg, house, techno) helped in the formation of a wider club culture which I discussed above. The soul/disco 'subculture' of the late 1970s on, catering for virtually any people aged from their teens to their early thirties, was based around dance musics which were largely absent from Radio One airplay. Pirate radio stations reappeared in the inner cities from the late 1970s to broadcast these musics – reggae, soul, funk, jazz–funk, from the early 1980s also hip-hop and rap, and from the late 1980s the many forms of post-house dance music. Despite opposition from both the record companies and the Home Office to stations which paid neither license fees nor royalties (opposition which included vigorous and repressive policing: raids leading to the confiscation of equipment and the arrest, fines and even imprisonment of those charged),[77] the pressure to provide airtime for these musics eventually led to the granting of licences to several new stations, including in London the former pirate station Kiss FM. One long-term effect of the cumulative pressure of club/dance cultures has been to change the nature of the pop charts, so that BBC Radio One, even though it is still wedded to the playlist, and though much of its programming is white-indie by derivation, now (late 1996) plays more black-influenced dance music than ever before.

## The jazz revival cycle

The visibility of black music and musicians was also improved by the 'jazz revival' of the 1980s. Jazz revivals are cyclical – and they always forefront the problems of defition and use which this chapter has discussed. The shadows of popular music have always included many who see jazz as an important art in parallel with classical music, and who identify with both this artistic status and its implicit remove from other musical forms in which the musician's creative freedom is curtailed. Jazz has attracted more than its fair share of the fantasy of opposition, the individualised, implicitly male, 'heroism' of the great artist working in defiance of social norms. This is a convenient view of themselves for lonely suburban men, not gifted with great social skills, but who can play a saxophone or trumpet – or who have record collections and opinions thereon.[78] It is a particularly important self-view for the professional musician, whose training may have produced a deeply alienated proletarian, a highly skilled worker with no control over the product s/he helps to create, and only a small proportion of the value s/he adds to it – a topic discussed in chapter 5. In this vision, the musician subject to the whims of the composer and/or conductor is liberated by jazz, whose emphasis on 'improvisation' is seen as truly creative. Musicians from many genres, therefore, respect jazz and its musicians, and have helped to sustain the mythology of their romantic/shamanistic cultural place.[79]

Jazz also has a shadow existence as an entertainment form, as good music to dance to, converse to, chat up to. The tension between art and entertainment has dogged jazz (as it has other forms such as opera) throughout its history. Many moments of public interest in jazz have enthused in its danceability – the rhythm or groove, rather than the technical ability of the soloists so revered by musicians. And indeed from the 1920s to the end of the Second World War the principal meaning of jazz was precisely as a form of dance music, if a dangerously eroticised one. The career of Spike Hughes helps to illustrate the ways in which jazz in pre-war Britain was caught. The Anglo-Irish Hughes was a bassist, arranger, composer and bandleader who worked in musical comedy (playing for several Coward shows); toured with Jack Hylton and with his own dance band; then in 1933 went to New York and recorded an album of his own compositions with American musicians, including Benny Carter and Coleman Hawkins. This, rather then being the beginning of a career in concert jazz, was the apogee of Hughes's career as a musician – because he did not see jazz as anything other than, in his words, 'a diversion ... an afternoon walk';[80] thereafter he worked as a critic for *Melody Maker* and wrote the first definitive history of opera at Glyndebourne.

Jazz is still used as dance music, as marching music, as background music – in the early 1990s, for example, 'acid jazz' became a catch-all label including a lot of soul, but also some music in which the rhythm section (bass, drums, keyboards) was produced by high-technology sequencers and samplers, while live soloists used traditional instruments (one example, guitarist Ronny Jordan's 1992 album *The Antidote*, charted). A subgenre 'jungle jazz' emerged, with soloists following the frenetic drums and dub bass lines of drum'n'bass (its title echoing the 'jungle music' played by the Duke Ellington band in 1920s Harlem). But more readily the 'acid jazz' label included almost any post-war jazz which people *could* dance to, including hard bop and various Latin confections. Jazz does not die, but is continually reconstructed, and every so often experiences a major 'revival'. 'Trad jazz', a form related to the early days of the music in New Orleans, was (re)constructed in the 1950s, and at its high point of popularity in Britain played its part alongside folk music in the CND moment of the early 1960s (and at many trade union marches thereafter – an odd conjunction, given the importance of the Communist Party to union militancy, and the Soviet hatred of jazz).[81] Meanwhile, at the same time that trad was accompanying CND, the 'modern jazz' of soul/funk grooves and the Hammond Organ-based sound made by players like Jimmy Smith was also popular in Britain – and gave the name 'modernist' to the 'mods' (this style was revived in the moment of acid jazz by the James Taylor Quartet). A more rebarbative and complex 'modern jazz', played by British musicians such as Mike Gibbs, Mike Westbrook, John Surman and Alan Skidmore, enjoyed a brief moment of relatively high presence in the early 1970s, as it drew on some of the instruments, influences and values sanctioned by 'progressive [rock] music' to negotiate a place in the public ear: this moment is discussed in chapter 3. Others, such as Evan Parker and Derek Bailey, moved away from the music's structural conventions and towards 'free' improvisation.

A generation later, around 1985, many young British jazz musicians emerged. The big band Loose Tubes, for example, shot to fame during a successful season at Ronnie Scott's club. Showing one of the common characteristics of such phenomena, the band was drawn in the main from college graduates bored with the disciplines of orchestral music; one of them resigned from full-time employment with the London Symphony Orchestra to join the band. However, Loose Tubes was in its first incarnation all-white and all-male. A group of young black musicians formed a rival big band, the Jazz Warriors, adopting both musical and ideological stances from the radical black American jazz of the 1960s (the music and politics of, among others, Eric Dolphy, Archie Shepp, Albert Ayler and the Afri-centric Chicago-based grouping the Association for the Advancement of Creative Music). In the saxophone section of the Jazz Warriors were Gail Thompson, Steve Williamson and Courtney Pine. Pine was then launched on a solo career; like Bob Marley with reggae, his name and his first album (like Marley's, on the Island label) were used to help to launch this jazz revival to a wider audience; both the album, *Journey to the Urge Within* (1986) and its single release, 'Children of the Ghetto', did well in the pop charts. Pine became for a while in some ways a 'pop star', rather as violinist Nigel Kennedy did – he was a curiosity, but an instant media personality, appearing on chat shows, modelling clothes, constantly pictured and interviewed. Behind him, a legion of young blacks put on zoot-suits and hung around looking cool.

This wasn't, precisely, aestheticised poverty *à la* Joe Harriott (or South African immigrants like Dudu Pukwana or Mongezi Feza), but commercial success: it must be seen that the 'yuppie moment' of the late 1980s associated with Thatcherism had opened the space for the expression of this young, black and upwardly mobile grouping – the first upwardly mobile generation of blacks in Britain. For a couple of years, black British jazz had a real social cachet, with advertising and television theme titles abundant, including credits music on the revived pop show *Juke Box Jury* and the first series of BBC 2's arts commentary programme, *The Late Show*. As it had been before the triumph of the electric guitar within pop, the saxophone became a cultural icon once more, signalling a successful, sexualised masculinity in a number of television adverts.

Another black grouping to benefit from the entrepreneurial ethos of Thatcherism, and to an extent working within the same African–American Heritage notions of black music, was Soul II Soul, the recording ensemble and record company led by Jazzie B. Again the symbols of modernity and the musical references to the 1960s mixed happily. Jazzie B's constant companion in the early days of Soul II Soul's success (at least when there were photographers present) was a mobile telephone, perhaps the ultimate sign of the new confidence of the business classes in the late 1980s, the (very brief) moment of 'enterprise culture'. Jazzie B's dedication to the idea of a specifically black capitalism, so redolent of the example of Berry Gordy, has in fact led him to set up his own label within the Motown Corporation in California. Again it must be said that the success of a black-owned British record company would have been unimaginable before Thatcherism; and ownership was crucial here. The chart successes of earlier black British performers such as soul singer Junior Giscombe and soul/funk bands Light of the World, Imagination and Incognito in the early 1980s was tempered by a (presumably) racist disbelief by the record companies in their abilities to produce long-term success.[82] Indeed, one implication of Jazzie B's move abroad in the early 1990s (with a recording studio in Antigua, as well as the deal with Motown) is that the British music industry is still fundamentally racist, hostile to and unwilling to invest in major black British talent;[83] though the success of Des'ree and particularly, perhaps, the blanket television promotion, in 1995, of the second album by Seal, signals, hopefully, a continuing decline of that negative and deeply stupid attitude.

## Let's mix again

Meanwhile the continuing and successful presence of black musics and musicians in Britain has prompted new waves of interaction within street-level musical culture. As Dick Hebdige has shown, the black British presence has stimulated cultural change since the 1950s. Simon Jones's book *Black Culture, White Youth*,[84] building on Hebdige's assumptions, demonstrates powerfully the continuing attraction of reggae culture on young whites who choose to move within it. There are white hip-hop bands like the Stereo MCs, to match the early 1960s white r'n'b movement. And there is a long tradition of 'mixed race' bands, from the Coventry two-tone bands like the Special AKA and Selecter and Birmingham's UB40 in the late 1970s and early 1980s, through Culture Club and the Thompson Twins in early 1980s pop, to more recent bands such as the Bristol-based Massive Attack, who use soul, jazz–funk and reggae samples as the bases for tracks which explore their places in the urban melting-pot (and include British folk-influenced as well as African, American and Caribbean musics).[85]

Both musical style and ethnic identity are in this mix, in a configuration of the city as a culturally interactive space which has affected people and their musics from all over the world. Apache Indian, raised in the Handsworth suburb of Birmingham, uses English, Punjabi and Jamaican patois interchangeably, rapping across language and dialect on the back of rhythm tracks which owe more to dance-hall reggae than to Indi-pop, for all their use of dhol and tabla drums. At the time of writing the most commercially successful of these syncretic adaptations is 'Bhangra', a form developed originally from a North Indian folk-music but now driven as well by the rhythms (and the technologies) of European/American dance music. Partly because of its continuing use of lyrics in Punjabi, Bhangra has a whole political economy, as well as a whole subculture, of records, videos and live concerts, often 'all-dayers' aimed at young people whose parents would not have the slightest interest in their attending concerts at night; many of those attending all-dayers are involved in a specifically urban masquerade, adopting the partygoer's identity for the daytime events, then removing make-up and changing clothing before returning to the supervision of their families. The gradual emergence of this music into general awareness, helped by the first dedicated television series in 1991 (if only, again, in a 1.30 a.m. Channel 4 'ghetto slot') promised much for the future interactive development of British pop.[86]

The promise was confirmed to an extent when in late 1996 'Dil Cheez', a Bally Sagoo track, sung in Hindi, entered the mainstream chart. Bhangra is not the only form to develop from within the British Asian communities; Najma Akhtar's careful fusing of the ghazal (Urdu ballad singing) style with rock and jazz rhythms and instruments has achieved commercial and critical success, and Sheila Chandra has recorded albums (for example, the aptly named *Weaving my Ancestors' Voices*)[87] which similarly explore and fuse the musics of her bicultural background. Bengali pop musics drawing on rock, rap and rave have emerged in East London, with the

band and associated DJs 'Joi' collaborating with musicians of the
older generation while fusing Bengali and rock rhythms;[88] the politicised rap of Fun'da'mental has asserted the confidence of the South
Asian presence in British life.[89]

Other communities (the Greek, Turkish and Cypriot, for example) have produced fusions of their own drawn from rap, rock and
their own rhythmic and harmonic systems; pressure from pirate
radio stations serving non-English-speaking publics in the cities
(broadcasting in Greek, Turkish, Punjabi and so on) has produced
licenses for new stations like Sunrise Radio, whose programming
includes a great deal of what is often called 'ethnic' music – the popular music of Greece or Cyprus, say – but also fusions of these with
the pop musics of other neighbouring cultures. The city maintains
its capacity to surprise, to transform what it contains, producing
new forms and new ways of consuming those forms. Through these
points of chance contact, mutation and development, music's living
history continues.

One conclusion to this chapter (though this is a story without, so
far, an end) might be once again to question the more consumerist
aspects of the ideas of young peoples' creativity offered by Willis.
The point is not peoples' ability to misread or otherwise reinterpret
the message from television programmes. This may happen, may
indeed contribute to the setting up of new small-scale local cultures
and codes. But more importantly, the city and the communication
technologies of the global village offer the spaces and soundscapes
in which people actively create, rather than just interpret, forms,
signs, meanings and the mode of production in which they are situated. Drum'n'bass is not an act of interpretation but of creation, and
that is why it is important. Through these connections and relationships 'the popular' now has to be defined, and – because of the
continued, relatively powerful position of the British music business
– the new resultant musics will be propagated world-wide, to form
new nodes of connection in their turn, in other urban spaces. There
is no conclusion to this chapter.

There is, however, another way in which a conclusion could be
written, which the next chapter will try to delineate. The continuing, selective, narrative offered here has been paralleled by consideration of theoretical developments. But these have until very
recently been sociological, or cultural in the broadest sense. Very
few discussions of popular music have broached the questions of

why musics sound as they do, and/or of the impact those sounds have on those who perform and listen to them – which, among other things, makes it difficult to address the question of the British-ness of any music beyond a swift glance at its performer's passport. Recently, however, this boundary has been crossed, and the next chapter will identify ways in which the study of popular music can be enriched by an emerging musicology, and will try to demonstrate the usefulness of such an approach to our examination of the float-ing signifiers of recent musical Britishness.

## Notes

1   T. Palmer, *All You Need is Love*, Futura, 1976, p. 15.
2   E. Lee, *Music of the People*, Barrie and Jenkins, 1970, p. 148.
3   D. CLarke, *The Rise and Fall of Popular Music*, Harmondsworth, Viking Penguin, 1995.
4   C. Larkin, ed., *The Guinness Encyclopaedia of Popular Music*, Guin-ness Publishing, 1994, comprised 14 volumes by that date; by contrast, D. Clarke, *The Penguin Encyclopaedia of Popular Music*, Penguin, 1989, P. Gammond, *The Oxford Companion to Popular Music*, Oxford, Oxford University Press, 1991, are single-volume compendia.
5   For the Benson orchestra see L. O'Brien, *She-Bop: the Story of Women in Popular Music*, Harmondsworth, Penguin, 1995, pp. 35–6.
6   S. Tracy, *Who's Who in Popular Music*, World's Work, 1984, p.1.
7   D. Russell, *Popular Music in England 1840–1914: a Social History*, Manchester, Manchester University Press, 1987, pp. 169, 182.
8   Compare, for example, R. Finnegan, *The Hidden Musicians: Music Making in an English Town*, Cambridge, Cambridge University Press, 1989; N. MacKinnon, *The British Folk Scene*, Buckingham, Open Uni-versity Press, 1993; S. Cohen, *Rock Culture in Liverpool: Popular Music in the Making*, Oxford, Oxford University Press, 1991.
9   One account which tries to do justice to this relationship and others which helped to structure the hegemonic American forms is P. van der Merwe, *Origins of the Popular Style: the Antecedents of Twentieth-Century Popular Music*, Oxford, Oxford University Press, 1989. My thanks to Ken Parker for referring me to this book.
10  Aspects of this connection are discussed in J.J. Beadle, *Will Pop Eat Itself? Pop Music in the Soundbite Era*, Faber, 1993, p. 39; M. Sinker, 'Music as Film', in J. Romney and A. Wootton, eds, *The Celluloid Juke-box*, BFI, 1995, pp. 107–8; A. Blake, 'The Echoing Corridor: Music in the Postmodern East End', in T. Butler and M. Rustin, eds, *Rising in the East: the Regeneration of East London*, Lawrence and Wishart, 1996,

pp. 197–214.

11  Studies include P. Bailey, ed., *Music-Hall: the Business of Pleasure*, Milton Keynes, Open University Press, 1987; J.S. Bratton, ed., *Music-Hall: Performance and Style*, Milton Keynes, Open University Press, 1989; for its traces into the twentieth century see R. Pearsall, *Edwardian Popular Music*, Newton Abbot, David and Charles, 1975 and Pearsall, *Popular Music of the Twenties*, Newton Abbot, David and Charles, 1976.

12  See the polemic by D. Harker, *One for the Money: Politics and Popular Song*, Hutchinson, 1980.

13  See M. Pickering and T. Green, eds, *Everyday Culture: Popular Song and the Vernacular Milieu*, Milton Keynes, Open University Press, 1987.

14  Palmer, *All You Need is Love*, p. 99.

15  A. Briggs, *A History of Broadcasting in the United Kingdom*, Oxford, Oxford University Press, 1995 edn, vol. 2, p. 85.

16  F. Beckett, 'Opportunity Knocks for the Young, Gifted and Black', *The Independent*, 6 December 1990; Blake, 'The Echoing Corridor', p. 200. My thanks to Helen Noake and Chris Cole.

17  This is woefully under-researched; see Russell, *Popular Music in England*, p. 72; two useful surveys are R. Pearsall, *Edwardian Popular Music*, Newton Abbot, David and Charles, 1975 and Pearsall, *Popular Music of the Twenties*, Newton Abbot, David and Charles, 1976.

18  Lee, *Music of the People*, p. 139.

19  Briggs, *A History of Broadcasting*, vol. 4, p. 692.

20  Russell, *Popular Music in England*, pp. 185–7; K. Prodger, unpublished, 1993 Open University project, 'The Involvement of Working People in Classical Music in the North-East Midlands, 1930–60'; R. Nettel, *Music in the Five Towns 1840–1914*, Oxford, Oxford University Press, 1944; Finnegan, *The Hidden Musicians*.

21  Russell, *Popular Music in England*, p. 92.

22  J. Lanza, *Elevator Music*, Quartet, 1995.

23  Briggs, *A History of Broadcasting*, vol. 3, p. 256.

24  *Ibid.*, vol. 3, p. 41.

25  *Ibid.*

26  Briggs, in his *A History of Broadcasting*, vol. 2, p. 32, indicates that the proportion rose throughout the 1930s.

27  Briggs, *A History of Broadcasting*, vol. 3, p. 253.

28  See M. Kohn, *Dope Girls*, Lawrence and Wishart, 1993.

29  Briggs, *A H istory of Broadcasting*, vol. 4, p. 684.

30  G. Boyes, *The Imagined Village: Culture, Ideology and the English Folk Revival*, Manchester, Manchester University Press, 1993, p. 213.

31  See A. Blake, 'Listen to Britain: Music, Advertising and Postmodern

Culture', in M. Nava, A. Blake, I. MacRury and B. Richards, eds, *Buy This Book: Advertising and Consumption since the 1950s*, Routledge, 1997.

32  N. Mackinnon, *The British Folk Scene*, Buckingham, Open University Press, 1993, pp. 45–6.

33  Karen Prodger in her Open University project (see note 20 above) suggests that the popular investment in classical music declined rapidly after the Second World War, and was very tenuous by the 1950s.

34  Martin Parker, 'Reading the Charts', *Popular Music*, vol. 10, no 2, pp. 205–18 (p. 206).

35  Compare the sad attempt by George Michael to remake his career. On the 1950s entertainers, see A. Medhurst, 'It Sort of Happened Here: the Strange, Brief Life of the British Pop Film', in J. Romney and A. Wootton, eds, *Celluloid Jukebox*, BFI, 1995, pp. 64–5, and M. Houghton, 'Billy Fury', in J. Aizlewood, ed., *Love is the Drug: Living as a Pop Fan*, Penguin, 1994, pp. 204–12; on the light music career see J. Rogan, *Starmakers and Svengalis*, Macdonald and Queen Anne, 1988, pp. 18–22; G. Melly, *Revolt into Style*, Harmondsworth, Allen Lane, 1969, pp. 26–9.

36  For continuities in the story of exploitation see Rogan, *Starmakers and Svengalis*; S. Garfield, *Expensive Habits: the Dark Side of the Music Industry*, Faber, 1988; F. Dannen, *Hit Men: Power Brokers, Fast Money and the Music Business*, Vintage, 1991.

37  For documentation of these court cases see Garfield, *Expensive Habits*.

38  The arguments in this section are compressed from A. Blake, 'Britische Jugend: Gibt es noch/British Youth: Does it Still Exist?', in N. Bailer and R. Horak, eds, *Jugendkultur Annäheurungen*, Vienna, Wiener Universitätsverlag, 1995, pp. 206–38.

39  Enthusiasts included William Mann, chief music critic of *The Times*, and Wilfrid Mellers; see A. Kozinn, 'Beatles as Classics', *BBC Music Magazine*, October 1995, pp. 33–7; and Kozinn, *The Beatles*, Phaidon, 1995.

40  Rogan, *Starmakers and Svengalis*, pp. 106, 127, 277.

41  First to recognise the teenager was M. Abrahams, in *The Teenage Consumer*, London Press Exchange, 1959. The academic response in Britain is a process described by some of its constituents: for example, D. Hebdige, *Subculture: the Meaning of Style*, Methuen, 1979; P. Willis, *Profane Culture*, Routledge and Kegan Paul, 1978.

42  S. Cohen, ed., *Images of Deviance*, Harmondsworth, Penguin, 1970; S. Cohen, *Folk Devils and Moral Panics: the Creation of the Mods and Rockers*, McGibbon and Kee, 1972; P. Willis, *Learning to Labour: How Working-Class Kids get Working-Class Jobs*, Saxon House, 1977. A useful critique of the last is B. Skeggs, 'Learning to Labour', in M. Barker

and A. Beezer, eds, *Reading into Cultural Studies*, Routledge, 1992, pp. 181–96.

43 See S. Hall and T. Jefferson, eds, *Resistance Through Rituals*, Hutchinson, 1976.

44 G. Marcus, *Lipstick Traces: the Secret History of the Twentieth Century*, Secker and Warburg, 1989; J. Savage, *England's Dreaming: the Sex Pistols and Punk Rock*, Faber, 1991; B. Watson, *Frank Zappa: the Negative Dialectics of Poodle Play*, Quartet, 1993.

45 P. Willis, *Common Culture: Symbolic Work and Play in the Everyday Cultures of the Young*, Buckingham, Open University Press, 1990.

46 Willis, *Common Culture*, pp. 101–3.

47 M. Nava, *Changing Cultures: Feminism, Youth and Consumerism*, Sage, 1992; A. McRobbie, *Feminism and Youth Culture: From Jackie to Just Seventeen*, Basingstoke, Macmillan; in particular McRobbie, 'Settling Accounts with Subcultures', reprinted in S. Frith and A. Goodwin, eds, *On Record*, Routledge, 1990, pp. 66–80; and Skeggs, 'Learning to Labour'.

48 See S. Garratt, 'All of Me Loves All of You: the Bay City Rollers', in Aizlewood, ed., *Love is the Drug*, pp. 72–85.

49 See, for example, H. Thomas, ed., *Dance, Gender and Culture*, Macmillan, 1993; and more specifically on dance and 'subculture', S. Thornton, *Club Cultures*, Cambridge, Polity Press, 1995.

50 S. Reynolds and J. Press, *The Sex Revolts: Gender, Rebellion and Rock-'n'Roll*, Serpent's Tail, 1995.

51 For an illuminating discussion of these issues, see J. Gilbert, 'White Light/White Heat. Jouissance beyond Gender in the Velvet Underground', in A. Blake, ed., *Living Through Pop*, London, Routledge, 1998.

52 I. Chambers makes some of these points in his *Urban Rhythms: Pop Music and Popular Culture*, Macmillan, 1985, pp. 187–9.

53 On this see also R. Dyer, 'In Defence of Disco', reprinted in Frith and Goodwin, eds, *On Record*, pp. 410–18.

54 S. Redhead, *The End-of-the-Century party: Youth and Pop towards 2000*, Manchester, Manchester University Press, 1990.

55 *Ibid.*, p. 25.

56 A. Melechi, 'The Ecstasy of Disappearance', in S. Redhead, ed., *Rave Off*, Aldershot, Avebury Press, 1993, p. 37.

57 T. Jordan, 'Collective Bodies: Raving and the Politics of Gilles Deleuze and Felix Guattari', *Body and Society*, vol. 1, no. 1, pp. 125–44.

58 For the purity debate and much else on the pharmacology of the rave phenomenon, see N. Saunders, *Ecstasy and the Dance Culture*, published by the author, 1995.

59 S. Redhead, *Unpopular Cultures: the Birth of Law and Popular Cul-*

*ture*, Manchester, Manchester University Press, 1995, p. 6.

60 *Ibid.*, pp. 6–7.

61 Narrated in, for example, D. Bradley, *Understanding Rock'n'Roll: Popular Music in Britain 1955–1964*, Buckingham, Open University Press, 1992; a useful personal account of a local scene is D. Lister, *Bradford's Rock'n'Roll*, Bradford, Bradford Libraries and Information Service, 1991.

62 Harker, *One for the Money*, p. 83.

63 Indi-pop is discussed illuminatingly in A. Durant, *Conditions of Music*, Macmillan, 1984, chapter 6.

64 An interesting account of the British blues scene and its development towards rock is D. Heckstall-Smith, *The Safest Place to Be*, Quartet, 1988.

65 C.S. Murray, *Crosstown Traffic: Jimi Hendrix and Post-War Pop*, Faber, 1989.

66 Guy himself, a Chicago blues musician, has been adopted in Britain; the 1991 album *Damn Right I've Got the Blues* (Silvertone Ore CD 516) used British guest stars such as Jeff Beck, Mark Knopfler and Eric Clapton.

67 L. O'Brien, *She Bop: the Definitive History of Women in Rock, Pop and Soul*, Harmondsworth, Penguin, 1995, p. 294.

68 Examples include the Beatles' 'I Call Your Name' and The Tornadoes' 'Blue, Blue, Blue Beat', both released in 1964.

69 A. Sherwood, interview on BBC Radio Three, 'Mixing It', February 1995.

70 See, for example, P. Fryer, *Staying Power*, Pluto Press, 1984; P. Oliver, ed., *Black Music in Britain*, Milton Keynes, Open University Press, 1991.

71 See the discussion in chapter 3 of Reynolds and Press, *The Sex Revolts*, on body, mind and bass.

72 This is the view of J. Hind and S. Mosco in their *Rebel Radio*, Pluto Press, 1985; but note the qualification offered in S. Barnard, *On the Radio*, Milton Keynes, Open University Press, 1989, pp. 40–1.

73 A useful account of the evolution of Radio One in relation to its less conventional programming is K. Garner, *In Session Tonight: the Complete Radio 1 Recordings*, BBC Books, 1993.

74 C. Loughran, 'Radio 1: Fall and Rise', *Ariel*, 5 December 1995.

75 Previous attempts to find the 'right' youth music TV format are discussed in Briggs, *A History of Broadcasting*, vol. 5, pp. 200–6.

76 Compare the relationship between pop and cinema explored in Romney and Wootton, eds, *Celluloid Jukebox*.

77 See Barnard, *On the Radio*, for a summary of these events and disputes.

78 See S. Frith, 'Playing with Real Feeling – Jazz and Suburbia', in Frith,

*Music for Pleasure*, Cambridge, Polity Press, 1988, pp. 42–58; E. Hobsbawm (writing as Francis Newton), *The Jazz Scene* [1959], Weidenfeld and Nicolson, 1989, pp. 222–3; and P. Larkin, *All What Jazz: a Record Diary, 1961–68*, Faber, 1970. D. Boulton, *Jazz in Britain*, W.H. Allen, 1958, provides an interesting overview of the late-1950s moment.

79   See the paper given by the musician Ken Hyder at the 1995 conference *Music and the Psyche* held at the City University, London.

80   D. Boulton, *Jazz in Britain*, p. 50.

81   Hobsbawm, *The JazzScene*, p. 245.

82   See, for example, Incognito, interviewed in *Music Technology*, vol. 5, no 10, September 1991, pp. 54–6.

83   The charge was repeated in a BBC 2 *Open Door* programme on 12 April 1991. When the magazine *Hip-Hop Connection* was launched in 1988, it had great trouble persuading advertisers that young black people (the magazine's target audience) had money to spend (personal testimony).

84   S. Jones, *Black Culture, White Youth*, Macmillan, 1987.

85   For example, Massive Attack's version of 'Home of the Whale', by Owen Hand, *Massive Attack e.p.*, Wild Bunch Records WBRDG 4. Compare the explicit multiculturalism of the British rap band The Brotherhood: 'One Mixed-Race, One Black, One Yid' on *Elementalz*, on Virgin Bitem, CDBHOOD1 7243 8 41324 2 2. For a genealogy of the urban mutations which helped to produce Massive Attack's particular mix, see P. Johnson, *Straight Outa Bristol: Massive Attack, Portishead, Tricky and the Roots of Trip-Hop*, Hodder and Stoughton, 1996.

86   Bhangra has yet to find its historian; one early approach is S. Bannerjee and G. Baumann, 'Bhangra 1984–8: Fusion and Professionalisation in a Genre of South Asian Dance Music', in P. Oliver, ed., *Black Music in Britain*. See also S. Sharma, J. Hutnyk and A. Sharma, eds, *Dis-Orienting Rhythm: the Politics of the New Asian Dance Music*, Zed Books, 1996.

87   S. Chandra, *Weaving my Ancestors' Voices*, Real World CDRW 24 0777 7 86722 2 7, 1992; more recently *ABoneCroneDrone*, Real World, 1996.

88   G. Lipsitz, *Dangerous Crossroads: Popular Music, Postmodernism and the Poetics of Place*, Verso, 1994, p. 119.

89   On this in general see Sharma, Hutnyk and Sharma, eds, *Dis-Orienting Rhythms*.

# 3

# The Romanticism of rock

British popular music, like the other arts, lives in the shadows cast by Beethoven and other artists of the early nineteenth century, who can over-simply be labelled 'romantic'. Descriptive sociology and critical journalism alike tends to reinforce this picture of great artists producing great music. It does so, routinely, at the expense of any analysis of the way music sounds; indeed, it is a constant part of the defensive elitism of most writing about popular music that it is a discourse which does not rely on neutral, routine analytical tools, but on engaged enthusiasm and writing skill. Fortunately, a counter-discourse of textual engagement has emerged in recent years. This chapter will examine the limits of the 'romantic' approach, and will go on to discuss the analysis of music. The emerging 'rock musicology' has concentrated on the music of the late 1960s, and I do so here. Tracing the interactions of jazz and rock at this point, I examine a specific set of sonic relations in a music which was trying to adapt Anglo-American and other forms in order to find a more authentic British voice.

It is this moment, the late 1960s, in fact, at which a canon of (largely white, male) 'rock' performers emerged, seeking new musical values and distancing themselves from the commercial hurly-burly of chart pop – and with them grew a school of journalism which was eager to canonise both their work and its own. The rock musician is shadowed by the Rock Writer, whose informed awareness of the music's subtleties and desire to discriminate among artists and their work is matched by a refusal of analysis; all of which is profoundly resonant with that anti-intellectualism of British cultural criticism which was identified in the introduction.

Rock writing romanticises both its subjects and the writers them-

selves. Its fans, obsessive worshippers of their heroes, often transfer
this obeisance when writing professionally, presenting themselves as
analogues of the talented people whom they discuss.[1] Take, for
example, Nick Kent's collected writings, *The Dark Stuff*.[2] On the
front cover a young, full-mouthed Kent stares vacantly out over the
words 'living legend of rock journalism', while on the back encomia
from Morrisey and Lou Reed are supported by Kent's modest self-
assessment: 'I happen to believe that *The Dark Stuff* contains some
of the greatest, most truly heroic stories of my time and generation
… and no one else has written them quite like me.' Whose tales have
been told by this sometime student of English literature? We first
meet Brian Wilson, who invented the aural Californication of 'surf
pop' with the Beach Boys, then became increasingly and obsessively
experimental, using new studio technologies to their limits on his
way to a sequence of drug-fuelled nervous breakdowns. Next stop
Jerry Lee Lewis, whose story Kent cheerily admits features 'madness, bigamy, religious mania, tragedy, psychotic arrogance, epic
violence and debauchery, drugs of every shape and substance, an
ocean of alcohol, wealth, corruption, damnation, probably even
murder'.[3] Then to Syd Barrett, the art-school whimsicalist who
wrote perfect psychedelic pop for Pink Floyd before collapsing
under the mental burden of the chemicals used in their creation.
Kent ascribes the following to Syd Barrett, cogently identifying crucial aspects of the emergent musical language of British rock:

> the quintessential marriage of the two ideal forms of English psyche-
> delia – musical rococo freak-outs joining together with Barrett's sud-
> den ascent into the lyrical realms of ye Olde English whimsical loone,
> wherein dwelt the likes of Edward Lear and Kenneth Grahame. Pervy
> old Lewis Carroll, of course, presided at the very head of the tea-
> party.[4]

But there is malice in wonderland; Barrett's descent into pharma-
cological catatonia involved sexual violence. And so on through
Brian Jones, The Rolling Stones, Lou Reed, Sid Vicious, Iggy Pop,
Shane McGowan, Guns'n'Roses, Happy Mondays, the Stone Roses,
Miles Davis and Neil Young, leavened by the not quite so twisted
lives and times (in these Kent chapters, at least) of Elvis Costello,
Morrissey and Roy Orbison.

Rock here is epic male creativity, its heroes emerging through
pain, debauchery and excessive behaviour to produce great art –

and in the cases of Jones, Wilson and Barrett, then collapsing. Both its primary creators and their shadows, the rock writers (certainly Kent himself), exist in this Faustian world of genius paying a high personal price in order to produce the goods. The details of the creative process are unimportant against this general sense of creative power achieved through rebellion against conformity. These musicians may not starve in a garret, but otherwise they are archetypes of the Romantic Artist: members of an elite of gifted individuals for whom normal social rules do not, cannot apply.

While concentration on the hotel-trashing, partying, drug- and sex-consuming of the band on tour makes rock biography interesting reading, it mystifies the production of music, identifying 'stars' whom we see at play rather than at work. This is the basic mode, for example, of *Hammer of the Gods*, Stephen Davis's biography of Led Zeppelin, which opens with the rumour, propagated early in the band's career, that they really had made a Faustian bargain[5] – a recurring claim, backed by Jimmy Page's interest in magician Aleister Crowley. While Davis provides a great deal of information about the band's emergence, and the development of 'rock' itself, from the British r'n'b movement, the story is one of personalities and their sexual and chemical excesses, rather than of musical decisions. We learn a little about Page's innovations in guitar technique and in recording – placing microphones twenty feet behind an amplifier (as well as the usual one just in front of the speaker cabinet) in order to achieve a more ambient, live-feeling sound[6] – but little else of how the band actually made its music. Even Page's innovative use of the quirky electronic instrument the Theremin is glossed over.[7]

This is not to say that *Hammer of the Gods*, or other books of the type, are of no use. Davis provides a cultural history of musical Britishness, rich in contextual detail. Led Zeppelin came from the British African–Americanism of the blues, but invested heavily in the mythologies of the Celtic and Scandinavian past and the post-colonial present of 'world music'. Even on the first album, recorded in a few days in 1968, 'Black Mountain Side' shows these investments, as Davis says: 'a modal version in mock-sitar tuning of an old English folk riff that had been played in clubs by a folksinger named Annie Briggs and recorded by Bert Jansch. A tabla player, Virami Jasani, was brought in to provide a ragalike rhythm track.'[8] As Elgar had done when writing his Celtic cantata *Caractacus*, the band depicted the historicised landscape they lived in. Many tracks were written and rehearsed in a Welsh mountainside cottage and recorded in a Hampshire country-house studio.[9] Led Zeppelin's most famous track, 'Stairway to Heaven', is a product of this multi-cultural investment, a tribute to a Celtic 'White Goddess' influenced by Robert Graves's portrait of the same,[10] and composed in a style related both to the madrigal and the hymn: the 'rock anthem' has deep British as well as American roots.[11]

Led Zeppelin, then, are at the same time paradigmatic Romantic monsters and typical British musicians of the twentieth century, playing with diverse aspects of their world-wide and local musical heritage. They therefore exemplify my argument that the study of British music-making and listening should reflect the move away from unitary models of musical history and towards the more inclusive, less linear and less categorically differentiated cultural history that this book is trying to offer and Led Zeppelin were trying to create. They are part of a particular moment in that history, 'progressive rock', which has recently become an object of academic study, and this chapter will examine that moment in this context.

### Studying popular music/ology: the emerging paradigm

The study of popular music has become a routine aspect of sociology and cultural studies since the pioneering work of Simon Frith in the late 1970s.[12] The academic counterpart to the rock biography places popular music in its context, exploring the relations between social and taste groups, but not analysing the music itself except at the most basic level of successively or synchronously available genres. As my introductory chapter commented, this is partly because the models of musicology, tied to the western classical tradition, were inappropriate.[13] Western notation cannot encompass the aspects of rhythmic interchange and groove, or vocal and instrumental timbre, which (as subtle deviations from the norm) are among the most important signifiers in a popular music most of which shares a limited number of harmonic and rhythmic models.

The usual starting-point for a *musicological* cultural theory of music is the work of Theodor Adorno, whose Freudian Marxism is a guiding light we have seen shining from the pages of Ben Watson's treatment of Frank Zappa. However, though they routinely confront his work as a starting-point for their own analyses, most writers on popular music remain blind to the value of Adorno's critique.

It is the product of a moment in which German Marxists became convinced that one reason for their master's failure as a prophet of socialist revolution within advanced capitalist societies lay in the success of popular culture. For the writers of the 'Frankfurt School', newspapers and magazines, film, radio (television was not around when these diatribes began) and popular music were all means by which the ideas of a ruling elite were perpetuated and transmitted as common sense, in the form of a 'false consciousness' which promised individual happiness from a very limited set of behavioural codes and life opportunities. The culture industries offered 'Enlightenment as Mass Deception'.[14]

Adorno applied the norms of this philosophy of disillusionment to music.[15] He argued that popular forms such as Tin Pan Alley songs and what he called jazz were instances of mass deception. Creating, through their lyrics and in jazz through the improvised instrumental 'solo', an idea of individual freedom, they actually demonstrate the opposite. Song structures, lyrics, the very notes of the solos themselves (however 'improvised' they may be) are, Adorno claimed, all constructed according to a small, endlessly repeated, set of simple formulae. Promising individuality and romantic fulfilment, they demonstrated instead the 'pseudo-individualism' of conformity. Everything about the music (the sounds of the instruments, the chords used by instrumental soloists, the chord sequences of the songs) underlined this conformism. Only European classical music which refused the easy relations of tonal harmony, the Modernism of Schoenberg and his followers, was acceptable to Adorno, because only this music presented an analogue of the pain and alienation of contemporary existence. Music must reflect the truth of its society: for Adorno, that truth involved a masochistic listening experience; since listening should induce pain, harmony must be replaced by (structured) noise. Aesthetics should not offer anaesthesia. Good music should sound how Adorno felt. Bad.

Critics have pointed out that Adorno did not actually like American popular music, whereas he was a fan of European classical music, as if this openly acknowledged taste disallowed his analytical capability; that he listened to comparatively little of it; and that what he did listen to was from a period when popular music *was* indeed formulaic, produced on an industrial basis, according to a limited number of repeated patterns, by a small number of companies.[16] From the 1950s on, popular music has become increasingly fragmented, such that the individualism offered by the ideology of capitalism is far more readily realisable within the many styles, the different age-, gender-, sexuality- and ethnicity-related popular musics currently in circulation. Popular music is now so fragmented, so lacking a uniform voice, that it cannot offer 'mass deception', but multiple possibilities and identities.

Adorno's elision of politics and personal taste is often rejected. Curiously, however, the same relation of taste and political reading is present in the work of most popular music journalists and academic critics. They have repeated Adorno's blanket condemnation of the relentlessly melodic and cheerful, and his blanket association of the noisy with the subversive–realist in their negative attitude to commercial pop and their heroic readings of rock, punk and so on.[17] For instance, in *The Sex Revolts*,[18] Simon Reynolds and Joy Press discuss issues of gender across a wide range of mainly Anglo-American popular music; but their focus is left-field, independent 'rock', rather than chart pop: the very music romanticised by Nick Kent. Teen bands (whose product surely has something important to say about the social construction of gender) are conspicuous by their absence; while of an artist often held up in cultural studies circles as an iconic post-feminist role-model, Madonna, they say

> Eminent musicologist Susan McClary has stoutly defended Madonna's songs and divined all manner of radicalism in their key changes and structure; for us, it's all too apparent that Madonna is a mediatician, not a musician, that in most of her music, for all its burnished state-of-art production, there's a lack of real grain and swing … An image-fascist, Madonna is the perfect MTV-age star, privileging eye over ear.[19]

In other words, her 'burnished' music isn't noisy enough. Adorno's values ride again. Good music must sound bad.

Another writer often considered central to a cultural theory of the arts is Walter Benjamin. Viewing the same phenomena as Adorno, the rise of a 'mass' culture fuelled by the media industries, Benjamin came to the opposite conclusion. Adorno had claimed that it was only the highly individualised activity of the composer in the elite tradition which could reveal the real conditions of contemporary existence and could, therefore, produce the alienation effect necessary for the transcendence of false consciousness. So for

Adorno there is still a place for the Romantic Artist. Benjamin, by contrast, argued that the mass production of cultural commodities had made the work of art more democratically available, and had thus removed from it the 'aura' of supreme individual creativity which had made the arts supportive of an elitist system by implying that only a privileged few could create meaningful work. Again, where Adorno assumed that the content of a work led unerringly to specific effects on the audience (the transmission and reception of false consciousness), for Benjamin the complexity of mass production and the easy availability of the resultant product both contribute to the removal of the aura, making it far easier for the' audience to act as participant in the creation of meaning rather than just the passive recipient of the messages intended by the author, musician or producer.[20] The film spectator, and by implication the listener to mass-produced popular music, is actively involved in the production of meaning.

These theoretical positions are routinely debated in writings on popular music, usually at Adorno's expense. But if we are to talk about music, response and meaning, we will have to follow his example and delineate which sounds are received in which ways in order to create which meanings. The difficulty of using notation and the techniques associated with musical analysis should not preclude the attempt. A 'popular musicology' which engages with music as text, rather than text about music, is indeed beginning to emerge.

David Hatch and Stephen Millward's pioneering *From Blues to Rock*[21] concentrates on the generic and the linear, as they trace the evolution of specific songs from others with the same or similar harmonic or melodic material. They argue that much pop can be divided into 'song families', giving as example the derivation of the Rolling Stones's 'Not Fade Away', via Buddy Holly, from an 'original' by Bo Diddley. As this demonstrates, much of the trajectory in this 'evolution' since the 1950s is a move from black American forms (blues, boogie, gospel and so on) into the mainstream of commercial pop. Hatch and Millward insist that although there was a tradition of popular songwriting which involved the use of sheet music, this 'Tin Pan Alley' model became less important after the impact of rock'n'roll in the 1950s, and eventually song*writing* was eclipsed by an oral tradition. But this is not an oral tradition in the sense of generations passing on their knowledge directly, as in some romantic constructions of folk-song: it is mediated through recording and radio broadcasting. People learn to become competent songwriters, they argue, by learning first to play what they can hear from recordings and/or the radio. Thus song families are generated and reproduced locally, nationally and transcontinentally.[22]

Hatch and Millward also chronologise sounds, such as the trace of hill-billy vocal delivery – characterised here as high, nasal and declamatory, rather than full-throated – which was first recorded in the 1920s, is then available to be copied by non-hill-billies, and can be heard again through Bob Dylan, David Bowie and Bryan Ferry, thence through punk and the New Wave (and, one might add, in the dulcet tones of Dire Straits' Mark Knopfler).

The authors are careful to point out, however, that recording and broadcasting technologies do not determine these lineages, however much they help to produce them. By the mid-1960s the technologies of the recording studio (specifically multi-track recording) gave musicians and producers the opportunity of making music which was less spontaneous, and could be both more considered, and on a larger scale. In many cases, they took the opportunities offered by the new technology, thus helping popular music to escape from the limitations of the blues, gospel and r'n'b traditions (and the 2.5 to 3 minute limit on the song implied by the 7-inch single) and offer instead music of high ambition – but, they argue, low achievement. They consider the turn taken by rock in the late 1960s to have been an aesthetic disaster.[23] This common valuation in writing on popular music reflects a paradigm shift, formed in the critical rewriting of music history with values consequent from the impact of punk, which seems to have survived in this age of relativism. Again, the parallels with Adorno's conflation of personal taste, political belief and aesthetic judgement are clear: noisy punk good, relatively consonant progressive rock bad.

So popular musicology here involves historical analysis of musical codes and their transmission through technology. Firstly an 'oral history', by confirming and reproducing families of songs based on recording and broadcast transmission, interrupts the smooth transmission of light music. Then studio technology increases both the creative potential of the writer and producer and the pace of development, leading to the fragmentation of popular music into styles and genres associated with individuals and schools of performance: the song-family trees grow more branches. Eventually (to qualify Hatch and Millward's position by reference to a more recent development), technology interrupts this model in turn by increasing the power of the machine over the musician – through sampling, for example – in ways which increase the power of the producer/composer. New technologies both increase the potential fragmentation of music and the possibilities of its reintegration through the combining and synchronisation of disparate matters. For example, the track 'Sadeness' on the Enigma album *MCMXC a.D.* (1991) rejoices in the combination of spoken and sung female lead vocal, sampled drum loops from 1960s soul records, a melody played via the keyboard whose sound is a sampled shakuhachi (a Japanese traditional flute – the sample is an Akai standard factory sample, and has appeared on tracks by many other artists), chord sequences played from synthesisers and the Gregorian Chant of a monastic choir.[24] While the monks who had made the original recording of the Gregorian Chant sued for copyright damages and sales royalties (and won), it was otherwise a successful new integration of musics; not just a collage, but a new polyphony of voices and sounds.

A similar stress to Hatch and Millward's, on the importance of broadcasting and imitation, occurs in Dick Bradley's *Understanding Rock'n'Roll*,[25] which deals with the growth of rock'n'roll in Britain. While this is more a cultural history than musicology, it is well informed by cultural theory; Bradley offers insight into the fusing of new black American and existing white-dominated popular codes which became pop music in the early 1960s. He argues that the meanings of sounds are culturally constructed from interchange across time and space, class and ethnicity. This calls into question any notion of 'authenticity', of true musical meaning belonging to one group of people or another. However, his account is informed by psychoanalytic theory, where some musicological absolutes may be discerned.

One category within psychoanalytic thought is its account of mental development from a state of 'prelanguage' or preconsciousness, in which sounds have not been differentiated into language/other; and a subsequent state, after the human subject has learned language, in which the mind has a clear division between subconscious and conscious patterns of activity. The implication is that the recognition of language displaces all other sounds to the subconscious.[26] Julia Kristeva has offered the division between 'semiotic' and 'symbolic' systems of signification. The symbolic is language-based and centred from the acquisition of language, which is associated with the acquisition of gender roles. This means that, in any current society, language reproduces patriarchal relations. The semiotic, although it only exists as a counterpart to the symbolic, is outside this linguistic paradigm, and can therefore present alternatives to it. Even words, if outside the norms of language use, can become sounds signifying something different – though it should be remembered that in this as in any other semiotic system, sign-worlds and their meanings only exist in relation to each other. What is called for is not regression to an absolute prelinguistic paradise, but recognition of another way of speaking/enunciating which embodies a difference in the present. In Kristeva's work, avant-garde poetry was a model for this semiotic subversion of patriarchal meaning.[27] Music can, clearly, act in this way, and can provide a different, arguably subversive, model of signification.

A well-known essay by Roland Barthes builds on this distinction between rationalised language and extra-linguistic musicality. In 'The Grain of the Voice', Barthes discusses the work of two male singers who perform a wide range of classical music.[28] The German Dietrich Fischer-Dieskau attempts above all to convey to the listener the meanings of the words: the lines of the music and his own physical pleasure in singing are sacrificed to the cause of clarity of diction. Barthes's sometime singing teacher, the Swiss–French singer Panzera, on the other hand, paid very little attention to the meanings of the words he was singing, giving himself over instead to the joys of the physical activity itself, producing a specific sound, the 'grain of the voice', which expresses a state of being outside and beyond language, embodied but not enunciated. Barthes called this state *jouissance* (usually, rather inaccurately, translated as 'ecstasy') as opposed to *plaisir* (pleasure). This bodily ecstasy was for Barthes a more genuine, indeed authentic, musicianship than the pleasures of the rendered text. Elsewhere in Barthes's work this juxtaposition was related to knowledge: we greet the recognised with pleasure, and the unrecognised with jouissance; the jouissant response then becomes an aspect of our response to the sublime, the terrifying, the unknowable. This is one reason for the power of audience identification with performers whose work denies the limits of rationality, whether piano hero Franz Liszt in the nineteenth century or guitar hero Jimmy Page in the twentieth. It also helps to explain the close association of such musical virtuosity with the occult; the Devil is here identified as the source of that which is opposed to the knowledge-based and rationalised egos of everyday life – and which resides in the unconscious.

Simon Reynolds has followed this Barthesian model and suggested that it is precisely the loss of rational, language-centred subjectivity, including the sublime pleasures/terrors of loss of (self-) control, that is at the heart of the power of rock music: it actually *bestows* a lack of control, enabling the listener to escape from the socially constructed repressions of everyday subjectivity.[29] Chapter 2 noticed some of the accounts of 'raving' which stress this escape from the everyday. Bradley's discussion of the arrival of rock'n'roll also moves in this direction, suggesting that this music offered a way out of the limited subjectivity which, among working-class and lower-middle-class people at any rate, constructs them as working to a limited set of ends such as career or livelihood.

There is a contradictory tendency, shown in Barthes's idea of 'grain', which implies that there is an authentic human truth to be found, and expressed, once we move outside language and into the body. It is difficult to hold to this approach while also arguing, as Bradley does, that the notion of authentic music – say, of an authentically 'natural' black musicianship – is itself a socially constructed category, like the category 'race' from which this position is derived.

To extend the point, the Kristevan model of semiotic meaning owes its origin to a specific moment within French feminism: its proposal that the semiotic order could be a refuge for the feminine. In music, awareness of extra-linguistic possibilities has to be tempered by the knowledge that music, though routinely 'feminised', offers no simple escape from patriarchal values. Bradley insists that the codes of the new popular music were gendered – specifically, they were codes of masculinity and male sexuality; this he offers (in a circular argument) as the chief reason why most people in the enormous number of beat groups in early 1960s Britain were male. The 'semiotic' vocalisations of Elvis Presley – the Brando-like mumblings or other speech-based vocal inflections, as well as the extra-linguistic whoops – were male speech-signs recoded as music. Not words, the dominant, the conscious of patriarchy, but sounds, its subconscious. They were the codes of a masculine irrational. Masculinity and rationality are not the same thing.

Indeed, according to *The Sex Revolts*, they cannot be. 'A sense of loss is intrinsic to the human condition',[30] it appears, because we all have to learn to leave our mothers. This is a bigger problem for males than for females; it leads, apparently, to all the psychic problems of the incomplete male ego: fascism, misogyny, cyborgism, the perpetual escape of life on the road and/or the search for a return to the womb are all represented in 'rebel rock'. Through these bold statements Reynolds and Press offer a useful alternative history of popular music, exploring the masculinity of most rock, but also paying special attention to musics which could be heard as a 'musique féminine'. Here, for instance, they speak in praise of dub: 'like ambient acid house, dub is wombadelic music: its bass penetrates your body, the music floats out to enfold you'[31] (the astute reader will have noticed the use of 'penetration' as well as 'enfolding', which underlines the difficulty of this reductive reading!); or again, of German experimentalists Can, 'despite the all-male personnel of the band, it is radically "feminine" music, embodying principles of flow and symbiosis into its structure, texture and aura'.[32]

Such analyses can show real insight. However, these moments of praise or blame often become a litany designed to uphold the theoretical matrix. As well as the troubling absence of music for puberty, questions of sexuality and sexual orientation are taken somewhat for granted. In a book which relies on Freud's model of original polymorphous desire and the construction of heterosexuality as only one of many potential moves away from that original positioning, there is no exploration of lesbian, gay and bisexual desires – or, a few token moments apart, of how these have affected, and continue to affect, the making and using of music. The equally important questions of class, ethnicity, regional derivation, the position of musics and musicians in relation to capital, the ability to play musical instruments or use specific musical codes, the very place of peoples and their musics in time – all are crucial to a nuanced understanding of any music, and they are not always addressed. John Street, a leftist critic, claimed that *Rebel Rock* was ultimately conservative.[33] Reynolds and Press agree – but in effect transpose the hyper-individualised, anti-social values of rock stars on to the social conservatism they themselves implicitly support. Hiding behind much of Reynolds and Press's denunciation of masculine rock rebellion lurks another demon, High Toryism, with its back-to-basics picture of the stable marriage and happy family. At the end of the twentieth century, as divorces sky-rocket and abused children cry, this fantasy won't wash. Bradley's book, by contrast, in which psychoanalytic models are a component, rather than the dominant interpretative matrix, offers more insight about the workings of music within society.

Psychoanalysis and cultural history have been joined by the work of writers with musicological/analytical skills. Robert Walser provides both a useful perspective on theorisations of gender and an impressive analysis of the playing of the genre in his book *Running with the Devil: Power, Gender and Madness in Heavy Metal Music*.[34] The basic component of heavy metal (HM) is the power chord, which is a symbol of stability, permanence and harmony on the one hand, and of overdriven, screeching excess on the other. This juxtaposition is crucial, as Walser argues that the analysis of popular musical discourses should revolve around the presence of 'horizons of expectation' for the listener, and, in, or across which utterances can be made, either confirming the genre (and the listener's pleasure in recognising it) or subverting it (thereby giving the listener the potential pleasure of the shock of the new). In other words, *plaisir* and *jouissance* are on offer again.

Walser insists that HM is 'heavy' because of timbre: the sounds of the instruments and the mix. Again we have Adornoesque values: this music is brutal, distorted, and always frighteningly loud; 'chain-saw guitar' is an apt journalistic cliché of the genre. The overdriven amplifiers sustaining chords indefinitely, the large drums making every kick (bass drum beat) into a sepulchral hammer-blow, the *noise* of it all. And yet it is a very particular, structured, noise. The classic power chord is based on the fourth or fifth, with resultant tones (due to the amplifier's distortion) which add low frequencies. As Walser says, the effect is like a very loud pipe-organ, with its sound reverberating around the space of a cathedral.[35] The vocal sound of HM is also particular: most of its lead vocalists are high tenors who can also sustain notes, use heavy guitar-like vibrato, and above all, they can scream.

Moving from sound to its disposition via harmony and rhythm, Walser notes the prevalence of modes in HM performance and composition, and details the ways in which knowledge of these is shared through sources such as *Guitarist* magazine: there is an information economy in HM, crucial to both connoisseurship and practice. Many guitarists also acknowledge the virtuoso performer/composers of the past (classical as well as rock) as forebears. Eddy van Halen and Yngwe Malmsteen (both European) look to J.S. Bach, Vivaldi, Paganini and Beethoven as well as earlier guitar heroes such as Jimi

Hendrix and Ritchie Blackmore (himself a Bach devotee) – and
Walser demonstrates these affinities, looking at the scores of the classical composers and then at transcribed guitar solos (using a modi-
fied version of Western notation), which use the same patterns.[36]

There is, of course, more to HM than the reworking of eighteenth-century music via overdriven amplifiers: Walser comments
on the social meanings of this music and, as his title suggests, specifically on the issue of gender. HM is played largely by men, who
share what he describes as the Orpheus problem – a problem we met
in eighteenth-century Britain. Orpheus must display supreme musicianship, including the public display of emotion. This outpouring,
however, will destabilise his masculinity. HM, therefore, for all its
patriarchal posturing, its 'cock-rock' antics, is threatened; a threat
often underlined/self-parodied by the dress and stage behaviour of
the performers, in which gender codes are routinely mixed, as in
bands such as Kiss. However, until the advent of MTV, argues
Walser, the form was enthusiastically followed only by males. Since
then, and especially since the appearance on MTV of the more
romanticised HM of Jon Bon Jovi (who does not exceed the usual
dress codes of gender and sexuality), the audience has shifted: HM
now plays to gender-balanced audiences.[37]

All the more reason, by their lights, therefore, for the concern
shown about the medium by right-wing American 'parents'. Thanks
to Bon Jovi and MTV, HM will now endanger teenage girls, who are
the centre of attention in any discourse of the family (and its subset
debates over abortion, contraception and so on). 'The family', as it
has since the 1950s, if not before, decodes as 'protection for teenage
girls from sexual knowledge and experience'. So HM has come
under sustained attack because of the eroticism, blasphemy and
devil-worship of some of its subject-matter. Rap, of course, has
come under similar pressure, and for similar reasons, in the name of
the family. Gender is an issue in rock music to more than sociologists. Indeed, in Walser's book, as in Bradley's and in *The Sex
Revolts*, it is an issue in musicology, in the make-up of sound as
much as in the surrounding cultural practices and reactions.

Alan Moore's *Rock, the Primary Text*[38] is, by contrast, a study in
aesthetics rather than social meanings. Moore argues that rock
musicology must pay attention to texture, sound manipulation and
performance practice. He describes what the instrumental and vocal
elements in rock music (drumkit, bass, guitars, lead and chorus

voices and so on) actually do; how songs are structured rhythmi-cally; and how vocal styles establish collective as well as individual personalities (so rock singers do not sound like soul singers or pop singers, not because their bodies are different, but because of a set of vocal techniques; in other words, different genres are learned and performed differently). When talking of harmony, he argues, like Walser, that all players, in accompaniment or solo, use modes as well as Western major/minor harmonies based on interchangeable tonic triads.[39]

Moore spends much of his time on the moment of 'progressive rock', c. 1967–74. As he sees it, progressive rock emerged from the commercial successes of Merseybeat. Record labels invested much of their profit in new recording studios and technologies and made deeper investments in the bands they signed, encouraging them to use the new studios, to experiment and to produce albums (rather than make three singles, with an album to follow only if they achieved success in the singles charts). While there was no one style to emerge from this moment of overcapitalised experiment, Moore identifies several features in the musics of the time:

1   The influence of the art college, whose students included John Lennon, David Bowie, Brian Eno and Malcolm McLaren.[40]
2   The continuing influence of black American forms, especially the blues riff, the repeated phrase played by bass guitar and other instruments, which both underpins the harmony and dri-ves the song forward: the blues riff is the crucial element of what was to become heavy metal.
3   The influence of jazz, especially the 'serious' concert music of 1940s bebop onwards (rather than the entertainment/dance musics of swing, jump and so on). This arty jazz is important in the music of British bands Van der Graaf Generator, If and Colosseum, as well as to American bands such as Blood, Sweat and Tears and Chicago.
4   The importance of improvisation, especially the guitar solo based on accepted formulae and predictable relations with the harmony: this owes much to the blues and jazz legacy, and it helps to create the deified rock instrumental performer, notably the guitar hero.
5   The influence of European classical music, and especially that of contemporary experimental Modernist composers: Berio and

Stockhausen were cited as direct influences on 'A Day in the Life' from the Beatles' *Sergeant Pepper* album, for instance.[41] Others (for example Nice and their successor Emerson, Lake and Palmer) performed covers of classical pieces arranged with solo spaces, much like the 'third-stream' jazz of the Modern Jazz Quartet; The Moody Blues, Deep Purple and others wrote and performed pieces for rock musicians and classical orchestra.

6  A related use of existing songwriting forms and traditions such as folk (important to Jethro Tull, for instance) and music-hall (used, for example, by the Beatles and the Kinks): Moore suggests that this, like the use of classical music, formed a partial *and quite deliberate* break with the domination of the USA.[42]

7  An ideological utopianism, whether expressed in the pacifism of King Crimson or Van der Graaf Generator, the Orientalised, Indian-related pseudo-Buddhism of Quintessence or the science-fiction utopianism of Hawkwind or pre-'Dark Side' Pink Floyd.

One important addition to this list is proposed by Sheila Whiteley, who also concentrates on the moment of progressive music in her book *The Space Between the Notes*.[43] Whiteley describes what she calls 'psychedelic coding': the relationship between sounds and the drugs taken by musicians.[44] Emerging in the mid-1960s, along with the use of the drug LSD, was a musical style which expressed the experience of taking it, and which she characterises thus: 'the manipulation of timbres (blurred, bright, overlapping), upward movement (and its comparison with psychedelic flight), harmonies (lurching, oscillating), rhythms (regular, irregular)'.[45] Both Jimi Hendrix and Cream's Eric Clapton tended to play solos which push irregularly against a regular beat. Whiteley argues that this performance style homologises the LSD experience of feeling different aspects of awareness move quickly in and out of focus: for example, '[Eric Clapton's] solo focuses on configurations of vibrant bent-up notes and sliding glissandi to effect a sense of 'tripping' around the underlying beat',[46] or again, in one of Jimi Hendrix's solos:

> while the lead break is fairly firmly metrical with most of the bars being in eighths or sixteenths plus ornaments, the occasional deflection of accents from weak to strong beats creates a feeling of being within a different time scale ... fed by phrasing and articulation ... the guitar meanders in an almost raga-like noodling around the notes.[47]

Again, in the early Pink Floyd gigs, oil-based light-shows replicated the visual experience of the acid trip even as the lengthy, monotonal, noise-affected structures of Pink Floyd's music replicated the aural experience of the trip – as more recently, one might add, the relaxed, shuffling beats of trip-hop offered a sense of fluctuating focus for the MDMA/'Ecstasy' taker. In these ways, Whiteley argues, by offering a psychotropic experience paralleling that given them by their favourite illegal chemicals, progressive bands and artists could connect with their unconscious, rather than their conscious and socially placed, selves. At the start of the movement, this was also presented in subversion of the norms of entertainment within capitalism. Many concerts were given free.[48]

Fear of subversion of both the economics of the entertainment industry and the ordered functioning of the rational mind, and thereby of the whole social order, lay behind much of the opposition to the drugs and the music (as it has more recently with media hype and legislation against rave culture, its chemical stimulants and its informal economy of parties and independently created music). However, the almost immediate commercialisation of the music and associated culture by record companies and producers of lifestyle aids undercut the early moment of free festivals and rage against the music industry. In America, Britain and elsewhere free festival 'love-ins' were replaced by 'cash-ins', festivals or other concerts from which entrepreneurs and musicians began to make money. The recording industry was also quick to respond to the music, with major labels signing the new bands and setting up new labels such as Harvest (EMI) and Vertigo (Philips) to accommodate acts unwilling to be associated with existing pop labels and selling the revolution as an aesthetic one (which it was), rather than the political transformation it had ambitions to become. Although there are exceptions, including the independent label Charisma, whose boss, Tony Stratton Smith, consistently made records he liked rather than records he or his advisers thought would sell, the music of the psychedelic era was for other companies a mere reordering of the consumer categories – a marketing opportunity.[49]

It was relatively easy to sell the new music as an aesthetic revolution because the industry had for several years been focused on the idea of young people as creative musicians, and psychedelia could be seen as a further step towards letting this creativity off the leash. Frank Zappa argued that 'if you want to come up with a singular, most important trend in this new music, I think it has to be something like: it is original, composed by the people who perform it, created by them'.[50] The rationale of ephemeral pop was being subverted, in other words, by particular individuals who could be drawn into the star system, portrayed as special, and then benefit from long careers: the new Romantic Artists, geniuses moving music in a new direction, who happily lined their own pockets and/or noses while so doing.

Rock musicians and critics argued for a new place for the music, on a par with the respect given to the classical music traditions and the more serious side of jazz. The musicians staked their claim by producing albums rather than singles; and often, linking the songs together as 'concept albums', searching for the status which was accorded to the long, integrated composition within the classical music world. After the early psychedelic moment, 'progressive music' was gradually differentiated from pop and from black musics, and this was reflected in niche programming on radio and television. The success of the Beatles' album *Sergeant Pepper's Lonely Hearts Club Band* (1967) led to the broadcasting of what had before this point been the values of a self-constituted elite: songs which pointed up the joys of LSD rubbed shoulders here with the rest of the Beatles' repertoire, mixing traditions from music-hall, the light entertainment of the 1930s and 1940s, r'n'b and the experimental music of the Modernist avant-garde. If *Sergeant Pepper* is the apogee of this tendency, its nemesis is an equally successful album, Pink Floyd's *Dark Side of the Moon*, which was at the top of the British album charts for two years from 1972. Here there is also generous experiment with sound, including use of minimalist synthesiser patterns and Modernist sound diffusion. But the celebration of the psychotropic which was in evidence in *Piper at the Gates of Dawn*, the album Pink Floyd were making in the same Abbey Road studio complex at the same time as *Sergeant Pepper* was being made, has given way, perhaps under the impact on members of the band of Syd Barrett's overdosing on that very psychotropic experience, which led to his mental breakdown. Instead, most prominent on *Dark Side* is a gloomy view of capitalism's effect on the individual – a gloom portrayed in a series of slow- to medium-paced 4/4 songs, and inexorably deepened by subsequent releases from Pink Floyd (and latterly Roger Waters, the originator of most of the band's material after Barrett's collapse) through the 1970s and 1980s.

In accounting for this disillusion, in the end Whiteley perhaps wisely ignores Floyd lyrics, but instead, unwisely, reproduces the politics of Richard Middleton and John Muncie, who in the early 1980s, writing units for the Open University's course on popular culture, were still trying to pull the rabbit of class-led revolution out of the hat labelled 'Britain's Future'. Indeed, towards the end of her book she quotes them to the effect that the counter-culture, including progressive rock, had

> diverted attention away from the structural inequalities of capitalist society: by criticising technology rather than the property-owning rich, by demanding quality in life rather than the satisfaction of basic needs and by elevating youth disaffiliation as the motor of social change rather than class conflict and struggle.[51]

This antiquarian fantasy about the nature of authentic politics has the unfortunate effect of drawing an interesting argument back into the world of British left(ish) academia, still using cultural analysis to tilt at the windmill of 'capitalism' and those enriched by it, and denying the effectiveness of any world-view other than its own model.

Not all commentaries on the progressive moment are quite so politically old-fashioned; the same interpretative starting-points can be used to propose more sophisticated political arguments. *Revolution in the Head: the Beatles' Records and the Sixties*, by Ian Macdonald, combines the social and contextual appreciation of the music of the 1960s with aspects of musical analysis. While this is not an academic text, it combines a careful, often detailed contextual examination of the making of all the band's generally released material with analysis of the tracks' sounds. Macdonald details the increasing complexity of the material, the band's move from the rock'n'roll derivatives through the influences of folk, music-hall and avant-garde/classical music traditions and the music of other bands such as the Beach Boys and the Incredible String Band, to the late 1960s anticipation of both heavy metal and folk/rock (which can be heard on the 1968 *White Album* – check, for example, the proto-HM 'Helter-Skelter' and the folky 'Blackbird', both with lead vocals by McCartney). All this is presented within an account of the band's rise, pomp and fall, which narrates the interactions of the main characters (John Lennon, Paul McCartney, George Harrison, Ringo Starr, Brian Epstein and George Martin) and their immediate and more general context (the political and economic changes of the 1960s).

Macdonald's account, like the more recent band biography by Alan Kozinn, idealises Lennon and McCartney as romantic artists.[52] He stresses their lack of musical education, their distance from the routinised procedures of any taught form of music-making. Like the Hatch and Millward examples, they taught themselves how to make music and could, therefore, he argues, be more fruitfully experimental than those who went to music college (many of whom became Prog Rockers). Macdonald also deals, throughout his text, with that other aspect of romantic artistry: the changing of the mind through drugs. He thinks that the music is influenced by whatever chemicals the band were taking – indeed, there is a veritable pharmacopia of creativity here:

> With *Rubber Soul*, the Beatles recovered the sense of direction that had begun to elude them during the later stages of work for *Beatles for Sale* and which, due to their indulgence in cannabis, almost completely evaporated during *Help!* Gradually realising, from Dylan's example, that they didn't have to separate their professional work from their inner lives, they consciously experimented in much of the *Rubber Soul* material, feeling their way towards a new style – one which, defining the second half of their career together, would be inspired by their encounter with one of the biggest influences on life and culture in the late Sixties: LSD.[53]

The progressive moment is here, as in Whiteley's text, identified as coming into existence through the increasing use of LSD. But what is it, in the Beatles' music? Macdonald offers the following:

> Knowing that their music's lack of institutional structure was chiefly what made it so alive and authentic, they kept it from becoming stale by constantly investigating new methods and concepts: beginning and ending songs in the 'wrong' key, employing modal, pentatonic and Indian scales, incorporating studio-effects and exotic instruments, and shuffling rhythms and idioms with a unique versatility. Forever seeking new stimuli, they experimented with everything from tape-loops to drugs and chance procedures borrowed from the intellectual avant-garde.[54]

All this was also, argues Macdonald, both a part of, and in a very important way a register of, a fundamental change which occurred during the sixties, the real meaning of that sociological concept of

'classlessness'. There was a 'revolution in the head', in which a society held together by the decaying vestiges of religious faith and
social class was replaced by an atomised and desocialised world
without shared values or consensus, an era of 'personal appetite and
private insecurity'.[55] LSD-inspired music is one of the watersheds of
this change towards a postmodern consciousness which has
replaced the politics of narrative with those of the sound-bite. For
all their complaints against it, therefore, the New Right's apologists
for market forces and meritocracy, which they proclaim to be hostile to the sexual and chemical hedonism of the 1960s, are themselves products of the new consciousness of this decade. It produced
the Beatles; it produced Thatcherism.

This argument could be compared with the cultural–economic
analyses of John Kenneth Galbraith on America and Anthony Sampson on Britain, with their emphases on the gradual erosion of the
social at the expense of the personal or familial;[56] however, as with
Jon Savage's account of punk, it places the burden of historical
change at the moment of the author's late adolescence. We read history through our memories, and our views of history's golden ages
and revolutionary moments remain coloured by memories of our
youthful years. But yes, deference did lessen; New Right Ideologies
stirred from the quasi-meritocracy of 'classless' swinging London;
and popular music assaulted head-on all and any notions about its
place in the world and the place of those who performed it.

This chapter will now attempt to build on some of the theoretical models explored here, while maintaining the focus on 'progressive music'. Much of British pop moved sharply, in the later 1960s,
away from the accepted formulae of pop success and towards the
experimental: there were experiments with studios and with the
new recording techniques (for example, Ten Years After, led by one
of the guitar heroes, Alvin Lee, produced in their second album
*Stonedhenge* (1968) a waxing which delighted in the effects offered
by stereophony, such as phasing and cross-panning – and listed
them all, track by track, on the back cover). Everywhere musicians
experimented with genres and ways of playing, with traditions of
musicality. Many of these move across African–American source-
material, both dependent on them (riffs, jazz-type improvisation)
and moving away from them (in engagements with classical, folk
and non-Western traditions). There emerged, in other words,

### 'Progressive music': the British moment

Whiteley and Moore's convention will be followed in dating the phenomenon from the Beatles' *Sergeant Pepper* album in 1967 to the December 1974 closing of the BBC Radio 1 'progressive strip' of programming from 6–7 p.m.[57] This, then, is another 'short decade', another '1960s' to follow the 'short sixties' of pre-Acid pop, 1962–67.

This is a music centred around UK bands, though Americans like Zappa, the French-based multinational band Gong (started by Australian ex-Soft Machine guitarist Daevid Allen, and later including guitarist Steve Hillage) and the German 'Krautrock' bands, especially Can, are afforded positive mentions in any account of the music – as here. Like it or not, progressive rock is as British as the Beatles, the Kinks and Britpop; and it is as concerned with British global/local musical development as the folk revival of the early 1900s or the pastoral symphonies of the 1920s and 1930s.

Nevertheless, there is a specific political moment here. The French near-revolution of 1968 and public demonstrations elsewhere in Europe and the United States articulated a widespread revulsion against the American war in Vietnam and its supporters in European governments, including the UK's – clearly the 'classless society' envisioned in the early 1960s was still, in fact, ruled by entrenched elites. The 'troubles' in Northern Ireland were part of this moment of reassertion of local politics against global tendencies. But manifestations of this age of protest were as often cultural as directly political. As soon as the Robbins universities were built, supposedly to produce the technocratic elite envisioned by Labour Prime Minister Harold Wilson, many of their students intervened to change the culture of those institutions towards a superficially more egalitarian culture; the university gig circuit which emerged at this moment remains important to rock. The mini-period ends in 1974 with another political crisis, as British Conservative Prime Minister Edward Heath was brought down by a series of miners' strikes.

America, then, is an ambivalent presence; and for all the continued interest in American music, many forms of popular and youth culture seek to distance themselves from American hegemony: 'Rebel Rock' in Britain was rebelling against this as well as against much else – just as British classical music had moved, early in the century, away from German hegemony and towards folkish national modalism (without escaping those German models altogether). A crucial part of the Moore model is that progressive rock involved new forms of musical engagement, many of which were no longer dependent on the simple American models of Tin Pan Alley or r'n'b songwriting. Instead bands blended ideas, musics and representations. Some of these involved a move towards quite consciously British-pop versions of classical music (Moody Blues) ruralism (Jethro Tull, aspects of Led Zeppelin's work), or more direct folkism (Fairport Convention, Pentangle) or neo-medievalism (the Strawbs, Jethro Tull). Following the Beatles' flirtation with a deeply Orientalised Indian spirituality, the Third Ear Band and Quintessence explored Buddhist or Hindu-ish mysticism: an engagement with the colonial past and the post-colonial present.[58]

The Anglo-American interaction also changed, moving from rock'n'roll inflected by British songwriting traditions to such phenomena as jazz/rock (with Manfred Mann Chapter III and If as counterparts to Chicago and Blood, Sweat and Tears in the USA) and the jazz revival (which involved convergence from the rock area by Soft Machine, and from the jazz side by Ian Carr's Nucleus, the Mike Westbrook band, and the work of John Surman; and from the States, the re-creation of Miles Davis as a high-tech jazz star able and willing to play rock circuit gigs such as the 1970 Isle of Wight festival, and then the setting-up of bands derived from the Davis ensemble, such as Joe Zawinul and Wayne Shorter's Weather Report, Chick Corea's Return to Forever, and the spiritual heavy metal of John McLaughlin's Mahavishnu Orchestra). There were experiments with various aspects of composed Western music: with electronics and the work of the post-war avant-garde European composers (the Beatles, Pink Floyd, Soft Machine), eighteenth-century 'baroque' composers such as Vivaldi and J.S. Bach (Nice, Curved Air, Deep Purple), and the American-composed minimalism of Terry Riley, Steve Reich and Philip Glass (Soft Machine, later David Bowie and Brian Eno). Finally, there were the beginnings of heavy metal (Black Sabbath, Deep Purple, Groundhogs, Free, Ten Years After, Led Zeppelin).

All this activity, and the cultural criticism which surrounded it, put bands on a pedestal very different from that reserved for teenyboppers or teenage rebels. Progressive rock was from the start a discursive object produced by music-press journalism which almost immediately brought into use the label marked 'romantic artist',

complete with the 'aura' which, according to Benjamin, could/
should be deconstructed through the mass production of art objects.
Almost from its appearance, then, there were attempts to put a critical distance between this music and the rest of the popular – a distance confirmed in 1969 when BBC Radio 1 introduced its 6–7 p.m.
'progressive strip'. Not all the critical response, though, was Kentish
romanticising. Edward Lee claimed in 1970 that

> 'Progressive Pop' has already become a separable form, which ... has
> only briefly been a mass music; that the nature of mass taste remains
> much the same is shown by the continuing popularity of Tom Jones
> and Herman's Hermits and by the rise of the [sic] Reggae. Moreover,
> 'progressive music' is no longer functional – its audience goes to listen
> attentively, not to dance. Most importantly, unlike all previous popu-
> lar music, it concerns itself with musical development, and not with
> the statement and repetition of a theme.[59]

This is not Dark Stuff, but sweetness and light. Far from the fans'
and rock biographers' creation of a Faustian music produced by
excessive masculinity, the weight of the Enlightenment bears heavily on this passage. Progressive rock is differentiated from the popular, because it is a music of rationality, of argument, of
development, rather than formula and repetition, a music which
demands and receives attentive listening from an audience of con-
noisseurs.

It has become routine to scoff at this attempt to erect an elitist
boundary.[60] Post-punk critiques of 'prog rock' constructed the concert status celebrated by Lee as a sign of failure.[61] Whatever, we are
back with the problem explored by Raymond Williams in *Culture
and Society*. Musicians and critics had the same problem as that
faced by the Romantic poets of the early nineteenth century, who
erected a theory of their own elitist position even as the new technology of the steam press helped them to become mass-sales successes. There is a new mass product, the 'rock' album, produced by
the new technologies of the recording studio. The instigators of this
new product are constructed as special people, and many of them
happily see themselves as creators, taking an elitist view of the public as mass, with their own role as sage, prophet or shaman.

A strange reversal happens to a popular music which had
descended from black r'n'b, and which still uses blues chord
sequences and riffs as the basis of much of its musical material. The

critics who see this music as 'art' tended to see soul and other black pop music as at best entertainment, tainted by commerce, tainted even by the shallow demands of danceable rhythm. This is the British ideology of 'pure art' again, like that offered by Williams's Romantics, or the obituarists of Karajan, or that maintained at events like the Aldeburgh festival: popular success, nay commerce itself, is dirty; so hide it, ignore it, or better still pretend it happens somewhere else.[62]

## Progressive jazz–rock

A typical musical process of the time is the mutual crossover between jazz and rock. British jazz in the late 1960s underwent one of its periodic revivals, and for the first time was seen as respectable enough to earn the support of the Arts Council.[63] Some jazz musicians wanted to work with the new instruments and techniques of rock. Many rock musicians, meanwhile, wanted to achieve some of jazz's new found respectability to give their music the cachet of seriousness and to validate their own abilities as improvisers, as the inheritors of the blues tradition which they themselves valued so highly.

The British jazz revival was led by young composers and arrangers like Mike Westbrook, Neil Ardley, Michael Gibbs and Graham Collier, and strong soloists such as the trumpeters Henry Lowther and Harry Beckett and saxophonists Mike Osborne, Alan Skidmore and John Surman. A subgenre of free improvisation, whose principal figures included guitarist Derek Bailey, saxophonist Evan Parker and drummers Tony Oxley and John Stevens, in contact with Continental Europeans like the Dutch drummer Han Bennink and the German saxophonist Peter Brötzmann, formed arguably the least Americanised 'jazz' there has ever been, a minority music owing much to the Maoist and Trotskyist fringe politics of the 1960s.

In the USA Miles Davis had used British musicians from this moment, guitarist John McLaughlin and bassist Dave Holland, in the making of a new jazz using electric pianos and organs for a contemporary-sounding rhythm section in which the chord-playing instruments could provide more sustained sounds than acoustic pianos or unprocessed electric guitars. That Miles Davis band employed minimalist repeated riffs, rather than the elaborate har-

monic progressions of hard bop, in a series of albums starting with
*In a Silent Way* (1969) and most influentially with the double album
*Bitches' Brew* (also 1969). The Davis band also used 'noise'. Moving away from the clarity of the cool, whether on the quintet sides
or those with Gil Evans's orchestration, and their careful, high-
fidelity recording values, the sound by the time of *Bitches' Brew* was
*noisy*: the rhythm keyboards, some using distortion pedals, cut
across each other rhythmically, harmonically and timbrally, constantly producing difference tones and unpredictable harmonics.
Though some of the acoustic instruments (for example, Holland's
bass and Shorter's soprano sax) are played and recorded straight,
like the keyboards, Davis's trumpet uses an echoplex tape delay, and
his hard-attack technique helps the effects unit produce 'distorted'
sound. In these ways the Davis band has *grain*, a particular *timbre-
signature* which rejoices in the physicality of sound in the same way
as Barthes's singing-teacher – for all that many of the sources of the
sound are electronic rather than directly embodied. Jimi Hendrix
and Jimmy Page were doing the same thing at the same time – indi-
vidualising the guitar's sonic capabilities through innovative physical techniques such as bowing, and through amplifier settings and
distortion pedals. The Nice's Keith Emerson began to torture his
keyboards as a routine part of his stage performance. *The Dark Stuff*
had an aural signature: for all its comparative harmonic sophistica-
tion, progressive rock was not all burnished clarity; noise, within a
Modernist aesthetic which Adorno would have recognised, was part
of the deal for many of its practitioners.

Following Davis's example, trumpeter Ian Carr's band Nucleus
attempted to crossover between jazz and rock; Nucleus's first two
albums, *Elastic Rock* (1970) and *Solar Plexus* (1971) featured the
rock guitarist Chris Spedding (auteur of the classic 1974 pop/rock
single 'Motorbiking'), and classically-trained oboist and pianist Karl
Jenkins, along with youngish jazz musicians keen to experiment
with instruments such as the electric piano and bass guitar (instruments subject to considerable hostility within the jazz world, with
its love of the 'authentic', defined in terms of tradition), and to solo
on riffs rather than chord changes. One example of jazz-based
crossover at work was Centipede, which released a double album,
*Septober Energy*, and played a few gigs, in 1971. The band's fifty
players (a hundred legs, thus Centipede) included classical strings,
rock and jazz musicians, with a number of vocalists from each camp.

Their music and lyrics were written by jazz musicians Keith and Julie Tippett, and the album was produced by Robert Fripp (a member of progressive rock band King Crimson), who also played on the gigs. The sleeve notes for the album were written by one of the band's three drummers, Robert Wyatt.

## The soft machine

Wyatt was at the time drummer and vocalist for Soft Machine, who formed in Canterbury in the mid-1960s, and started their recording career as an experimental rock band – one of the experiments being that they were usually without a guitarist (during one of the exceptional periods they used Andy Summers, later to achieve fortune with The Police, on guitar). The band toured thereafter with a changing line-up of bass, keyboards and horn-players all from the fringes of jazz. This signals their particular place in the Anglo-American dialogue. Named after a formulation for the human body by the American writer William Burroughs, they were a part of the early link with Jimi Hendrix and LSD-psychedelia, and part of Hendrix's very British take on popular music; he played rhythm guitar on some of their early recordings, and they supported the Experience on their tour of the States in 1967. At this point they were playing songs with a Syd-Barrettish whimsy, many of which can be found on their first two albums, and which were written by their then bassist Kevin Ayers. Tension in the band between this English–pastoral–eccentric songwriting and interest in abstract formal structures and modes of improvisation led Ayers, and three years later, Wyatt, to leave; the latter with a clear distaste for what he called the 'formality required of an established concert band'.[64] (Ayers continued to work as a songwriter in the jazz–rock area of progressive rock, his eponymous band including composer David Bedford, saxophonist Lol Coxhill and young bass guitarist Mike Oldfield, a product of the King's School, Canterbury.)

Soft Machine were joined by a more accomplished bass guitarist and composer, Hugh Hopper (again a middle-class Canterbury contemporary). The growth of their music from that early, Britpop–whimsical project of songwriting-with-interludes involved several, simultaneous directions: a move into abstraction, away from vocals and lyrics; a move towards longer pieces, using the repetitive rhythmic 'minimalism' pioneered by Terry Riley, Steve

Reich and others, as much as narrative tonality; tape experiments and noise, influenced by Riley and Reich, but also by Continental avant-garde composition; and a move towards jazz improvisation, including the 'free jazz' pioneered by John Coltrane and others and extended in scope by Continental European musicians. The band negotiated with the British jazz revival, using some of the revival's key players; after a period as a trio, they used an occasional horn section, and included saxophonist Elton Dean as a permanent member in the early 1970s. In later line-ups could be found oboist and keyboardist Karl Jenkins and drummer John Marshall, who had both been founder-members of Nucleus. Soft Machine's lingering career ended with a virtuoso guitarist (Alan Holdsworth, once of Gong) rather than saxes, in the front line.

In 1967 Soft Machine had been signed by CBS, in a British equivalent of their relatively adventurous policy of the time in the United States. As the line-up and musical direction of Soft Machine changed in the direction of more complex, wordless music, Robert Wyatt formed an offshoot, Matching Mole (also signed to CBS), which split up when Wyatt was confined to a wheelchair after an accident. Having already in his Soft Machine days made a tepidly jazzy solo album (*The End of an Ear*, 1970) Wyatt went on to make two powerful solo albums, *Rock Bottom* and *Ruth is Stranger than Richard*, for the Virgin label. His subsequent career has included work with jazz composer Mike Mantler and with ambient–postmodern–techno–trance–rock band Ultramarine. Other projects impossible without Soft Machine include the whole genre of quietly pretentious and occasionally politically radical music known as Canterbury Rock: bands like Henry Cow, Hatfield and the North, National Health, Phil Collins's muso work-out Brand X, and even, to stretch a point, that under-achieving wonder of the mid-1980s, Man Jumping, who reworked the electronic, experimental, jazz and minimalist connections and added a then-trendy taste of world music.[65]

Soft Machine were the only outfit who could conceivably have been characterised as a rock band, who have played at the Proms – in a late-night concert, following a programme of Modernist music played by the London Sinfonietta, in August 1970. Wyatt's sleeve-note for the album of this performance is disarmingly defensive:

> We was invited by Tim Souster, who had an evening using the hall to do what he liked with. I believe he'd heard our second LP, asked us on

the strength of that. He discovered us on the way to discovering Motown. Via the Who, I think. Anyway it was brave of him to invite us despite the withering contempt of the posh music establishment. Before our bit, I went out the back for a quick fag and then the door-man didn't want to let me back in. 'I've got to play in there', I said. 'You must be kidding, son', he said, 'they only have proper music in there.' Not that night they didn't.[66]

Nevertheless, for all the fuss, this was probably the only moment at which such a gig (that is, from a band identified as 'rock') was possible. What marked Soft Machine c. 1970 was a clear engagement with a Modernism which fitted rather well with Proms director Sir William Glock's Reithian vision of music (discussed in chapter 1).

Soft Machine's Prom performance started, the players still off-stage, with a tape which processed various looped and reversed key-board patterns – the minimalist-inspired opening of Mike Ratledge's tune 'Out-bloody-rageous', which can be found on the *Third* album, released at the time of the concert. While the tape is running, the musicians emerge, plug up, tune and so forth; the tape settles into a groove picked up by bass, drums and electric piano before Dean's alto sax, spikily aggressive through its direct pickup (a contact microphone on the instrument's neck, rather than a sep-arate microphone on a stand), plays the angular melody line. The band then stumbles uncertainly towards the first organ solo, using Ratledge's pet distortion-pedal sound: noise/grain is here individual expressivity. The tempo picks up for a brief alto break, then settles back through a contrapuntal duet between alto and piano over a C minor 7 pedal-bass for the second part of Out-bloody-rageous's written material. Dean then solos over the pedal while Wyatt works up a head of steam; again the tempo falls before a brief coda leads to the free-improvised start of the next piece, Hopper's 'Facelift'. Hopper's pedal-distorted bass riff restores order for the alto and organ to play another angular tune followed by an E minor blues chord-based organ solo space. Again here the playing is tentative, nervous (stoned?), and it is a relief to get to the next free-form sec-tion, in which all improvise around an E pedal. 'Facelift' ends with an E-Lydian-mode riff in 7/4 over which Dean lets go, playing con-fidently for the first time, twenty minutes into the gig, then a repeat of the unison melody. A drum solo links to a set of portentous chords laying out the B/A minor-based harmonic structure of the final piece, part of Ratledge's 'Esther's Nosejob', from the band's

*Volume 2* album. An organ solo and brief passage involving wordless vocal breaks from Wyatt leads, through yet another angular melody–duet (this time between organ and bass guitar), into a more relaxed two-chord (A/C) solo space for Dean's saxello. Then we are out of tempo for a longer section in which Wyatt's wordless voice, then drums (both through an echoplex), ride over gently pulsating bass and minimal interjections from the others, before a rushing snare pattern leads to a fast and rather more tightly played angular arrangement, around D, which ends the gig.

This performance, the band's publicity high-spot, was not the musical highlight of a career which involved many tours and albums and a dozen radio sessions, most for the Radio One John Peel programme.[67] Wyatt's departure, followed a year later by that of Dean and the arrival of Jenkins and Marshall, led the band firstly in a minimalist/cool-jazz direction, at its best on the *Six* album of 1973; thereafter it moved slowly towards a McLaughlinesque, guitar-led fusion, in a series of albums for the EMI Harvest label. The band's last album, *Land of Cockayne* (1981), a semi-concept album written by Jenkins, makes a final circular connection with the milieu of whimsical Englishness in which the Softs' Canterbury rock had been born.

Wyatt's subsequent career has been mentioned above. Hopper, too, remained on the fringes of art-rock, while Marshall and Dean went back to the jazz circuit. Jenkins and Ratledge moved into the more lucrative world of television advertising, forming a successful company. Jenkins has launched a third career on the back of this second one; some of his advertising music, scored for orchestral instruments, has led him into the Classic FM chart, with the album *Adiemus: Songs of Sanctuary* and its follow-up, the cod-baroque *Palladio.*[68] Jenkins's sleeve-note to *Adiemus* illustrates how far he has come from the hard-edged cool of *Soft Machine Six*:

> What was appealing was to write an extended work which came from the European classical tradition, but where the vocal sound came from 'world' or 'ethnic' music. The music was fully scored, in the time-honoured classical tradition, for female choir and orchestra ... We wanted the choruses to sound 'tribal' ... the more reflective pasages were intoned in a Celtic or ecclesiastical manner.[69]

The move is, it seems, from a Modernism which valued experiment within an avowedly 'progressive' mode, to a postmodern and post-

colonial integrationism in which African and Celtic inflections are
subordinated to the dominant mode of Western composition.
Whether this eclecticism has reintegrated classical music or
destroyed it, and indeed whether Soft Machine were a jazz band or
a rock group, or merely underplayed both forms, they have meanwhile taken their place in the pantheon of British pop history in the
postmodern form of sample. 'Moon in June', sampled from a 1969
John Peel session, can be heard as the base track for 'Clunk Click',
from British rap band The Brotherhood's *Elementalz*, an album
which also samples a classic King Crimson offering ...[70]

## Colosseum

In the case of Colosseum we have a simpler narrative, if again one
which involves the development of an Anglicised and Europeanised
voice from African–American sources. The development was from
the suburban connoisseur's versions of African–American music –
blues, and the funkier side of modern jazz, via the British blues-
based bands John Mayall's Bluesbreakers and the Graham Bond
Organisation, connections which had also helped in the formation
of the Yardbirds, Led Zeppelin and Cream. Members of Colosseum
had also played with two of the earliest British soul bands, Geno
Washington's Ram Jam Band and the outfit led by singer Chris Farlowe. One line-up of the Bluesbreakers, which toured the USA in
1968 and recorded the influential album *Bare Wires*, brought
together drummer Jon Hiseman, saxophonist Dick Heckstall-Smith
and bass-player Tony Reeves, all of whom set up Colosseum with
organist Dave Greenslade and guitarist James Litherland. Immediately the band sought for a differentiated voice: the first, 1968
album, *Morituri Te Salutant* ('We who are about to die salute you',
the gladiators' greeting to the emperor as they paraded before battle in the Colosseum in Rome) uses, as well as the blues, which is the
starting-point for five of the eight compositions, a J.S. Bach chord
progression (the same chord sequence used by Procol Harum on
'Whiter Shade of Pale') and the Japanese pentatonic 'soft scale'.
This first album, on the Philips Fontana label, is characterised by relatively long compositions (there are four five-minute tracks per
side), jazz and blues-influenced improvisation; half the tracks are
purely instrumental.
The second album goes further in this direction, the eponymous

instrumental *Valentyne Suite* taking up the second side. Side one features one blues plus three very different tracks: firstly the power trio of 'The Kettle'; next, the reflective 'Elegy', which features a gem of a soprano sax solo by Heckstall-Smith and the accompaniment of a small string ensemble arranged by jazz composer Neil Ardley, whose horn arrangements also accompany the other tracks on the side, 'Butty's Blues', and 'The Machine Demands a Sacrifice'. The lyrics of this latst number, by the then fashionable poet Pete Brown (who was lyricist for Cream, leader of two bands, the jazzy Battered Ornaments and the more poppy Piblokto! and dedicatee of a track on John McLaughlin's 1969 album *Extrapolation*) are printed inside the gate-fold sleeve along with a note by Hiseman which opens thus: 'The Valentyne Suite has the feeling of a love affair, the sort which flares up hotly and then consumes itself. Each of its three themes had been with us some time before the Grand Design was revealed.'

Let us examine this Grand Design. The following remarks, in conjunction with the accompanying charts, attempt an analysis of the Suite. Instead of using aspects of conventional notation to describe the pitched and harmonic relations of the piece, I have provided a linear narrative of the intensity of the sound, delineating aspects of the mix (balance and effects), the activity level of the drums, the moments of low and high energy such as thematic statements, individual solos and collective improvisation and the role of the backing musicians in relation to thematic statements and solos. Much of this is impossible to delineate using either conventional notation or descriptive words alone.

The Suite is characterised throughout by a hesitant, ambiguous attitude to tonality. There is nothing here of the limited and confident use of the blues, or of the straightforward narrative tonality of that Bach chord sequence, which had characterised much of the first album. Although the modality of the English musical Renaissance is sometimes suggested, the suggestions are never confirmed; there are also reminders of that attempt, on the first album, to use the Japanese 'soft scale'. Like the progressive moment as a whole, as seen by Moore, and like the Beatles as identified by Macdonald, the band seems to be questioning both the Anglo-American tradition and the tonality established at the time of the Enlightenment – and looking elsewhere for an identifiable voice.

The band had, in fact, already found its 'grain', its particular tim-

**Chart 1** Colosseum: *Valentyne Suite*, section 1.

| structure | intro | A | B | A | B | C | B | C | D | E | playout | link |
|---|---|---|---|---|---|---|---|---|---|---|---|---|
| key | F#/F | Fmin | F#/F | Fmin | F#/F | F#/F | F#/F | F#/F | F to Cmin | Cmin7th | Cmin7th | Bb |
| tempo | | | | | | | | | (free time) | | | |
| density | | | | | | | | | | | | |
| brass | | | | | | | | | | | | |
| tenor sax | | | | | | | | | | | | |
| soprano sax | | | | | | | | | | | | |
| organ | | | | | | | | | | | | |
| piano | | | | | | | | | | | | |
| vibes | | | | | | | | | | | | |
| guitar | | | | | | | | | | | | |
| bass | | | | | | | | | | | | |
| drums | | | | | | | | | | | | |
| time | | | | | | | | | | | | |

The vertical index for Charts 1–3 does not represent either pitch (as in conventional notation) or volume, but '*intensity*', which encompasses the level in the mix, timbre and performing style, and use of effects, of the individual track. All these levels of intensity together produce the *density* of the piece as a whole – which, as the density graph indicates, is not simply dependent on the number of instruments playing, or the tempo. In the individual instrumental tracks, shaded areas represent improvised passages.

bre-signature: overdriven organ and a gritty tenor sax sound combine in the middle of the pitch range and the middle of the mix, with busy drumming commenting and solid bass underpinning the groove, while the guitar is used as an occasional instrument and solo voice rather than the rhythm power-house. The Suite begins with this sonic combination. Over a floor-tom roll, the organ arpeggio in F sharp is joined by a slow, rising pentatonic scale played by organ and tenor sax. At the top of the scale the note is held and repeated, with the snare-drum joining the pitched instruments to drive their rhythmic emphases forward, in an immediate reminder that Hiseman is the leader of this particular band, and is nowhere restricted to the role of accompanist. The snare-driven repeats lead to a chord change to F minor, over which the first section's theme is played, snare and organ crisply rattling out the off beats for eight bars [A], before the F sharp–F tension is explored [B], with solo vibes (over-dubbed by Greenslade) filling over the chords. The same is repeated, with guitar and organ providing the fill, before a third-time chorus [C] reintroduces the tenor sax and, mixed very much in the background, the Ardley-arranged brass section. [B] and [C] now alternate, with Heckstall-Smith's tenor and soprano saxes (not over-dubbed, but played together à la Roland Kirk) bringing the energy level down to [D], in which the soprano sax improvises floridly over a pedal F held by Greenslade's piano, sustained by arpeggiated chordal work very much in the style of McCoy Tyner with the later John Coltrane quartet, and Hiseman using tympani sticks on toms and cymbals in the manner of the same quartet's Elvin Jones. Tension is increased by the increasing level of activity among all three, with soprano sax and tom rolls leading the change to a C minor 7 pedal. From this emerges an unaccompanied organ pedal riff, over which Greenslade solos with stops, Leslie cabinet and amplifier settings all designed to produce distortion when chords are played. Hiseman's aggressive snare pattern, now with conventional drumsticks, signals the return of the rest of the band, with tenor sax doubling the organ-pedal riff alongside the bass guitar, as the organist uses splash chords and pitch control along with the structured distortion to heighten the solo's expressive intensity. As the snare drives along in fast triplets, with the ride cymbal maintaining the basic pulse (a virtuosic inversion of normal percussive practice), the section ends with a return of the opening pentatonic scale, and the suite continues straight into the second section.

This is harmonically the most interesting part of the Grand Design, based around a very ambiguous C/D/A/G cycle, with no clear establishment of either a tonal, modal or even major/minor hegemony on the basis of those root notes. Instead, the optional nature of the available 'blue notes' is stressed both by the organ, which first plays the principal theme, and by the presence of a small mixed-voice choir (arranged by Ardley), wordlessly articulating voices whose tone is straight from 1960s easy listening (examples would be the Ray Conniff Singers, or the Swingle Singers, who had sung ba-ba-baroque on the hit album *Jazz Sebastian Bach* in 1964).[71] After the chord sequence's first appearance, the tenor sax solos over a further four cycles with choir, and then with the band alone – with

**Chart 2** Colosseum: *Valentyne Suite*, section 2.

| structure | A2 | A2 | A2 | A2 | A2 | A2 | A2 | link |
|---|---|---|---|---|---|---|---|---|
| key | C/D/A/G.......................................................... | | | | | | | Bb/C/D/A/G |
| density | | | | | | | | |
| tempo | | | | | | | | |
| choir | | | | | | | | |
| tenor sax | | | | | | | | |
| soprano sax | | | | | | | | |
| organ | | | | | | | | |
| bass | | | | | | | | |
| drums | | | | | | | | |
| time ......... | | | | | | | | |

the energy level here raised by a gradual acceleration in tempo, as well as by thicker accompanying chords and more polyrhythms, with increasing independence for drums, bass, organ and guitar, while the tenor sax is joined by soprano again. The introductory pentatonic scale reappears, leading to a brief linking passage in which riffs played in unison by organ and tenor sax, interspersed with drum-breaks which gradually slow the tempo again, are mixed through an increasing level of 'phase' (a slight delay in signal across the two speakers, resulting in an unfocused sound); a final, strongly phased drum-break leads to the third section.

Tenor sax and guitar announce a strong theme, not quite pentatonic now, but in the closest the European tonal system gets to it, in C harmonic minor [A3], while the soprano sax echoes it in parallel fifths – again, like the choice of key, an unsettling harmonic device whose ambiguity is heightened by the guitar's addendum to the main theme [B3] and the following passages for brass section, this time in parallel fourths, and for organ [C3], stressing the flattened second of the scale. Organ and then double-tracked, duetting bass guitars, take solos over a single chorus of [B3], before the guitar, its sound processed firstly through strong reverb and then wah-wah

**Chart 3**  Colosseum: *Valentyne Suite*, section 3.

| structure | A3 | A3 | B3 | C3 | B3 | C3 | B3 | B3 | B3 | B3 | B3 | B3 | D | E | A3 |
|---|---|---|---|---|---|---|---|---|---|---|---|---|---|---|---|
| tonality | Cmin | G/C/F/C................................................. | | | | | | | | | | | G/C/F/Cmin.................. | | Cmin |
| density | | | | | | | | | | | | | | | |
| tempo | | | | | | | | | | | | | | | |
| brass | | | | | | | | | | | | | | | |
| tenor sax | | | | | | | | | | | | | | | |
| organ | | | | | | | | | | | | | | | |
| piano | | | | | | | | | | | | | | | |
| guitar | | | | | | | | | | | | | | | |
| bass | | | | | | | | | | | | | | | |
| drums | | | | | | | | | | | | | | | |
| time | ....................................................................................................................................... | | | | | | | | | | | | | | |

pedal, leads the band through several cycles of [B3] towards a collective, accelerating improvisation which finally breaks down over a sustained C pedal, slowing to a portentous drum and cymbal-roll punctuated by open fifths on the bass guitar, before a repeat of [A3], complete with its unsettling parallel harmonisation, brings the Suite to an end.

This is as close as Colosseum got to the 'concept album'. It is very much concept jazz–rock: for all the neo-classical pretension the band is also echoing Duke Ellington, who often used the notion of the suite to link together longer compositions. For Hiseman, though, the move was part of a search for a new language: the blues and jazz were seen as too American and too limited in appeal, and 'prog rock' was one way to create a new and indigenous music which straddled the worlds of composition and improvisation. He insisted that the band's writers, Geeenslade and Heckstall-Smith, aimed for complexity; one track was rehearsed for six months before performance, something unheard of in the blues bands they had all played in during the 1960s.[72]

The rest of the Colosseum story, however, involves the failure of the band's attempt to produce an autonomous, instrumental music, with its own harmonic language, from within this jazz–rock moment. After beginning to experience lukewarm audience responses on tour, Hiseman felt that Colosseum needed a front-line vocalist, and hired Chris Farlowe, with whom he and other members of the band had worked. The results can be heard positively on *The Daughter of Time* (1970 – also featuring Clem Clempson, a stronger guitarist), but less so on the 1971 double album *Colosseum Live!*; attempted crowd-pleasing, featuring long solo spots, was characteristic of stage performances by many of the bands of the time, but worked less well for Colosseum than for many others. As they relied for day-to-day income on tour audiences (album sales never covered advances), this was a real problem. Reeves, Clempson, then Farlowe, drifted away, and the band folded in 1971. Although Hiseman went on to make more straight-ahead rock with Tempest and Colosseum II, he also continued to play jazz–rock as a member of the United Jazz Rock Ensemble and Paraphernalia, led by his wife, the saxophonist Barbara Thompson – a band, formed in 1975, which had much success in Europe in the early 1980s. Dave Greenslade formed a band of his own, then, like Ratledge and Jenkins from Soft Machine, found a career in studio film/TV music; Dick Heckstall-Smith still performs on the British jazz circuit.

## Other 'progressive' movements

There was more to the search for a new music and new musical status than the attempted rapprochement with jazz–rock. Folk–rock created another form of distinctive musical Englishness (and Irishness, with the band Tir Na Nog reworking the music, as well as the legends, of Irish culture; and Welshness, with the rock band Man proudly constructing their own Welsh identity, with a splendid map of Wales on one of their gatefold album sleeves). Bands like The Incredible String Band, The Strawbs, Renaisance and Barclay James Harvest all came in different ways from the folk revival of the 1960s, as did Fairport Convention and Pentangle, who from the same direction attempted an 'electric folk'. So, in the end, did Jethro Tull, who rode on the first wave of commercial success for 'progressive rock' in the late 1960s (with the hit single 'Living in the Past', which peaked at no. 3 in the charts in May 1969, still, as far as I know, the only British Top 20 single ever in 5/4 time). The use of tradition here is not only in the use of songs or song-families, *à la* Hatch and Millward – indeed, in their early moment of triumph Jethro Tull were not particularly folky, for all their leader Ian Anderson's unusual use of the orchestral flute as solo instrument. But different though they were, all these bands tended to use an Anglicised folk-song voice, a nasal voice via not Hatch and Millward's hill-billy, but folk-song and medieval and/or Tudor sources, a vocalisation worlds away from the fuller sound of the blues singer, the full-throated scream of emergent heavy metal or the delicate, understated humour of the singer/songwriter.

As with the orchestral folk of Vaughan Williams and others, this folksy ruralism existed within the usual paradox of high-technology, high-investment musics whose very existence relied on the facilities of the city. Unsurprisingly this paradox led to commercialised showmanship: Jethro Tull always were, and the Strawbs became, stadium bands. One ex-Strawb, Rick Wakeman, went on to become a fully-fledged, or rather fully-caped, keyboard wizard (and therefore Romantic Artist), with Yes. Wakeman then had, and still has, a solo career, airing such masterpieces as a suite called 'The Six Wives of Henry the Eighth' (using that crucial historical moment of Englishness, the Tudor period, again). His stage act reworked the Lisztian showmanship of the flying cape and matching, swirling hair, as he moved between the racked ranks of massed keyboards. Wakeman's solo projects apart, there is less abstraction in this aspect of the music than there was in jazz–rock, in the sense that comparatively little of it is purely instrumental; these bands tended to have strong vocalists, and to write songs, but long songs, with instrumental interludes and solo spaces: songs with lyrics, even narratives, which routinely escape the moon/June of pop romance – if only to produce an alternate banality.

There are strong continuities in this music, and not just with various traditions: the 'dinosaur generation' is not yet extinct. And to support them, and to keep alive the memory of those who have slipped from the (zimmer-) frame, there is a magazine culture (for example, *Mojo*) catering for thirty/forty-something nostalgia for that moment of progressive rock. Here we are back with that continuous theme of the book: people inhabit modernity through tradition, often constructing tradition themselves through micro- or mini-cultures (such as magazines or, in the case of wealthy rock

stars, the occupation of the land); its narratives provide the continuities otherwise lacking in lives addressed by the maelstrom of
continuous change.

But there is more to continuity than texts or tours by the Rolling
Stones. David Brackett argues that since all those 1960s musicians
moved in their different directions away from Anglo-American pop,
a value-system negotiated in the 'progressive' moment, an aesthetics of popular music inflected by high culture has been available to
popular musicians and audiences; he takes as his prime example the
career of Elvis Costello.[73] In the work of figures like Robert Fripp,
Brian Eno, and even David Bowie, we hear a different kind of continuity, one which is more active in its own deconstruction/recon-
struction: musics of development, over the whole of the musicians'
careers so far. These figures emerged from the progressive moment;
they have continued to work within and to transform it. All have
worked together. Fripp and Eno in particular, however, have
attempted to work against its most restricting convention: they have
refused the mantle of Romantic Artist, producing minimalist
musics, experimental musics and (quite deliberately) background
musics. Bowie has been more ambivalent here (as with everything
else), living the life of the star-in-general. But his music has developed, and continues to do so, from a base which was always questioning, experimental; and this experimentalism has been
recognised by other musicians. The Bowie/Eno album *Low* has even
formed the basis for a composition by the American minimalist
Philip Glass, the *Low Symphony*.[74] Fripp has worked with the minimal and with 'ethnic' musics, consistently experimenting and, it
seems, following a volition other than the purely commercial. He
turns up, for instance (sampled, but from a dedicated session) on the
1994 Future Sound of London album *Lifeforms* – an album some
would characterise generically as 'ambient techno'.[75] Eno, of course,
patented the term 'ambient music' to describe the music he made for
airports (for example): music whose function was to provide a
sound in a place, and not to be listened to *per se*.[76] Here, too, there
are continuities with the ambient music of the 1990s.

Narratives constructed by criticism have tended, in their search
for authentic value and/or the tastes of the young, to ignore continuities, and we should note here that though the experimental
jazz–rock of Soft Machine and Colosseum's more muscular
jazz–rock faded, progressive music as a whole did not stop, or even

petrify. As well as the touring dinosaurs, a relatively new band, Pen-dragon (taking its name from an aspect of the Arthurian legend) has made ten albums since the 1980s, complete with neo-classical orchestrations and Tolkienian lyrics. Meanwhile, after the entry point of Britpop, with its reworking of pop *c.* 1965, in 1996 Kula Shaker, a band in their very early twenties, charted with singles owing much to the sounds of the prog rock short decade – sitars and tabla underpinned mystical lyrics drawn from Hindu sacred texts, while critics fought over whether the band's guitar licks had been lifted from Carlos Santana or Dave Gilmour. A new post-colonial Britishness charted, the white versions this time alongside tracks by British Asian artists such as Bally Sagoo and Jyoti Mistra.

Meanwhile in the dance music scene (which included Bally Sagoo's Hindi film-music mixes) there had been attempts to pro-duce a hierarchy of value, ordering the musics and their sub- and micro-genres into categories headed, among other things, 'intelli-gent'. It is worth asking, therefore, the following question:

### 'Ambient' and the dance scene: progressive music again?

'Ambient' emerges from a more general dance-music culture. Let us accept one convenient piece of terminology, and use the word 'rave' to cover musics for dance which have evolved since the 1980s through, among other progenitors, the Chicago house scene, Northern Soul and the Ibiza– and Goa–Metropolitan connection, and which have involved Italian, German, Dutch and Belgian musics as well as those made in Britain and the USA. Ambient is a subgenre of this, and one which stresses listening rather than danc-ing – but is it a return to 'progressive music'? Some of the origina-tors of acid house in America certainly thought of British rock as an inspiration; Marshall Jefferson claimed that he was 'trying to get a mood or something, like the old Black Sabbath records, or Led Zep-pelin', while Larry Heard, another pioneer, was into Yes, Rush and Genesis.[77]

Rave music has been around long enough to accumulate journal-ism and a little academic criticism; we must survey the state of play. Jon Savage, editing *The Hacienda must be Built*,[78] offers a many-voiced narrative which has become part of the myth of Manchester, in which rave derives from existing forms of nocturnal activity such as Northern soul. There is a story here, of the continuities with the pre-rave dance scenes, which is a powerful alternative to the conventional narrative of British pop, one which demotes the punk in which Savage also believes strongly.[79]

As I mentioned in chapter 2, Steve Redhead's work has reconfigured cultural theory away from some of its fixations on internal elites and class politics. In discussing the rave phenomenon, Redhead argues that no linear model can encompass what happened in the cultures of young people in the 1980s. Like Savage in *The Hacienda Must Be Built*, Redhead claims that 'Acid House' had forebears in the Northern soul dance movement and post-punk warehouse parties, as well as the relatively well-known moment of Balearic Beat hitting south London *c*. 1987 as people returned from their holidays. And it did not have a linear trajectory thereafter, with Acid House devolving into many musical styles and tendencies, and the rave party phenomenon drawing in teenagers, football fans, 'New Age' followers of all ages and twenty-something media folk, to parties which were often run by entrepreneurs who occasionally dignified themselves with the term 'Thatcherite', for all that their activities annoyed many of the good lady's followers.[80]

The collective book from the Manchester Centre for Contemporary Culture, *Rave Off* (1993),[81] attempts to come to terms with the phenomenon. Several points emerge from the book's six chapters:

1   The Thatcherite enterprise culture – an ambivalent relationship; money is made, but from things the morality of most New Right conservatism cannot accept.

2   The acceptance of European culture and the mingling of British and European cultures (with, of course, the usual American models) continues to produce the musics of rave. This is not British or Anglo-American, but Euro-American music.

3   Similarly, the continuing mix of black and white musics and musicians, producing new sounds, new fashions and new body-styles is crucial to rave and its musics; the positive identification of young black British people as such, and their interaction with whites, offers a strong contrast with the continuing racially separate ghettoisation of America. (The comparatively integrated form, jungle, which began to taste commercial success after *Rave Off* was in print underlines the point.)

4   Connections with the mid-1960s and those first experimental moments of progressive rock are important; there are acknowl-

edged inspirations, as between Pink Floyd and the Orb; as well as musical connections with sound sources and genres, there are similarities at the events, with sounds and lights once more combining in an analogue of chemically induced changes in consciousness (now reinforced by the use of computers to generate images and fractal patterns as well as music). There are also philosophical and political connections, with the 'New Age' being signalled in the early 1990s through high-technology music and images, just as the 'Age of Aquarius' was in late 1960s rock.

5    There are similar, severe, public reactions to the dress, drugs, music and parties. And consequently a similar politicisation of young people, because their ideas of having a good time are being resisted. (The book went to press before the drafting of the Criminal Justice Act, which has made virtually any gathering potentially illegal.)

Rave cultures exist in a society whose analyses can no longer bear the class-based, left/right divisions which drove subcultural theory in the 1970s. A libidinous musical culture which is always already part of the world of information technology cannot be reduced to questions of class, gender or ethnicity. Instead we should think about hybridity, liminality and the borderlines between peoples and their cultures as the places from which new cultures, new identities, perhaps even new centres emerge. In the Ecstasy-fuelled passages of the rave, analysis of the body and its capacity for both making and using music rests on those borderlines.

One previously firm borderline between mass and elite music has already been shifted irrevocably, in that we have a music of mass consumption, much of which is wordless, and in the rest of which words are relatively unimportant – the voice is used as a musical instrument. As recently as 1987 Simon Frith was writing confidently that most popular music had words and would continue to do so, though he also explored the gendered grain of the voice – something which survives in much dance music, though the voice's centrality does not.[82] The moment of progressive rock (jazz–rock especially) went some way towards this 'abstraction', and dance music has confirmed it. So a moment in which semiosis displaces symbolism, in which music tends, collectively, to the *jouissant*, occurs in mass-embodied music now, as against then in the elitist-listener's music of prog rock. The semiotic order, in most dance musics, displaces the symbolic order of (patriarchal) language through a wordless address to the body.

In the related issue of the part played in this culture by drugs, we recognise one of the archetypical patterns of Romanticism, and connect that archetype with the LSD-inspired music of the 1960s. In its use of psychotropic drugs like Ecstasy, rave culture is deliberately attempting to exceed the norms of Enlightenment rationalism. Ecstasy and similar little helpers change perception of time, space and personality, down to and including the complete, if usually temporary, deconstruction of the ego. Similarly, in the use of a music characterised by repetitive beats, profound low frequencies, high volume and often intense speed – as with hard-core techno and jungle/drum'n'bass – there is a breakdown of the normal bodily responses, including mental responses, to sound. The music provides an analogue of the drug experience. *Space and time as perceptual conditions, even the very possibility of thought as we know it, are altered by this experience*, as they are intended to be. The force of this music is such that it displaces individuated identity, including what we would conventionally think of as memory. It produces a music, an experience, of the perpetual present. People rave *in order to* lose their minds. It could, on the other hand, be proposed that the collective delirium achieved at a rave is not the negation of thought, but a new form of mental activity – new collective memories are created in clubs, through the combined operations of psychotropic drugs and loud repetitive music. The many albums of club mixes celebrating events such as Cream and Renaissance are a mnemonic, a memory-regenerator, for these events; an aural photograph.

Meanwhile, new technology and the 'New Age' have come together. At club-like events like London's Megatripolis, information and entertainment were combined, in lectures known as the Parallel University: here New Age scientific information and 'traditional' medical/medicinal and other knowledge-systems coexist and develop mutually and happily, as the microprocessor and its abilities are spiritualised and ritualised through music, image and dance. Megatripolis offered a language of the self, as actualisable/improvable through dance, technologies, therapies and alternative knowledges.

If so, it is not entirely new in the 1990s, though a history of alternative music-led consciousness within Britain would have to be a counter-history written across lines of awareness, as in Greil Marcus's *Lipstick Traces* and George McKay's *Senseless Acts of Beauty*; in each case the historian draws connections between present and past of which the present actors are unaware. It was not the 1960s but the 1900s which saw the first large-scale turn, in Britain, to Indian mysticism, notably under the influence of the Theosophical Society, founded in 1900. Gustav Holst's Hindu opera *Savitri* (1916) is a product of this moment; Rutland Boughton's setting of Rabindranath Tagore's 'Sacrifice' was performed at his Glastonbury Festival in 1918. There are strong similarities, for example, between the 1990s New Age vision of music and that proposed by the composer and Theosophist Cyril Scott. In his *Music and Modernism* Scott identified an 'astral body … composed of a very rare form of matter, and … susceptible in the highest degree to vibratory influence, just as it is susceptible to alcohol, opium, hashish and other pernicious poisons'.[83] This anticipation of the ego-dissolving music of the 1990s rave or of the 1960s Third Ear Band was written in 1917. Compare Peter Dawkins, writing in 1996 in the booklet presented with the *Megatripolis* CD collection: 'rhythm is the driving power of the creative life force … by following the vibrations of nature, we can constantly give regular impulses of energy and love-light to the world and to our own lives'.[84] Compare also this assertion by composer and psycho-acoustician Michael McNab, writing of the recognition of fractal patterns in computer music: 'there is a physiology-based common ground for musical aesthetics'.[85] In the 1920s, following a suggestion by the Russian composer Scriabin, Cyril Scott had explored the possibilities of multi-media shows in which the body would be addressed by light and colour as well as by sound and vibration, convinced that a music tuned to the body's receptors and combined with shifting patterns of colour would help achieve a higher consciousness. Scott was, therefore, anticipating the physiological and mental effects of rave musics: 'the swifter the vibratory rate inherent in such music, the more potent the effect … on the emotion-bodies of its listeners … music which expresses nothing directly can have a moral and spiritual effect on its listeners'.[86]

All is not new in the New Age. How, though, do musics known in shorthand as ambient fit into the overall pattern? A first suggestion would be that most rave is more like pop, music for ephemeral use, while ambient is for relaxed contemplation, more like the concert music of prog rock. While there are fewer concerts (as in sitting down, concentrating and listening), ambient is arguably at its best in the 'chill-out' room of a club.

There are also biographical continuities across time and genre. Categories such as 'intelligent techno', 'intelligent drum'n'bass' or especially 'isolationism' indicate that some of the makers of this music see themselves, and are seen, as people apart. The phrases 'total genius', and 'fairy-tale symphonies', taken from reviews reproduced on the jacket of a trippy dance music CD by BT,[87] indicate the presence of the Romantic Artist. The Aphex Twin (Richard James) is another candidate for the term. The Twin is a one-man British Kraftwerk, the man in the white suit working in the lab late one night, twiddling knobs – playing machines he has often built himself, rather than buying the latest Japanese box like the rest of us. He thinks that he creates the most important and meaningful music currently being made – and has said so. Some incautious music press critics have tended to agree with him – reporting that some of his music is revealed through lucid dreams (which was how archetypical Romantic Richard Wagner started his *Ring* opera sequence).[88] Individualised creative masculinity rides again in the creation of this image of Aphex Twin as the latest Great Musician. The pretension even in the title of the CD *Ambient Works Volume II* (1994) is obvious. Even the connections with the contemporary classical world, so important to the prog rockers, are repeated here; Philip Glass, the minimalist composer of the *Low symphony* based on Eno and Bowie's work, has also co-produced music with Mr Twin, commenting favourably on 'his ability to dream and imagine'[89] – while avant-gardist and mystic Karlheinz Stockhausen, iconically important to the dance-music generation, has commented (unfavourably) on his work, suggesting that it is harmonically and rhythmically limited.[90] But history does not simply repeat itself: the different names/titles he has used for various projects and the lack of any 'star' stage presence act against Richard James's construction as a Romantic Artist, for all that in the confessional world of Aphex Twin, the Dark Stuff is postmodernised into a lucid dream, and music into a trick of the memory.

The success of rave in destabilising the egos of its users does not mean that relationships between music, memory and place have been disrupted altogether. The music of the Aphex Twin is in fact

post-colonial in construction, as Kodwu Eshun has argued.[91] While
the music of urban Britain, from Glaswegian hard-core techno to
Bristol trip-hop, articulates the new physical, economic and social
conditions of the land without music, there has been at least one
attempt within the field of dance music to rework national traditions through the new technologies.

'When we write songs, we think of landscapes.' That Elgarian
remark is attributed to Ultramarine.[92] The band is, at first listening,
a typical high-tech duo, employing banks of samplers, sequencers
and mixers to create layered, trancey, dub-influenced dance music.
But their stage act (and recordings) also include live performance,
using guitars, saxes and even that rhythm-generating dinosaur
which was extinct long before dance music evolved, a drumkit.
Their second album, *United Kingdoms* (1993)[93] displays the vestiges
of other traditions. Two nineteenth-century songs, the folkish
weaver's protest-song 'Kingdom' and the later, equally politicised
music-hall parody 'Happy Land', appear in tranced-up mixes; it
produces a very similar effect to Elgar's insinuation of folk-music
and madrigal styles into *Caractacus* (discussed in chapter 1). This is
one specifically national tradition, in its radical version, rather than
the sanitised folk of Cecil Sharp. There is another: the voice used to
sing them is that of Robert Wyatt, and the instrumental line-up
includes the soprano sax of another late 1960s jazzer (and occasional performer with Soft Machine), Jimmy Hastings.

The archive of recorded music, including Wyatt's voice, is not
here a postmodern plaything existing outside narrative, but a set of
historical documents to be reworked and interpreted through per-
formative scholarship. The memory is in the machine, but people
still push the buttons, and Ultramarine's humanisation of
techno/dub moves it towards the mainstream which has been occu-
pied, for example, by Leftfield, while simultaneously connecting it
with that moment of 1960s counter-culture through which a new
national popular music emerged. A soundscape is preserved
through the sampler as well as through the lives of its participants,
and the ghosts of the past sing on in the machines, as they do
through the voices and personalities of Britpop.

Soundscapes and technoscapes are deliberately spatialised con-
cepts, acknowledging the spatial relations of contemporary culture.
As I have argued throughout, musics made through the technologies
and spaces of the city are often expressive of the rural, from the folk

revivals and Elgar's Malvern wanderings to the Kinks' (North Londoners all) creation of themselves as members of the Village Green Preservation Society. Music may be metropolitan in creation, but it is often realised elsewhere in performance, especially at the many festivals which celebrate music in Britain. Ultramarine's acknowledgment of landscape is important; music is located in relation to an imagined geography, and often expresses that geography. The next chapter explores further the spatial realisation of music, its relation with place, in twentieth-century Britain.

## Notes

1   See, for example, J. Aizlewood, ed., *Love is the Drug: Living as a Pop Fan*, Harmondsworth, Penguin, 1994.
2   N. Kent, *The Dark Stuff: Selected Writings on Rock Music 1972–1993*, Harmondsworth, Penguin, 1994.
3   *Ibid.*, p. 76.
4   *Ibid.*, p. 103.
5   S. Davis, *Hammer of the Gods: the Led Zeppelin Saga*, Sidgwick and Jackson, 1985, p. 10.
6   *Ibid.*, p. 54.
7   Those interested in Page's use of the instrument (or anyone else's) may consult the Theremin page on the World Wide Web: http://www.Nashville.Net/~theremin/Tbands.html.
8   Davis, *Hammer of the Gods*, p. 53.
9   *Ibid.*, pp. 92–8.
10  R. Graves, *The White Goddess*, Faber and Faber, 1948, rev. edn, 1952.
11  Davis, *Hammer of the Gods*, p. 107.
12  S. Frith, *The Sociology of Rock*, Routledge, 1978, reprinted in a second edition as *Sound Effects*, Routledge, 1984.
13  R. Middleton, *Studying Popular Music*, Milton Keynes, Open University Press, 1990.
14  T. Adorno and M. Horkheimer, 'Enlightenment as Mass Deception', in their *Dialectic of Enlightenment*, Allen Lane, 1973.
15  See, for example, T. Adorno, *Philosophy of Modern Music* (1941), Sheed and Ward, 1973; and Adorno, *Introduction to the Sociology of Music* (1962),. New York, Seabury Press, 1976. Adorno's classic 1941 essay 'On Popular Music' is reprinted in S. Frith and A. Goodwin, eds, *On Record: Pop, Rock and the Written Word*, Routledge, 1990. Useful treatments of Adorno's work on music are Middleton, *Studying Popular Music*, pp. 34–63; P. Martin, *Sounds and Society*, Manchester, Manchester University Press, 1995, pp. 75–125; and M. Paddison,

*Adorno's Aesthetics of Music*, Cambridge, Cambridge University Press, 1993.

16 See, for example, D. Harker, *One for the Money: the Politics of Popular Song*, Hutchinson, 1980, p. 40.

17 See, for example, T. Bloomfield, 'Negative Dialectics in Pop', *Popular Music*, vol. 12, no. 1, January 1993; this approach is discussed in C. Hamm, *Putting Music in its Place*, Cambridge, Cambridge University Press, 1995.

18 S. Reynolds and J. Press, *The Sex Revolts: Gender, Rebellion and Rock-'n'Roll*, Serpent's Tail, 1995.

19 *Ibid.*, p. 322. Compare my article defending her musicianship, A. Blake, 'Madonna the Musician', in F. Lloyd, ed., *Deconstructing Madonna*, B.T. Batsford, 1993.

20 These arguments are at their most concise in W. Benjamin, 'The Work of Art in the Age of Mechanical Reproduction', in Benjamin, ed. H. Arendt, *Illuminations*, New York, Schocken, 1969.

21 S. Hatch and D. Millward, *From Blues to Rock: an Analytical History of Popular Music*, Manchester, Manchester University Press, 1987.

22 The importance of changing forms of transmission is also argued by former Henry Cow guitarist Chris Cutler, whose *ReR Quarterly* is a repository of Out-Rock and Art-Rock of many ages. See also P. van der Merwe, *Origins of the Popular Style*, Oxford, Oxford University Press, 1989, pp. 181–5.

23 Hatch and Millward, *From Blues to Rock*, pp. 147–70. See also I. Chambers, *Urban Rhythms: Pop Music and Popular Culture*, Macmillan, 1985.

24 Enigma, *MCMXC a.D*, Virgin 262 029 – PM 527, 1991. The Akai shakuhachi sample can be heard, for example, on Richard Grey's mix of Marshall Jefferson, 'Open Our Eyes', on the first of a three-CD set, *Megatripolis*, Funky PCD1, 1996. The track is discussed by D. Laing in his 'Sadeness, Scorpions and Single Markets: National and Transnational Trends in European Popular Music', *Popular Music*, vol. 11, no. 2, 1992, pp. 127–40.

25 D. Bradley, *Understanding Rock'n'Roll*, Buckingham, Open University Press, 1992.

26 A useful account of this body of theory is in R. Lapsley and M. Westlake, *Film Theory: an Introduction*, Manchester, Manchester University Press, 1988.

27 Kristeva's position is commented on in R. Coward, *Female Desire*, Paladin, 1984 and T. Moi, *Sexual/Textual Politics: Feminist Literary Theory*, Methuen, 1985.

28 R. Barthes, 'The Grain of the Voice', in *Image–Music–Text*, ed. S. Heath, Fontana, 1977; a version may be found in S. Frith and

A. Goodwin, eds, *On Record: Rock, Pop and the Written Word*, Routledge, 1990, pp. 293–300. See the discussion of this essay in
A. Durant, *Conditions of Music*, Macmillan, 1984, pp. 90–2.

29   S. Reynolds, *Blissed Out: the Raptures of Rock*, Serpent's Tail, 1993.

30   Reynolds and Press, *The Sex Revolts*, p. 79.

31   *Ibid.*, p. 178.

32   *Ibid.*, p. 189.

33   J. Street, *Rebel Rock: the Politics of Popular Music*, Oxford, Blackwell,
1986; for example, p. 197.

34   R. Walser, *Running with the Devil: Power, Gender and Madness in
Heavy Metal Music*, Hanover, New England, Wesleyan University
Press, 1993.

35   See also R. Palmer, 'The Church of the Sonic Guitar', in A. de Curtis,
ed., *Present Tense: Rock & Roll Culture*, Duke University Press, 1992,
pp. 16–36.

36   See especially Walser's third chapter, 'Eruptions, Heavy Metal Appro-
priations of Classical Virtuosity', pp. 57–107 of his *Running with the
Devil*.

37   Compare J. Gottlieb and G. Wald, 'Smells like Teen Spirit: Riot Grrls,
Revolution and Women in Independent Rock', in A. Ross and T. Rose,
eds, *Microphone Fiends: Youth Music and Youth Culture*, Routledge,
1994.

38   A.F. Moore, *Rock, the Primary Text*, Buckingham, Open University
Press, 1993.

39   Compare the claims that pre-industrial Western popular music was
modal rater than major/minor, and that this heritage is still present in
today's popular music, in P. van der Merwe, *The Origins of the Popular Style*, Oxford, Oxford University Press, 1989, pp. 118, 175, 181.

40   Compare S. Frith and H. Horne, *Art into Pop*, Methuen, 1987 and
G. Marcus, *Lipstick Traces*, Secker and Warburg, 1989.

41   See I. Macdonald, *Revolution in the Head: the Beatles' Records and the
Sixties*, Fourth Estate, 1994; G. Martin, *Summer of Love: the Making
of Sergeant Pepper*, Pan, 1995.

42   The suggestion is supported by U. Fiori, 'Popular Music, Theory, Practice, Value', in *Popular Music Perspectives 2*, Exeter, 1985, pp. 13–23.

43   S. Whiteley, *The Space Between the Notes: Rock and the Counter-Culture*, Routledge, 1992.

44   See in general on this H. Shapiro, *Waiting for the Man: the Story of
Drugs and Popular Music*, Quartet, 1988.

45   Whiteley, *The Space Between the Notes*, p.4.

46   *Ibid.*, p. 11.

47   *Ibid.*, p. 20. Compare the new complexity composer James Dillon's
justification of his attitude to pulse, or lack of it, in his own music: 'You

don't have to keep stating pulse. This idea actually came from Hendrix … He has this inbuilt clock which allows him to ignore pulse, he plays with it all the time … to bend and shape the song form – rubato, stealing time …' (from interview with Ben Watson, *The Wire*, August, 1996, p. 39).

48  See M. Clarke, *The Politics of Pop Festivals*, Junction Books, 1982.

49  For Stratton Smith's life and work listen to V. Stanshall, 'Eulogy', *The Charisma Poser*, Virgin CD 7423 8 39171 29, 1993.

50  Whiteley, *The Space Between the Notes*, p. 27.

51  *Ibid.*, p. 110. Compare D. Harker, *One for the Money: the Politics of Popular Song*, Hutchinson, 1980, p. 109.

52  A. Kozinn, *The Beatles*, Phaidon, 1995, for example, pp. 7–9.

53  Macdonald, *Revolution in the Head*, p. 145.

54  *Ibid.*, p. 111.

55  *Ibid.*, p. 13.

56  For example, J.K. Galbraith, *The Affluent Society*, Harmondsworth, Pelican, 1962; A. Sampson, *The New Anatomy of Britain*, Harmondsworth, Penguin, 1988.

57  See K. Garner, *In Session Tonight: the Complete Radio 1 Recordings*, BBC, 1993, pp. 77, 84–5, 94.

58  E. Said, *Orientalism*, Vintage, 1984.

59  E. Lee, *Music of the People*, Barrie and Jenkins, 1970, p. xi.

60  Scoffers at prog rock include various contributors to the 'A to Z of Prog', *Wire*, no. 133, March 1995, pp. 28–32 and no. 134, April 1995, pp. 32–5; Chambers, *Urban Rhythms*, pp. 90–117; Hatch and Millward, *From Blues to Rock*, chapter 6.

61  For example, J. Street, *Rebel Rock: the Politics of Popular Music*, Oxford, Blackwell, 1986, pp. 191–2.

62  As Dave Harker claims in his *One for the Money*, Hutchinson, 1980, this position could not have been made truthfully even in the seventeenth century.

63  A product of the moment is R. Cotterell, ed., *Jazz Now*, Quartet, 1976.

64  R. Wyatt, liner notes to the 1992 reissue of his first solo album, *The End of an Ear* (1970), Sony CDL 743005-2. Compare the liner notes to the Soft Machine's John Peel sessions, *Strange Fruit*, Strange Fruit CD SFRCD 210, 1990. Ben Watson identifies Canterbury Rock as 'art-rock' in differentiating it from the more pompous Yes and ELP; see B. Watson, *Frank Zappa: the Negative Dialectics of Poodle Play*, Quartet, 1994, pp. 210–11.

65  For a brief history of Man Jumping, see A. Blake, 'Not enough *Noise*: Man Jumping, piece by piece', in Blake, ed., *Living Through Pop*, London, Routledge, 1998.

66  Wyatt, liner notes, *Soft Machine Live at the Proms*, Reckless Records

Reck 5, 1988.

67 Soft machine's Peel sessions may be found on Strange Fruit records SFRCD210, 1990.

68 *Adiemus: Songs of Sanctuary*, Virgin VP CDVEX 925, 1995; *Palladio*, Sony Masterworks CD SK 62276, 1996.

69 K. Jenkins, in sleeve-notes booklet to *Adiemus*, p. 12.

70 The Brotherhood, *Elementalz*, Virgin BiteM CDBHOOD1 7243 8 41324 2 2, 1996.

71 J. Lanza, *Elevator Music*, Quartet, 1995, pp. 117–18.

72 D. Heckstall-Smith, *The Safest Place in the World: a Personal History of British r'n'b*, Quartet, 1989, p. 131. A useful typology of these attempts to find a new language is P. Prato, 'Musical Kitsch: Close Encounters Between Pops and the Classics', *Popular Music Perspectives* 2, pp. 375–86.

73 D. Brackett, *Interpreting Popular Music*, Cambridge, Cambridge University Press, 1995, chapter 5, pp. 159–98.

74 P. Glass, *Low Symphony*, Point music CD 438 150-2, 1993.

75 Future Sound of London, *Lifeforms*, Virgin CDV 2722 7243 8 39433 2 6, 1994.

76 Narrated in B. Eno, *A Year with Swollen Appendices*, Faber, 1996, pp. 293–7.

77 D. Toop, *Ocean of Sound: Aether Talk, Ambient Sound and Imaginary Worlds*, Serpent's Tail, 1995.

78 J. Savage, ed., *The Hacienda Must Be Built*, Manchester, International Music Publications, 1992.

79 See also S. Thornton, *Club Cultures*, Cambridge, Polity Press, 1995, chapter 1.

80 For example, David Gill, Leeds fanzine editor, quoted in J. Miller, *Vox Pop: the New Generation X Speaks*, Virgin Books, 1995, p. 113.

81 Redhead, S., ed., *Rave Off: Politics and Deviance in Contemporary Youth Culture*, Aldershot, Avebury Press, 1993.

82 S. Frith, 'Why do Songs have Words?', in A. Levene-White, ed., *Lost in Music: Culture, Style and the Musical Event*, Routledge, 1987, pp 77–106.

83 C. Scott, *The Philosophy of Modernism in its Connection with Music*, Kegan, Paul, Trench, Trubner & Co., 1917, p. 101. Compare Inayat Khan, *Music*, Claremont, Calif., Hunter House, 1988, written in the early twentieth century: music 'creates also the resonance which vibrates through the whole being, lifting the thought above the denseness of matter; and it almost turns matter into spirit, into its original condition, through the whole harmony of vibrations tracking every atom of one's whole being' (p. 92).

84 P. Dawkins in *Megatripolis*, Funky PCD1, 1996.

85  M. McNab, 'Computer Music: Some Aesthetic Considerations', in
    S. Emmerson, ed., *The Language of Electroacoustic Music*, Macmillan,
    1986, p. 153.

86  C. Scott, *Music: Its Secret Influence Through the Ages*, 2nd edn, Rider
    & Co., 1950, pp. 106–7.

87  BT's *ima*, eastwest CD 0630-12345-2, 1995, a waxing which was
    voted album of the year by readers of *Muzik* magazine.

88  See, for example, R. Young, 'Aphex Twin and the Music of Dreams',
    *The Wire*, no. 134, April 1995, pp. 28–31; Razor, 'Aphex Twin', *The
    Lizard*, no. 4, April–May 1995, pp. 42–4; Toop, *Ocean of Sound*, pp.
    208–16.

89  R. Blaine, 'Dynamic Duo', *Future Music*, October 1995, pp. 64–7. An
    extract from the collaboration was presented on the issue's free CD; it
    can be heard in full on the Aphex Twin album *I Care Because You Do*.

90  In D. Witts, 'Advice to Clever Children', *The Wire*, no. 141, November
    1995, pp. 32–5, Stockhausen admonishes Aphex Twin for indulging in
    'permanent repetitive language'. Stockhausen's new importance can be
    gauged by the interview 'Björk meets Stockhausen', *Dazed and Con-
    fused*, no. 23, August 1996, pp. 42–6.

91  See Kodwu Eshun's reading of rave/techno in *Modern Review*,
    August–September 1994, pp. 1–2.

92  C. Larkin, ed., *The Guinness Who's Who of Rap, Dance and Techno*,
    Guinness Publishing, 1994, p. 336.

93  Ultramarine, *United Kingdoms*, Blanco y Negro CD 4509-93425-2,
    1993.

4

# The landscape with music: local, national, festival

### Celebrating place

The larger cities may be crucial to the genesis of new musical forms and the preservation of the most expensive older ones (such as opera) but the propagation of music takes place throughout the land, both in small-scale local events and in the concentrated celebrations of the music festival. Without the festivals at Cheltenham and Edinburgh, Glastonbury and Reading, the musical nation would be very differently imagined, and its history would be very different.

This chapter is, therefore, a historical geography, focused around the place of the festival in British musical culture. I will examine ways in which, through modernity's creation of traditions as well as through the technologies of postmodernity, cultures have been drawn together, held together, created and re-created through music. There is also a more general argument, about the role of culture in a present which has seen the power of the state diminish. As states withdraw from the administration of spaces, this diminution is part of a radical reconstruction of the relationship between people and the spaces they inhabit and move through; culture helps to fill the gap left by the withdrawal of the state. Music exists in space as well as time, but it exists contingently; the current changes encourage a look back at the ways in which music has helped the imaginary representation of land and people in Britain.

George Lipsitz has argued that 'while the nation-state recedes as a source of identity and identification, popular culture becomes an ever more important public sphere'.[1] Drawing on the work of Arjun Appadurai, Lipsitz claims that transnational capital has worked with as well as against patterns of migration; with the development and use of new technologies of communication and the creation of new multilingual spaces and continuities, not only the nation-state but the 'country' may be an obsolete formant of identity. Instead of conceptualising countries, Lipsitz remarks, we should think about 'ethnoscapes, mediascapes, technoscapes, finanscapes, ideoscapes: through which we can all inhabit many different "places" at once'.[2] We would add, as he does, *soundscapes*; but these are not the undifferentiated products of musical forms. The global availability of musics such as Rai and Reggae have meant not the presence of a series of universal signs or the creation of universal cultures, but their incorporation into syncretised local cultures. This process should be seen, Lipsitz argues, as a sphere of democratic cultural interaction which has to a certain extent replaced the 'political' in its traditional sense.

The focus here is on the music festival – at which such moments of mutual enrichment of the local by musics from elsewhere are commonplace. Opening remarks on the nature of festivals and their relation to places, including the idea of carnival and its implications, are followed by consideration of the very different ways in which festivals are organised and of their performers and audiences, from the local to the global. The festival is ostentatiously spatialised in many dimensions, and by looking at small-scale as well as large festivals we can attain some understanding of the ways in which 'the land without music' has in the twentieth century characterised itself as precisely a musical land: a sounding landscape, or soundscape, whose historical continuities and vertical connections have been and are vital to the continuing reconfiguration of the musical. This notion applies as much to the urban as to the rural, though it is sometimes difficult to delineate the boundaries between the two; music in the postmodern city forms an important part of the construction of boundaries of identity and place, and the festival is a specifically focused example of this construction. The chapter ends with an examination of arguably the most influential British classical music festival, the BBC Proms, and the place of this festival in the national culture.

## Festival as carnival

Festivals, however genteel and well-behaved, have to be seen first and foremost as an aspect of carnival, a time during which normal rules of social hierarchy and acceptable behaviour were suspended or inverted. Our ideas about carnival owe much to the work of the Russian critic Bakhtin, who located his explorations of this phenomenon in the Europe of the early modern period (the sixteenth and seventeenth centuries), associating it with the writings of the French proto-novelist Rabelais, and arguing that local carnivals have declined in number since the triumph of bourgeois culture.[3] The popular culture of the Middle Ages and the early modern period has been analysed in the work of many historians of Europe, who have interrogated various moments of popular excess.[4] Through study of the legal and other records of such events they have pieced together a model of popular culture and of the importance of carnival within it.

Bakhtin argued that carnival took place at specific times (normally religious festivals, such as Easter) and in specific spaces – usually the public spaces of the town or village, such as the village green or market square. In these locations, and for an agreed period of hours or days, the normal flow of time was interrupted by what he called 'sacred time', during which 'the world was turned upside down'. In other words, the normal hierarchy of power-relations was inverted – people without power were crowned, while those with power became their servants. Bakhtin insisted that this reversal of power was paralleled by a difference in the prevailing modes of discourse. In normal times, the world was explained through a set of monological discourses. Monological explanations are unitary and closed, offering a single set of interpretations and incorporating, indeed justifying, the existing power-structure. They were carried principally by the Church and the law. In sacred time, however, the peoples' voices were heard, and monological discourses were replaced by dialogical interpretations of the world, which allowed for open-ended debate, interpretation and celebration, rather than official explanation. Carnival has almost disappeared as a general aspect of European culture, but aspects of these dialogic interpretations survive in popular song and in the behaviour of the crowd at some sporting events; Bakhtin also pointed out that some subsequent types of literary text, such as Modernist poetry, are also dialogical or open-ended, rather than the monological texts of the closed end ('happily ever after'). High culture becomes, in this account, a ghostly analogue of the popular, in an argument which is roughly contemporary with Adorno's justification of elitist art.

Other writers have developed these arguments about the loss of early modern culture. In their influential text *The Politics and Poetics of Transgression*,[5] Peter Stallybrass and Allon White argued that in Britain carnival was in decline from the seventeenth century onward, in retreat firstly from the more puritanical versions of Christianity which triumphed in the civil war of the 1640s, then from the time-discipline demanded by the machine-driven work of the Industrial Revolution. But carnival did not disappear altogether. Gradually fairs and circuses were marginalised and quite literally driven to the periphery of working-class culture, the seaside resorts built for working-class recreation (places like Cleethorpes, Southend and Blackpool).

In another influential book which I read as a complement to Stallybrass and White, *The Fall of Public Man*,[6] Richard Sennett has argued that the nature of peoples' interaction in public changed, becoming quieter, more mutually respectful and less openly emotional (including less violent). In particular, he argues, during the eighteenth century the 'masquerade' element of public life diminished. In the aristocracy and middle class, men ceased to wear make-up, flamboyantly coloured clothing and wigs. Women of these classes continued to dress up, but were not encouraged to go out; the home, the 'domestic sphere', became seen increasingly as 'woman's place'. These important aspects of culture, and in particular the stress on the material pleasures of the body and the pleasures of role-playing in public, were 'repressed'; but this repression has never been total, even for the middle class: Stallybrass and White, and Sennett, would agree with Bakhtin that traces of the carnival recur even in some ostentatiously 'high cultural' products, in literature, music and surrealist art. There were also strong traces of the carnivalesque in popular cultural forms such as music-hall and pantomime (which, unlike forms like opera, always allowed for a certain amount of public participation) and, of course, spectator sports in which (whatever the discipline displayed, or not, by the players) the crowd could and did behave drunkenly, abusively and sometimes riotously. Music competitions involving choirs and brass bands were often closer to the last than to the decorous audience of today's choir or band concert.

This, then, is an important legacy of the festival, in which place is both celebrated and transformed, its usual roles and functions added to or changed by the addition of new roles, people and performance. Since the eighteenth century at least, there have been important festivals in Britain organised around music and musicians; in the present century their number has become legion – and it continues to increase. Many musicians, bands and even orchestras spend their entire summers festival-hopping. There is an associated industry of programmes and souvenirs, catering and accommodation, which mean that festivals contribute to their local economies in such a way as to compensate for the disturbance and disruption caused by the events themselves, and this economic compensation has often led to local councils setting up, subsidising and helping to administer festivals on the grounds that they are good for local communities (though many of the people of Edinburgh, and the rural neighbours of the Glastonbury festival, would no doubt have their own, rather different views on the matter certainly in the case of Edinburgh, the city's holiday patterns have changed since the growth of the festival and its massive fringe, with many natives escaping for a fortnight).

Why should festivals be both so attractive and so repulsive? There is more going on here than a simple rejection by local people of anything which disturbs their lives. Festivals are a concentrated form of cultural celebration, drawing together the people of a locality or nation and/or the people interested in a certain type of work. Because of the carnival connection, celebration is of itself a difficult notion (particularly difficult for British inheritors of a legacy of puritanism). 'To celebrate' almost always involves an excessive transcendence of routine behavioural norms: drink, drugs, sex and verbal or even physical violence become foregrounded (though it is of course the case that this type of hedonistic celebration is in far more open evidence at the Glastonbury festival than at the Three Choirs festival). Furthermore, in almost all cases, there is the direct paradox that in the very mobile late twentieth century, festivals which may have originated in the desire to celebrate localities and work which reflects them, which may be based around local venues and around the talents of local people, cannot be local, cannot be restricted to residents, any more. In almost any festival (exceptions are mentioned below), the very rumour of a series of events will produce a large inflow of visitors with habits and hierarchies of their own. This invasion may be signalled by the temporary difficulty in finding car-parking space; by the noisy presence of a rave party in a neighbouring field; or by the impossibility of moving in the streets of a town such as Edinburgh at festival time without being accosted by a comic, a mime or someone advertising the shows put on by a young dance company.

Festivals, then, are upsetting, turning the world upside down even when they are formally set up to mark the most 'serious', high-culture-validated, musical, theatrical and artistic products – as was originally the case with the events at Edinburgh. From the outside, because of this general disruption of everyday routines, any festival will carry the marks of carnival. From the inside, too, even the most serious usually have their moments of carnival, spaces and events in which the world of the *festival itself* is turned upside down: moments called the 'festival fringe' or some such appellation. The Edinburgh 'fringe' is now a festival in its own right, arguably more important than the official festival, and certainly one of the most important British spaces in which young performers and/or radical work is/are displayed. More routinely, the music festival associated with the Henley Regatta – which relies on partnership between business sponsorship and local government organisation – includes a street festival of clowns, jugglers and public dressing-up, as well as a more decorous programme of (mainly classical) music.[7]

Carnivalesque fringes are virtually ubiquitous. Rock festivals, featuring numbingly long lists of bands often tediously convinced of the seriousness of their project, now as often feature stand-up comics to provide light relief. One such, or rather one such team, Newman and Baddiel, rather overran their place in the rock hierarchy in the early 1990s, moving from supporting rock acts to headlining gigs of their own in rock venues – and went on a rock-style tour, including appearances at Wembley Arena, to underline the point. For a brief moment their success was taken as confirmation of the 'Death of Rock': comedy was apparently to be one of its replacements. Perhaps in the end, however, the momentary success of this enterprise only served to confirm the continuing health of the medium it parodied, as (in a pastiche of the death of a rock band) the comedians announced that they no longer liked each other, split up, and one of them went on to present laddish programmes about association football.

What, then, does carnival/festival mean? It can be argued that carnival subverts accepted values, overturning hierarchies of status, taste and behaviour and offering new ones (or none at all); it can as easily be argued that by offering a limited time and space for subversion, after which everything reverts to the pre-carnivalesque order, carnival actually reinforces the primacy of the values it upsets. This is, unsurprisingly, as true in the world of classical music as it is of rock. At the Southern Cathedrals festival, in which for three days every summer the choirs of Winchester, Chichester and Salisbury cathedrals meet to perform sacred choral music on a larger scale than their routine daily performances of Evensong and Matins, there is a late night 'fringe' event devoted to the performance of poetry and music far removed from the seriousness of most church music. Season ticket prices include this fringe event, which is attended not by a separate audience but by many of the patrons of the festival's more routine offerings. Again the emphasis of the Southern Cathedrals festival fringe is on humour, usually including parody of the officials and musicians involved in the main events – and usually presented and performed by some of those officials and musicians themselves. Here, too, jazz and light music can make their presence felt. The festival fringe here clearly gives audience and performers alike the chance to unwind from the seriousness of the work they have been drawn together to celebrate; it does not, in the end, threaten those values, but reinforces them – as does the festival as a whole.

## Festival as circus

One of the most important components of the festival is an idea which is often seen as the companion of the carnival and is often an important component of any area's carnival time, but is a separate entity: the circus. The circus is, in Western culture at least, a legacy of ancient Rome, where entertainers of every sort formed troupes for public entertainment, and where this was encouraged by the state in a way which Adorno would have recognised as the promotion of mass deception. The connections with present-day sport are clear; those with music will be teased out. The Roman idea of public entertainment included gladiatorial confrontations, in which the loser was often killed, and confrontations between groups of professional killers and groups of heretics (for example, Christians), in which the heretics were slaughtered. But there are also connections with other forms of public entertainment, including all matters theatrical and musical. The crucial notions of circus as they relate to the musical world are these: circuses are professional (performers are paid); they are nomadic (performers travel the world to greet their public, rather than wait for the audience to come to them); and – a related, if more arguable point – they are not representatives of any one nation-state or other political grouping, in the ways in which touring state orchestras or troupes of folk musicians can be. Indeed Charles Dickens used the independent travelling circus in his 1854 novel *Hard Times* as a positive counterpart to what he portrayed as the dehumanising evil of industrial society. International musicians on the circus tour are for this reason especially important carriers of cultural difference, agents of the transformation of local cultures in the sense proposed by Lipsitz and others.[8]

Circuses were once local, or at most national, phenomena, though they were always considered to be an internal social Other. They also tended to be seasonal, until the technologies of travel made them fully international. Music-hall performers and opera singers were in demand, but would often perform for 'seasons', such as the pantomime season in midwinter, or the holiday months. Since the development of air travel, and especially since the introduction of the Boeing 747 'jumbo jet', however, sporting and musical circuses have become fully international. So travelling rock musicians and opera stars, like many sports performers, are parts of an international circus, professional nomads plying their trade round the world, their lives organised by agents and promoters, with comparatively little sense of nationalised selfhood. The British-born rock musician David Bowie lives (that is, has his principal home) in Switzerland; the German-born composer Hans Werner Henze divides his time between homes in Italy and England; but both constantly travel the world, making new musical and other projects, as, in effect, circus artists. The massive growth of the festival circuit, in Britain as elsewhere in the world, is a consequence of this – a consequence of the development of air travel.

This point should remind us that music is part of the global entertainment business, and that there are close links between international capital and the international music and festival circuit. When this chapter was first drafted, several well-established British rock bands, including Dire Straits, Pink Floyd and the Rolling Stones, were involved in multinational touring programmes. These tours are not simply for display or entertainment, but are efficient ways of generating profit. In most cases companies are set up for the duration of specific tours. Teams (often upwards of 200) of set-builders and sound personnel, personal assistants and managers, travel with the bands, and are paid as full-time employees for the duration, which in the case of Dire Straits was the best part of two years. Monies from tickets, merchandise, performing rights and associated album and video sales can be considerable, which is one reason for U2's dispute with the PRS performing rights collection agency. U2 are of the opinion that PRS is an inefficient collector of the money due to them as performers of their own songs; they wish to charge the venues at which they perform directly, and bank the money immediately – and claim that had they done so on their most recent world tour they would be several million pounds better off. (This greed is not universal in the rock world. In a similar but inverted dispute, Pearl Jam challenged the Ticketmaster concert agency to reduce the inflated ticket prices the agency has charged – though both examples indicate that when the circus comes to town and everyone wants a piece of the action, someone, somewhere will make some money, often at the expense of both performers and public.)

Of course, international performing circuses are not quite the same thing as carnivals or festivals. But without the possibility of the international circus, the possibility given by the comparative ease of travel, the festival as we know it would not exist. The festival, including its possibilities for carnival, is at present largely dependent on the circus.

## Festivals in Britain

Carnivalesque occasions were not necessarily popular festivals organised from the bottom up. Among the most important ancestors of the current festival were the Tudor, Jacobean and Caroline masques, which started as court entertainments, but which during the early years of the seventeenth century were deliberately expanded until they included, at some level of spectatorship or participation, much of the population of London. Though masque routinely involved transgressive dressing and behaviour, it was equally routinely supportive of the state. Dance and music were important parts of the whole, and the attention of many court composers such as Thomas Campion and William Lawes (and of poets such as Ben Jonson and architects/designers such as Inigo Jones) was given to the creation of suitable music for this massive, participatory public entertainment in which professional participants, courtiers and members of the public played parts.

We may ascribe a similar role to the Handel festivals of the later eighteenth century, through which much of what we now think of as 'classical music' came into existence. Through these festivals new class alliances were permitted and symbolically celebrated, and the power of the state was reinforced, as a chain of like events spread through the larger towns of the nation[9] – a process which was then repeated in the nineteenth century as organisations like the Huddersfield Choral Society increasingly involved working-class people. Handel, though every bit as German as the British royal family, came to share that family's surprising ability to symbolise Britain and Britishness. Handel's music is still used *ad nauseam* in television's documentary and other commentaries on royalty, and on Heritage Britain generally – and has become more generally associated with things monarchical. The Disney cartoon *The Lion King* (1994) shadowed this usage, as the death of the older lion king was accompanied by a cod-Handelian slow movement; in an arguably less excusable anachronism, no doubt aimed at American sales, the music of Handel, arranged by George Fenton, was used throughout the British film *The Madness of King George* (also 1994). (This is only a partial anachronism, of course. In George III's time Handel was a revered figure already celebrated in festivals; however, George's court would have been more routinely used to the music of contemporaries such as J.C. Bach and Haydn – none of which is evident from the film score.)

This national use of music may be festive and may create a sense both of space and time, but is surely not transgressive. As was argued above, even the most openly world-inverting festival celebration can serve to confirm the values it inverts; here the values and hierarchies are not subverted (though there is often a deeply unoffical 'fringe' to royal occasions; the silver jubilee of Queen Elizabeth II, held in 1977, an official festival if ever there was one, involved Handel's music *ad nauseam* once again, but it also called forth the acidic deconstruction of the Sex Pistols' single 'God Save the Queen' and the equally acidic pro-punk commentary of Derek Jarman's film *Jubilee*). There are, however, important points to be made about public participation even in the most routine and official of festivals. As I argued in chapter 1, in Britain, where the status of the music profession has never been particularly high, and where during the nineteenth century the profession was finally feminised, much suspicion has surrounded the shamanistic role which has been more willingly afforded musicians elsewhere. The role of the amateur choir was in part to offset this suspicion by offering to its participants the opportunity of displaying, in public, precisely the kind of ecstatic communication which brought the musical profession under suspicion. In this no doubt comparatively mild way, the public display of emotion, including properly spiritual ecstasy, was brought into the public sphere from which it had been banished, and whose banishment was reinforced by various laws of the 1840s against gambling and duelling. It is especially important that women were members of these choral societies; here is one point of re-entry for middle-class women and for the expression of the emotions into a public sphere from which both had been purged earlier in the nineteenth century.

There were also, however, choirs from which women were excluded: the cathedral and Anglican church choirs, which had their own festivals (including the very long continuity of the Three Choirs festival, so important to composers like Elgar, Holst and Vaughan Williams, and from which the Southern Cathedrals festival derives); and the male-voice choirs of the working-class communities, most obviously in Wales, around which an instant tradition was created. Here, as with the other great male working-class musical phenomenon, the brass bands, the festival celebration tended to involve competition. The first brass-band championship is roughly contemporary with that other great symbol of working-class competitiveness, the Football League, which was founded at Lytham St Annes in 1882. Like music-hall, football soon became a professional, circus sport. Brass bands however, (like male-voice choirs), remained amateur for rather longer. Bands tended to be associated with villages or with workplaces (for example, the GUS Footwear band or the Grimethorpe Colliery band, which won the national brass band championship for the last time in 1992, when the pit which had given the band its name was threatened with closure).

The competition festival has, in the twentieth century, expanded to include classical music performance, with the Leeds Piano competition and Cardiff Singer of the World perhaps the best-known British examples of contests designed to find the best performers. These are international festivals, open to all comers, from which the winner will proceed to join the international circus as a recording and recital star. At national level, the BBC television Young Musician of the Year contest, and a Radio Two equivalent for light music performers, have launched a number of promising careers.

Classical music has become one of the most routine high-prestige components of Festival Britain. At both local and global levels, the music festival, and the festival with high musical content, have provided work for the international and national music circuses. This does not only mean the big cities or established performers. At Aldeburgh on the Suffolk coast the Britten–Pears foundation continues the work of the founders, bringing international and nationally-known artists to Snape and Aldeburgh; there is also a well-established tradition of masterclasses and other performances by young performers at this event, and the foundation does some work to support the work of younger composers. In the Orkneys, composer Peter Maxwell Davies has founded the St Magnus festival, which routinely involves both local and international performers, often performing work by Davies and others written specifically for mixed amateur–professional, local–global performance (as were some pieces by Britten, such as the pro–am opera for the whole community, *Noyes Fludde*, which was created specifically for Aldeburgh). Even in festivals such as these, however, tensions remain between local people and the invading audiences: the organisers, perhaps unwittingly, do not often enough see the danger of creating a 'local community' which is class-specific, or at best earnings-specific.

### Festivals in rock

This injunction now also applies to what we can call the established, perhaps even the establishment, rock festival. Prices at festivals such as Glastonbury and Reading are quite high enough for the organisers to make a comfortable profit, and for the principal catchment audience of students, whose financial situation has deteriorated rapidly in recent years, to think twice before attending such events. While these festivals now offer a wide range of music and associated entertainment (the 1980s moment of indie-rock as an index of student appeal having passed, and the audience for popular music no longer being addressable in coherent categories of class, gender and age-specific taste), their coverage in the broadsheet newspapers, as events with appeal to people from their late teens to their forties, would seem to confirm their status as established. They are carnivalesque moments, yes, for the many thousands who throng south and west at the appropriate times, but carnivalesque only in the temporary, status-quo-confirming sense outlined above.

However, Glastonbury, Reading and more recently the Phoenix (at Stratford-upon-Avon) are the inheritors of a movement which purported to be more permanently subversive, and whose ramifications are examined below. These festivals exist, whether consciously or not, as part of a tradition of carnivalesque activity which to some extent fits the model of resistant subculture discussed in chapter 3. For thirty years now, rock festivals have been the site of social anxieties and moral panics around drugs, sexual behaviour and noise. They have been the subject of parliamentary investigation, legislation and litigation. They have claimed the attention of police and local authorities. Everywhere they have been proposed, there has been local opposition; in the summer of 1996, for example, an attempt to set up a new festival in the Hampshire countryside (in the absence that year of the Glastonbury event) failed in part because of the opposition of the majority of the comparatively few local residents, while the summer dance event 'Tribal Gathering' also found it difficult to find a site, due to local opposition.[10]

Despite such opposition, rock festivals have become established. The origins of the Reading event are in the 1950s, when the Marquess of Bath, eager to earn enough money for the upkeep of his massive home at Longleat, ran jazz festivals based on the annual event at Newport, Rhode Island. Six hundred people attended the first of these in 1956; four years later there were ten thousand – and crowd disturbances, which caused the Marquess to turn his park over to the less dangerous practice of displaying wild animals. A festival was set up to maintain the new tradition, first at Richmond and then at Reading. By 1965 this had become a pop, not a jazz, festival, and attendances were over thirty thousand (jazz festivals still abound, notably at Crawley in Sussex and Brecon in Wales). In 1968 the 'Reading' event was held at nearby Sunbury.[11] It has since become equally important to the music business as a promotional tool and to fans as a celebration of late summer, just before the new term at school or university.

While Reading and, from 1971 onwards, Glastonbury, were locating themselves in the calendars of the nation, they were subject to official scrutiny. A succession of Home Secretaries set up committees of investigation to try to control events which many Conservative voters in particular thought of as anathema. The investigators did not, however, take a uniformly hostile position – each investigation came out in basic support of the festival idea. In 1973 the first of these, the Stevenson Committee, proposed a set of guidelines for the holding of festivals, attempting to regulate access, safety and so on. The Committee's preamble was clear: 'pop festivals are a perfectly reasonable and acceptable form of recreation';[12] while in 1976 a Department of Education working group concluded that

> free festivals … are developing an interest in a number of activities – for example, theatre, folk-dance, mime, rural arts and crafts, alternative technology and experimental architecture … we think that festivals can offer useful experience to young people, in living away from the facilities of wider society.[13]

Until the passage of the 1994 Criminal Justice Act, in fact, the law was on the side of those who wished to assemble in large numbers and listen to music.

Meanwhile, however, a movement had started which did not particularly want to be a perfectly reasonable form of recreation. This was the forebear of the culture at which the Criminal Justice Act was aimed. Early 1970s Windsor festivals, begun in the Great Park as an assertion of the right to hold a free festival in a public place as close as possible to one of the private spaces of the British monarchy, were deliberately combative and politicised events, and after the 1974 event a local action group, acting with the police, went to court (that is, the law courts!) and prevented another. Likewise Rochdale's Whitworth festival, begun in the early 1970s as a hippie-ish northern Glastonbury (reviving a medieval fair first held in 1251) and appropriated first by punks and then by the beginnings of the traveller movement, was also characterised by battles against local people and the police – as well as by a wide mix of entertainment, including theatre and musics including folk as well as rock.[14]

The Whitworth festival came to an end in the early 1980s, after mounting police interference. The official toleration of alternative and free festivals had worn thin by this time. At the height of Thatcherism's attempt to create a counter-culture combining rampant free-market capitalism with conservative 'family values', such old-fashioned counter-cultures were seen as unnecessary competition. During the highly confrontational miners' strike of 1984–85, free festivals (and another part of carnival culture, football fans) were the targets of government ire – and direct action was taken against them by an almost militarised police.[15]

One legacy of *all* this activity – the legal and the illegal, the free and the commercial – was the realisation that the festival can become a site of political activity. In their different ways the 1971 concert for Bangladesh organised by George Harrison, the 1985 Live Aid concert and subsequent phenomena such as the concert for Nelson Mandela, campaigning tours such as Rock against Racism, the Anglo-Irish Fleadh held annually in North London and the gay, lesbian and bisexual celebration, Pride, all have built on the notion of a popular festival as a way of proposing, trying to create, a truly vital cultural politics, one which has involved thousands of people and their pleasures, generating a far greater level of enthusiasm than other political events.

This may be one of the reasons for the suspicion in which such events have been held by politicians. Pre-industrial revivals, allying aspects of high-technology popular music, medieval craft fairs and the travelling circus do seem to add up to a collectively desired alternative society, an imagined community whose parameters are only realisable through such forms of interaction. The urban equivalents – spaces such as Megatripolis, with its stalls selling alternative diets, therapies and knowledges alongside the dance-halls and chill-out rooms of the club scene – are engaged in a similar process of reimagining the world. This is not, for all the connections with historic British forms of anarchism and socialism, necessarily an alternative to capitalism; it is in many ways an *alternative capitalism*, one which takes ecological values as seriously as it does innovation, customer satisfaction and profit.

But whatever the political economy, this is a world which imagines itself spatially as well as culturally. It imagines a landscape with music. The powerful symbolism of Stonehenge, around which mid-1980s battles were fought, can stand for the importance of landscape to this alternative history. For alternative history is part of the agenda here. As George McKay has identified, the folk-inflected rock festivals of the 1970s and after were proposing a new Albion, a landscape with music which looks 'back' to an imagined pagan Celtic past, to the fire festivals and the celebration of the seasons and to the use of identified and historicised sacred sites, such as Glastonbury – and at least one of the makers of high-technology dance music quoted by McKay, Mark of Spiral Tribe, claims that 'techno is folk music'.[16] They are thus, like the Glastonbury festivals run by Rutland Boughton in the early years of the twentieth century (festivals which performed his Celtic–Wagnerian operas), involved in a historic imaginary which stretches back through the long history of Arthurian literature and music, and including the work of twentieth-century writers like John Cowper Powys and T.H. White, to propose an imagined rural, mystical and at least semi-pagan Britain.[17]

Here we return to a paradox which this book has consistently identified. The festivals are patronised both by the comparatively few 'New Age' and by vast numbers of commuter-wage travellers, piling out from the cities to indulge in a touristic creation of paganism, celticism and so on. But, as I have stressed throughout, the history of popular culture is too concerned with small radical elites and not enough with the weekenders, and even for them the point stands. The historic agenda is that, like Bax and Boughton, they are working with an anti-Anglo-Saxon past; so this may be 'English' in its desire for a certain landscape, but it is *against English Establishment history*, with its celebration of Empire and Little Englishness. This is a long way from the conservative celebration of the Last Night of the Proms (and its touring versions, discussed below); yet one text held in common is William Blake's 'Jerusalem'. This is a British culture, riven with paradox.

What, then, can we make of festivals held in *urban* space, such as those held annually in East London, Brighton or the Edinburgh Fringe? All partake of that mixed-media folkishness identified (and welcomed) by the Department of the Environment in the mid-1970s. Although the Albion agenda may be as important here as it is to the rural festivals, there is, of course, much to celebrate in the inner cities as precisely the points at which the imagined Little England breaks down, and new populations and new cultural forms are constantly emerging. Where the landscape of Albion outside the cities is in fact owned by a comparatively few very rich people, landownership and use are important but less all-encompassing issues in urban areas. The cities are patchworks of small private and public spaces, a grid of ownership and responsibility which makes such events as the Telegraph Hill festival (discussed below) easier to make and promote than would be an equivalent around a rural village. Through events like Fleadh and Pride this patchwork of personal and collective identities can be played on and reworked in a celebration of the fluidity, the inner space, of the metropolitan experience.

One important example here is the carnival properly so-called, its nomenclature and many of the practices surrounding it derived from the cultures of the Caribbean. The best-known of these, the (West London) Notting Hill Carnival, is often called the 'biggest outdoor festival in Europe'. Here, for a weekend in late August, narrow streets are jammed with hundreds of thousands of people listening and dancing to bands and sound systems, looking at or taking part in costume parades and floats, and getting or being stoned. The event is heavily policed, and public anxiety has often focused around perceived problems of 'race' and crime, problems which led in the early 1980s to a rerun of the late 1950s confrontations between gangs of young men in Notting Hill, arguably the first 'race riots' in Britain; in recent years, however, a more professional management and an enforced virtual curfew has dramatically lowered the instance both of black–police confrontations and of robbery. Notting Hill Carnival, too, is heading away from the 'subversion' of open criminality and towards the establishment of its image as both tourist attraction and one which offers residents and participants a moment of dialogical reversal of routine power-relations within an otherwise monological world.

Meanwhile a whole skein of 'invisible' festivals has developed to celebrate the cultures of British Asian populations. Hindi film festivals, like Bhangra events, are massively popular and successful; yet for all their commercial success, they remain peripheral to mainstream awareness. At least one recent event, featuring Bombay film stars, filled Wembley stadium, but was neither previewed nor reported in mainstream arts or news coverage. These events, rather more than the travellers' free festivals, are truly counter-cultural. Nevertheless, as celebrations of the continuing identity as internal Others of their participants, they are hardly turning the world upside down; they, too, in their way, are 'established', reconfirming rather than subverting the identities of participants and audiences.

So too is the annual round of events in which musics from the world's folk cultures are performed and celebrated, though the cultural agenda here has shifted markedly since the establishment of folk festivals such as the Cambridge and Whitby events, and the slightly more rocky Copredy Festival, in which an Oxfordshire village annually plays host to some 17,000 visitors. Folk music, once locked into the sterile pursuit of 'authenticity', is now more open; 'folk roots' are acknowledged in musics from bluegrass to Bulgarian choral; the continuities and connections among Scandinavian and Eastern scale patterns, the dialogue between Irish and African–American musics, and so on, indicate that while folk does indeed preserve and maintain traditions, it also proposes an alternative internationalism and soundscape–landscape, escaping from the domninant musical languages of Anglo-American rock and Western classical music. Again, folk deals with landscape, and here there are still links to the West Country (including Glastonbury) of Cecil Sharp's heyday, with even Reading on the edge of Wessex, the imaginary heart of England since its invention by the novelist and poet Thomas Hardy.

One of the largest of these folk-ish events is the WOMAD (the World of Music and Dance) festival, currently held at Reading under the aegis of Peter Gabriel (sometime frontliner for Genesis), who has sanctioned, encouraged, and often himself produced many recordings of these performances. In one important sense WOMAD, however 'serious', and however much it serves to perpetuate an established category of commercially inferior musical Otherness, does serve to turn the world upside down, blending and juxtaposing musics and musicians in absolute opposition to the two major tendencies still operating within the music business: to promote the African–American and/or the Anglo-Saxon as the paradigms of commercial viability and to emphasise technology as opposed to human performance in the making of music. This eclectic mixing also serves to undermine one of the sub-tendencies within music of all sorts, the primacy accorded to the supposed 'authentic' as opposed to the mixed. In these ways WOMAD, too, however much it is itself 'established', performs a valuable counter-cultural role.

### Local festivals: the expression of containment

Given the above arguments about transport, audiences and performers, we have to ask: are such things as local festivals truly possible? In fact small-scale local festivals do exist, ranging in scope from the annual village 'fete', which might have an accompanying musical evening, to the local single- or three-day event, in which the small-scale and local are so much the driving force that their emergence on to the national/global stage is unlikely.

The Winchester Hat Fair first took place in 1985 – in a supposed revival of a medieval fair. Despite local opposition to a noisy popular event based in and around the streets of this overwhelmingly middle-class Cathedral town, a *modus vivendi* grew, and the fair is currently a festival of street theatre, comedy and music which provides as much entertainment for children as for adults.[18] The Hat Fair is in some ways a genuine, and unique, celebration of difference, and of the abilities of local people, which marks the area out as still having some cultural autonomy; the travelling players who converge on the town act in subordination to a local organising and co-ordinating committee which defends the fair year-round from its remaining local opponents. For those opponents, Winchester's autonomy is meaningless; for them it has no specific landscape, soundscape or theatrescape; it is imagined as a quiet retirement area, or a suburb of London, tied by road and rail links which make daily commuting possible, and by cultural links which have gradually effaced the local differences which the fair (and opposition to the M3 motorway) has tried to reinstate. The opposition to the fair signals a reluctance to embrace difference and particularity, and a reluctance to embrace the community spirit within which these differences are celebrated.

So local differences are not merely subsumed within some Home-Counties megalopolis of endless cultural repetition. Indeed, one can argue that, even as global culture has succeeded, for example, in siting a McDonalds take-away in the up-market London area of Hampstead (not to mention Winchester itself), so local cultures have also succeeded in providing differentiation within cities, towns, and even boroughs.

The Telegraph Hill festival is an even more recent phenomenon than the Hat Fair. First run in October 1994, it provided a series of events for and by the people of this quiet and relatively prosperous group of South London streets. Aimed at the thirty-something generation, people for whom the attractions of the local rock venue (The Venue) and football-ground (Millwall FC) had diminished with age/time, and their young families, the festival utilised local performance spaces, encouraged artists to open their bedroom studios and provided live poetry, adult and childrens' drama, dance and music workshops and rock, classical and jazz musics. The final

event was a party which included the usual sardonic carnivalesque–comedic look at the event as a whole, a brief, relatively structured jazz performance and a jam session in which members of the
audience participated in the music, playing as guests with an *ad hoc*
band, or performing, *en masse*, well-known songs with kazoos.
Almost everything at the festival, in fact, was performed by local
people, many of whom were professionals in their fields. All gave
their services free. The organisers of the event, a committee under
the auspices of the Telegraph Hill Conservation Society, sold tickets
and leafleted. Attendance at all events and associated activities was
excellent, and it seems possible that the festival, which has been
repeated, will become a semi-permanent fixture. Here is a genuinely
local celebration, one which covers a very wide range of activities,
partly because of the concentration of talent in the area, and which
could, therefore, remain local. Participants were agreed that problems might begin to arise if and when fees were paid to participants,
and that therefore in order to cover costs, performers guaranteed to
fill venues would be booked. Meanwhile, the postmodern geography of London had been changed once again, by an assertion of the
value of the local, small-scale production of culture by and for the
community.

## 'The nation' in the classical festival

Classical music festivals remain high-status events, usually supported by local and national arts councils and businesses. And they
are legion. A brochure distributed with the *BBC Music Magazine* in
March 1996 listed 172 summer festivals throughout Great Britain
and Northern Ireland. Since the rise of the Handel festival, they
have been important in the construction of national identities, and
this applies to comparatively local events like the Three Choirs festival as it does to events held in the big cities. It would be a mistake,
however, to suggest that an easy, coherent fit between nation and
identity was or is possible through the classical music festival. We
find on examination a patchwork-quilt of differentiated musics,
audiences and expectations, between which there is considerable
tension. The (official) Edinburgh festival, for instance, is a project
which began in the immediate post-war years in the same concilia-
tory, Eurocentric and forward-looking, but Reithian, spirit as the
Arts Councils (Reith was, of course, a Scot). Yet while there has

always been a place for new Scottish music, including Gaelic and Lowland folk-song as well as new work by Scots composers, there has always been concern that there was too little emphasis on the Scottishness of the celebration, and too much reliance on basic cosmopolitan repertoire.[19]

There are, of course, many festivals which present all the appearance of coherence, relying on a mix of traditional repertoire and newly commissioned work which, it is hoped, will fit with the existing repertoire: the Huddersfield choral festival, for example. But Huddersfield also hosts, in the late autumn, one of the more important of the European festivals of contemporary music, and here the tensions are extreme. Many of the elements identified in chapter 1 – Modernism, in the overdetermined form of 'new complexity', propounded by such stalwarts of the internally subdivided bar as James Dillon and Brian Ferneyhough; minimalism and especially the 'faith minimalism' of Henryk Gorecki, John Tavener and Arvo Part; and the postmodern 'new tonality' of Mark-Anthony Turnage, Judith Weir and others – are presented in the same performance spaces, to the annoyance, even the anger, of those who believe in one form or another as the bearers of absolutely correct musical value. The Huddersfield festival of contemporary music would seem to indicate the problems Modernist music still faces: moving outside the known semi-private space of mutually recognised expertise and into the wider imagined community necessarily involves a loss of the purity and rigour which has marked that music. For minimalists and postmoderns, on the other hand, there is a struggle to join the knowable community of Modernist musicians: to have the music they have identified with and created validated by an audience of critical *cognoscenti*. Here there is very little notion of music for an undifferentiated (or even a differentiated) 'general public'. Anoraks all round.

On the face of it, no such tensions are present at the Edington 'festival of music within the liturgy'. The vicar of Edington, a Wiltshire village with a particularly magnificent fourteenth-century priory church, initiated this week-long summer celebration of sacred music in 1956, using choristers on holiday from Salisbury cathedral. Since then it has expanded to include three choirs: one, the Nave Choir, of boys and men; one, the 'Consort', of young men and women; one, the 'Schola Cantorum', of men only. The singers attend at their own expense; they, and many attending the festival, are put up by 'host families' in the surrounding area. Entry to all the services and celebrations is free, and there are no tickets except for the central social event of the week, a supper which is also the festival's very careful 'fringe' – while the guests dine, male voices sing light music from well outside the liturgy (staples of classic popular song, for example, 'A Nightingale Sang in Berkeley Square'). The music is presented for the most part quite literally 'within the liturgy', the context of the services for which the music was originally intended; and so it will be heard not in concert, but at celebrations of the Eucharist, at Matins, Compline and Evensong. In recent years BBC Radio Three has broadcast one of the week's Evensongs.

The services are quite deliberately Anglo-Catholic. Ornamental vestments are worn by the priests, and the air is thick with incense. The nation imagined here is intensely conservative – an aspect of the heritage culture vision promoted by John Major, of old maids cycling to communion. It is, therefore, at the same time a very conservative event, a long way from the nation created under Thatcherite Conservatism, and a very long way indeed from the Church of the inner cities and the rural poor. It is a nation imagined as highbrow, middle-class, with a strong, if deeply implicit, component of gay masculinity, above all perhaps 'well-educated' in the traditional classics/humanities sense – and therefore able and willing to engage with the best liturgical music from Continental, as well as English, church traditions (though the festival also includes contemporary music, occasionally commissioning it). Indeed, in its implied ecumenical yearning for reunion with the Roman Catholic Church, this is both deeply English and implicitly a festival of Anglo-European amity.

A Continental echo of this wish is provided by the 'Night of the Proms' concert phenomenon. Begun a decade ago by the Belgian company Prommusic, this annual pan-European tour takes a classical orchestra plus MOR rock/soul performers such as Al Jarreau and Bryan Ferry to venues in Spain, Germany, Switzerland, France, Belgium and Holland. Popular classics based on the format of the Last Night of the Proms form the centre-point of the evening, providing an ersatz patriotism – an association which was strong enough for one political party in the German election of 1994 to adopt 'Land of Hope and Glory' as its campaign theme-song. Here the European middle class can respond to a British format, in an analogue of the cultural Europhilia of the Edington festival.[20]

A very different middle-class nation is proposed in the outdoor Proms promoted every year by the Royal Philharmonic Orchestra, the most populist and least heavily subsidised of the London orchestras. At country-house sites like Herstmonceux Castle, Longleat and Petworth, the orchestra provides evenings of 'Prom Classics'. Early in the evening, some of these classics are European, but the orchestra ends by turning to the heavier fare of patriotic tunes with increasing audience participation. There is usually on these occasions a miniature last night of the Proms, in which Elgar's 'Pomp and Circumstance March no. 1' (in its guise as 'Land of Hope and Glory'), Parry/Blake's 'Jerusalem' and Arne's 'Rule Britannia' are sung by all present, before the evening ends with a firework-display accompanied by the music of the adopted musical patriot, Handel. The audience dresses for the occasion in Union flags and items of apparel based thereon. Here the lower-middle-class sings and jives along to a musical Englishness which is in some ways the analogue of the Englishness of the magazine *This England*; the music of late Empire is charged with the historicised nostalgia of heritage culture for the mainly white audiences who attend and who profess no love of things European. The RPO's gig at Longleat and the festival at Edington are very close geographically, but in different cultural, and therefore national, worlds: the communities imagined and represented by these festival soundscapes could not be further apart. Are they brought any further together by the Proms themselves?

### From coherence to divergence: the Proms

The Proms, the series of concerts organised by the BBC and held every year at the Royal Albert Hall, and which celebrated its first hundred years with two special seasons of retrospective and commissioned work in 1994 and 1995, holds these two imagined nations in tension. The 'Last Night' provides the model for those populist RPO outdoor concerts. The Last Night's music is programmed around the sequence of British imperial melodies, Elgar's 'Pomp and Circumstance', Arne's 'Rule Britannia', and Parry's 'Jerusalem', with the series' first conductor, Henry Wood's arrangement of sea-shanties a reminder of the connections between trade, empire and naval strength which created British imperialism. On the face of it, then, this is a deeply anachronistic musical celebration of the nation as an expanding, capitalist and imperialist power. The crowd sings along, flags are waved, television presenters make trite remarks, and everyone goes home happy. Many at the BBC have been unhappy with this unveiled jingoism, and have attempted to change it.

The Last Night is a moment of internal carnival, the built-in fringe of a serious event, when the world is turned upside down and the audience participates directly in the music-making – but it is not the only carnivalesque moment in the festival. There are others, notably the Viennese Night, when 'lighter' music, this time dance music of the later nineteenth century by the Strauss family and others, allows for a less serious approach from the audience. The Viennese Night, however, is less stable than the Last Night; both have been threatened over the years, but while the Last Night has remained relatively intact, on occasion the waltz programme has been altered, even dropped. Writing in the prospectus and programme guide for the 1980 series, the then director of Radio Three and planner of the season, Robert Ponsonby, reasoned thus:

> We have converted the Viennese Night into Operetta Night. We were not convinced that we were always doing justice to the dance music of Vienna or that this tradition was still particularly vital. Moreover, it effectively excluded complete operettas from the Proms. So, taking advantage of the Offenbach centenary ... we aim to establish Operetta Night, so that we can accomodate not only French, but also Viennese and English operetta in future.[21]

The quota-system implied by the juxtaposition of 'either' Viennese waltzes 'or' French operetta in a two-month series which has plenty of room for both has never in fact become open policy, and programming has fluctuated over the years – though there have been, as it happens, too few operettas, as well as too few waltzes. Ponsonby's comment signals one of the continuing concerns of the administrators of the Proms series: the question of authority.

The relationship with the audience is partly a function of the Proms' success. While the attendance for straightforward classical concerts at London's Festival Hall has been in decline since the late 1970s, Prom audiences have actually increased, and in the early 1990s were averaging over 80 per cent of potential ticket sales. Commentaries have consistently celebrated the audience's relative youth and enthusiasm, and planners of other concert series have employed opinion pollsters, PR consultants and others to try to attract the same people to their events – with comparatively little success; while the BBC has reacted with concern at any suggestion that the demographic profile of the audience is changing (due to student poverty, for example, as at the Glastonbury rock festival). The Royal Philharmonic Orchestra's announcement, in 1994, that it intended to hire the Albert Hall and to broadcast concerts with accompanying visual stimuli on cable television signals one further attempt to capitalise on the success of the Proms.

For the BBC's planners, however, the audience's task remains one of passive acceptance of their enlightened programming. This leads to conflicts of authority. In the 1977 prospectus Robert Ponsonby announced the basic principle of the event, a statement informed by the classic Reithian assumption: 'The programme policy remains unchanged: discriminatingly to balance the best of what is familiar with what we believe to be the best of what is not, whether it is new or old.'[22] The audience, without autonomy, is hailed into position as the receiver of what is thought by those in authority to be the best. Members of the audience, however, have minds of their own. Indeed, it has often seemed to the planners that some of the audience was only interested in the relative frivolity of the Last Night. In 1950 the BBC Symphony Orchestra's concert manager wrote: 'Some attempt must be made to curb the increasing hysteria of the audience, and the only way that I can see is to present a less frivolous type of entertainment.'[23] In 1953 proposals to drop the Wood sea-songs were rejected after vigorous public debate;[24] in 1969 'Land of Hope and Glory' was dropped, and again after much lobbying, reinstated the following year.[25] In 1982, the year of the Falklands conflict (and the consequent re-election of what had, immediately before that conflict, been a deeply unpopular Conservative government), the celebrations at the Last Night were particularly strident. Robert Ponsonby was shocked, on conversing with various people attending the year's Last Night, to discover that they had not attended any of the rest of the season's concerts, but were simply there on the one night, to wave flags and give voice to 'Rule Britannia'. Many were relatively unconcerned with the discipline of listening, and joined enthusiastically in the performance of the other pieces, with whistles and hooters, rather like a football crowd, with its very similar use of song to establish collective identity – truly a moment of carnival.

Writing about this in the 1983 prospectus, Ponsonby commented sadly that 'it seemed that those concerned had missed the point of what is essentially a musical occasion ... and not an extra-musical jamboree in its own right'.[26] In an attempt to curb this 'extra-musical' frivolity, a ballot for last-night tickets was instituted; henceforth tickets could only be bought by those who had attended some or all of the other concerts. This draconian move did not solve the troubled relationship between planners and audience. A decade later Ponsonby's successor, John Drummond, writing the 1993 prospectus, was moved to appeal to Prommers to 'let the music end before the cheering starts'.[27] This was followed in the programme guide by a dedicated article, 'Handy Hints', written by David Harman, which explained the etiquette of Promming, from patient queuing to that all-important question of audience response time.[28] The authorities continue in their attempts to control the audience of whom they claim to be so proud. In 1995, in a deliberate gesture of contempt for the last night and its audience, retiring director John Drummond programmed 'Panic', a Modernist piece for alto saxophone, drumkit and wind instruments by Sir Harrison Birtwistle. The audience in the hall, already smarting under Drummond's insistence that they listen quietly, tolerated the piece; from the wider community of watching licence-payers, BBC switchboards were jammed by people trying to complain.[29]

In 1994, the hundredth year of the festival, the programme guide resonated with the series' history, with articles in the catalogue celebrating venues like the Queen's Hall and conductors such as Wood and Sir Malcolm Sargent. Here too, however, the crisis of authority was present. We were told how the repertoire has changed; how the blend of light music and classics gave way first to a mix of (mainly German) classics and contemporary (mainly English) music, then the same classics with harder European and American Modernism. Concerts replicated these moments in an aural history of the event. But the impression remained that the BBC has often commissioned and performed difficult-sounding work because Aunty thinks it is good for us; and that while there has been much exposure for British, European and American Modernist music, since the war a generation of British composers has remained under-represented. 1994 there was a concert performance of Ethel Smyth's opera *The Wreckers*, arguably a tokenist gesture aimed at placating both traditionalists and feminists (the magnificent pro-feminist peroration after this performance, by radio announcer Natalie Wheen, was the broadcasting highlight of the season).

Lobby groups have been debating the direction of the Proms since the BBC assumed control of them in 1926: both within and without the BBC, they pose another threat to the authority of the planners. Recently, the argument that the Proms should be a more representative, and more British music festival, a case made eloquently in 1981 by composer and sometime BBC producer Robert Simpson,[30] has been joined by claims that it should perform music for middle-brows, for whom the early operas of Richard Strauss are about the limit in experimental composition.[31] The Proms have survived earlier partisan furores: pressure-groups for British music (or music by women, or Asian or African Caribbean music, or jazz) have consistently been ignored or patronised by tokenism, such as the 1992 appearance by a steel band, which performed outside the hall and was the only concert in the season not broadcast on Radio Three. Post-colonial Britain was, apparently, adequately represented by the European tradition up to and including Modernism, and if listeners didn't like it, they could switch off.

Now, however, they can switch over; since the success of Classic FM and the chart success of music by Tavener and Gorecki, Radio Three's attitude to its listeners has come under more consistent attack, and the Proms are as open to criticism as the rest of the network. This crisis of authority is signalled in John Drummond's introduction to the 1994 prospectus, with its defensive, ironic reference to the days when 'new music was likely to be British rather than by nasty old foreign atonalists',[32] and an equally defensive essay by Stephen Walsh on three of these foreign mischief-makers, Schoenberg, Berg and Webern, which claims without much substantiation that their music is no longer a 'problem'.[33] Furthermore, Drummond remarks,

> the example of Henry Wood has been an encouragement and an inspiration to those of us who have followed. I hate to think what he would have made of the current fashionable idea that 'easy listening' is the standard by which we should judge music. Great music deserves an effort on the part of the audience, and cannot be served up only in bite-sized chunks.[34]

As usual, the case here is asserted, not proven – no attempt is made to substantiate the point of view in a series which actually included as part of its historicist celebration a 'Wagner Night' in which extracts rather than complete scores were performed, with no apparent ill effects on either audience or performers. In some ways here we are back with that question of authority and audience discipline (and certainly with the Reithian agenda); but intertwined with it is the battleground of current identity politics: the question of Britain and Europe. The Proms since the 1960s, and the directorship of Sir William Glock, have been Eurocentric rather than Anglocentric; which is offensive to many of the proponents of British music – the historian Corelli Barnett, for example – who are also 'Eurosceptics', seeing a culturally integrated Europe as some kind of evil German master-plan. But there is a genuine problem here as (if?) Britain approaches European unity. Can there be a separate British national culture in a European Union? And if so, how should it be represented by the BBC?

There is no question that the Proms are, and have been throughout their first hundred years, routinely celebrated as a unique national festival. Their own textual construction, in fact, is as a backbone of a national musical heritage. The texts of the Proms – histories, celebrations, catalogues, programmes of individual events – play a part in this continuing narcissistic delight. So it is worth paying some attention to the programming of the series. I have concentrated on the period from 1974 to 1994, which coincides with my own (very sporadic and selective) attendance at the Royal Albert Hall and other venues. In Table 1 I have categorised programmes according to the age of the piece being performed, the nationality of its composer and in the case of music written *after* the Second World War, its character as either Modernist 'New Music' or music relatively reliant on tonality and pre-serialist techniques. All prewar music by established Europeans is categorised as mainstream. This is a personal categorisation, and leads to what many will see as anomalies. So the music of, for instance, Schoenberg, Berg, Webern, Stravinsky and Bartok is classified as mainstream European, for all its rebarbative implications for the Classic FM listener; perhaps most controversially, I have decided that the post-war composer Olivier Messiaen's work owes enough to tonality to be categorised as mainstream.

The tendencies are clear. Support for new and recent British work has remained fairly constant, but the concerts are not and never have been a haven for the new and experimental. Programming of

**Table 1** *Proms contents over 21 years*

| date | Ger./Aus. | Other | New | Old | Brit. | Britnew |
|------|-----------|-------|------|-----|-------|---------|
| 1974 | 80 | 49 | 7 | 25 | 28 | 17 |
| 1975 | 70 | 54 | 11 | 55 | 19 | 28 |
| 1976 | 68 | 48 |  | 17 | 27 | 24 |
| 1977 | 72 | 48 | 11 | 13 | 22 | 18 |
| 1978 | 65 | 54 | 8** | 3 | 23 | 13 |
| 1979 | 67 | 48 | 10 | 24 | 19 | 22 |
| 1980 | 70 | 60 | 13 | 38 | 23 | 17 |
| 1981 | 84 | 40 | 10** | 20 | 15 | 23 |
| 1982 | 62 | 60 | 11** | 20 | 19 | 22 |
| 1983 | 71 | 55 | 8** | 20 | 15 | 19 |
| 1984 | 63 | 54 | 16** | 54 | 17 | 25 |
| 1985 | 71 | 73 | 14** | 2 | 12 | 15 |
| 1986 | 57 | 73 | 9 | 14 | 15 | 20 |
| 1987 | 50 | 91 | 9 | 48 | 27 | 18* |
| 1988 | 64 | 70 | 11 | 34 | 38* | 10* |
| 1989 | 73 | 81 | 13** | 5 | 25 | 15 |
| 1990 | 65 | 82 | 8 | 21 | 26 | 9*** |
| 1991 | 64 | 56 | 13 | 9 | 28 | 31 |
| 1992 | 66 | 92 | 16 | 11 | 14 | 17* |
| 1993 | 72 | 85 | 16** | 15 | 21 | 18 |
| 1994 | 71 | 86 | 6** | 4 | 40 | 27 |
| 1995 | 69 | 83 | 27 | 11 | 15 | 19* |

Ger./Aus.: German and Austrian, eighteenth century–1945.
Other: Other European and USA, eighteenth century–1945.
New: European (including German), world, and USA, post-1945.
Old: Pre-eighteenth century British and European.
Brit.: British music, eighteenth century–1945, in traditional style.
Britnew: first and early performances of post-war British music.
*: includes jazz.
**: includes Indian, Thai, or Korean.
***: includes steel band.

*Source:* compiled from BBC Proms prospectuses, 1974–95.

early, jazz and world musics remains tokenist. Although the core of the programme remains music from the European tradition, Austro-German work has received consistently less emphasis over the period; this applies to avant-garde work as much as to the Bach to Brahms mainstream (for example, performances of Stockhausen's work, routine in the early 1970s, are a rarity twenty years later).

Tables 2 and 3 examine the change in status and appearance of the prospectus. Over the years what was once a very plain catalogue has become an increasingly bulky magazine, a publication with its own Reithian 'mission to explain', trying to reach an audience which does not already know the music and how to discriminate. In 1974 the prospectus was exactly that, a 66 page catalogue with a brief introduction by the chief planner, 28 advertisements, and the concert listings, which were printed without comment (presumably on the assumption that the potential audience was familiar with most of the music, or at least the names of the composers and the styles in which they worked). By 1994 there were 132 pages, with as well as the introduction, 66 advertisements, and 9 specially commissioned articles – on the event's history, on the artists and composers featured at this year's festival, and on music old and new. The prospectus is now supplemented by the BBC Music Magazine, an informative but relentlessly lower-middlebrow publication which is also designed to make classical music more accessible (here, too, there are a few token pages on jazz). The BBC has played its part, an honourable one, no doubt, in the commodification of classical music.

Whatever we make of this process of commodification and neo-Reithian explanation, the continuing success of the Proms is undoubted. The range of programming has remained wide, and the audiences have grown, even during a time of continuing recession. But there remain acute problems in the way in which the programmers have seen music. In these twenty years of continuing post-colonial transformation, it is disturbing that the event still only programmes non-European musics at the tokenist level of the annual appearance of Indian or Javanese performers[35] and that gestures towards jazz, such as the 1987 appearance by Loose Tubes or the 1994 concert by the Wynton Marsalis band, have also remained tokenist – for all the obvious debt to the jazz tradition by composers like Milhaud, Stravinsky, Walton, Turnage and so on, who have been more adequately represented. While there are also good arguments for the inclusion of more British traditional music (it is hard to imagine, for example, why only one Bax symphony has been performed in the last twenty years), they pale before those for jazz – or

**Table 2** *Proms prospectus changes shape: the advertisers*

| date | pubs | recs | hi-fi | BBC | fest. | c & a | inst. | bus. | ed. | others |
|------|------|------|-------|-----|-------|-------|-------|------|-----|--------|
| 1974 | 7 | 1 | 4 | 3 | 5 | 1 | 1 | | | 3 |
| 1975 | 4 | 2 | 1 | 4 | 3 | 1 | 2 | 1 | | 3 |
| 1976 | 4 | 2 | 2 | 4 | 5 | 1 | 3 | 1 | | 3 |
| 1977 | 3 | | 2 | 3 | 6 | 1 | 3 | 2 | | 4 |
| 1978 | 4 | 2 | 2 | 4 | 5 | 1 | 3 | 1 | 1 | 4 |
| 1979 | 4 | 2 | 2 | 4 | 5 | 1 | 4 | 1 | 1 | 2 |
| 1980 | 7 | 4 | 9 | 6 | 10 | 1 | 5 | 25 | 1 | 3 |
| 1981 | 5 | 4 | 13 | 11 | 8 | 1 | 3 | 10 | 1 | 4 |
| 1982 | 7 | 5 | 12 | 8 | 5 | 1 | 2 | 8 | 2 | 4 |
| 1983 | 2 | 3 | 13 | 7 | 3 | 1 | 1 | 9 | 2 | 4 |
| 1984 | 5 | 5 | 10 | 8 | 9 | | 4 | 11 | 1 | 5 |
| 1985 | 7 | 4 | 13 | 6 | 7 | | 4 | 8 | 1 | 4 |
| 1986 | 7 | 3 | 10 | 6 | 7 | 2 | 4 | 11 | 3 | 4 |
| 1987 | 3 | 3 | 10 | 6 | 7 | 1 | 9 | 10 | 2 | 6 |
| 1988 | 5 | 3 | 8 | 2 | 8 | 2 | 9 | 16 | 3 | 11 |
| 1989 | 2 | 3 | 8 | 4 | 2 | 4 | 8 | 14 | 5 | 7 |
| 1990 | 6 | 1 | 7 | 4 | 4 | 3 | 5 | 13 | 5 | 6 |
| 1991 | 5 | 2 | 6 | 4 | 4 | 1 | 2 | 14 | 5 | 5 |
| 1992 | 5 | 5 | 7 | 5 | 7 | 1 | 1 | 11 | 14 | 2 |
| 1993 | 6 | 1 | 4 | 6 | 8 | 1 | 2 | 12 | 17 | 2 |
| 1994 | 9 | 2 | 3 | 5 | 7 | 3 | 1 | 11 | 23 | 2 |
| 1995 | 4 | 3 | 3 | 7 | 7 | 3 | 3 | 10 | 21 | 3 |

pubs: publishers.
recs: record companies.
hi-fi: hifi companies.
BBC: BBC programmes and events.
fest: other festivals.
c & a: charities.
inst.: musical instrument manufacturers.
bus.: corporate business adverts.
ed.: educational institutions.

*Source:* as for table 1.

for certain 'popular' musics (such as ambient techno) which are now arguably closer in attainment to aspects of contemporary classical music than they have been since the late 1960s, when Soft Machine made the only appearance so far representing 'rock'.

**Table 3** *Proms 1974–95: prospectus contents*

| date | intro. | pp. | articles | Proms | cost (£ sterling) |
|------|--------|-----|----------|-------|-------------------|
| 1974 | 2 | 66 | 1 | 55 | 0.20 |
| 1975 | 2 | 68 | 0 | 57 | 0.30 |
| 1976 | 3 | 64 | 2 | 56 | 0.30 |
| 1977 | 2 | 68 | 2 | 55 | 0.40 |
| 1978 | 1 | 76 | 3 | 55 | 0.50 |
| 1979 | 2 | 72 | 5 | 54 | 0.60 |
| 1980 | 1 | 108 | 8 | 57 | 0.80 |
| 1981 | 2 | 96 | 7 | 56 | 1.00 |
| 1982 | 2 | 96 | 5 | 57 | 1.00 |
| 1983 | 2 | 84 | 5 | 57 | 1.00 |
| 1984 | 2 | 96 | 5 | 59 | 1.25 |
| 1985 | 2 | 88 | 3 | 60 | 1.25 |
| 1986 | 1 | 108 | 11 | 60 | 1.25 |
| 1987 | 1 | 120 | 9 | 66 | 1.50 |
| 1988 | 3 | 132 | 10 | 69 | 1.50 |
| 1989 | 3 | 126 | 10 | 68 | 2.00 |
| 1990 | 3 | 126 | 9 | 66 | 2.00 |
| 1991 | 3 | 122 | 10 | 66 | 2.50 |
| 1992 | 3 | 122 | 10 | 66 | 3.00 |
| 1993 | 3 | 122 | 10 | 66 | 3.00 |
| 1994 | 3 | 132 | 8 | 68 | 3.50 |
| 1995 | 3 | 132 | 10 | 70 | 3.50 |

intro.: number of pages of director's foreword.
pp.: number of pages in prospectus.
articles: number of articles.
Proms: number of concerts.

*Source:* as for tables 1 and 2.

At this point the question of technology becomes as important as that of form – we are dealing with a very particular soundscape here. Sounds work in space – or not; the Royal Albert Hall is a very particular type of space, wholly unsuitable to some musics because of its unwieldy acoustics and difficult to rig for electronic music because of its size and because of the age and condition of the current electronic infrastructure. While the BBC performs miracles in getting the hall to sound more or less acceptable for straight orchestral music, for those involved in multi-channel mixing and diffusion the hall presents additional problems, including that of its wiring. Experienced live-act sound designer Michelle Reynolds, fitting out the hall for a gig featuring singer Lisa Stansfield accompanied by a ten-piece band and forty-piece orchestra, opined in 1994 that 'It's the worst place to rig ... we were told that they had improved the cable run, but it is absolutely dreadful.'[36]

At the height of Glock's stewardship, new music could be performed in a more intimate space, the Roundhouse. Some electro-acoustic music, including music for tape alone, was 'performed' there. Very little has been performed or relayed at the Proms since this venue became unavailable. Leading electro-acoustic composers such as Jonathan Harvey have been allowed some access to the facilities of the Royal Albert Hall, but on the whole the 'new music' created for the Proms has been for that living museum, the orchestra. This has made it far more difficult to integrate the more experimental high-technology 'classical' with their equivalent 'popular' musics. That one performance at a Prom by what could be called a rock group, Soft Machine, in 1970, followed a concert by the Modernist orchestra the London Sinfonietta, in whose programme there was an electro-acoustic element, a piece by Tim Souster. A return to this blend of technologies would help to build the generic bridges implicit in postmodernity's compression of value-difference, and without which even the Proms may lose its way as a unique generator of enthusiastic audiences for classical music.

In order to face this question head on – as, for instance, the programme planners at London's South Bank complex are having to do, in the face of declining audiences for classical music – the planners will have to decide how they see value in relation to conflicting viewpoints. Among these are, firstly, the argument that in an age of relativism, the generic mix of programming could and should be broadened. This is the direction in which the South Bank is moving, with a mix of classical concerts and popular musics, both during the summer months, when the venues are competing directly with the Proms, and during the rest of the year, when they are 'only' competing with cinema, West-End theatre and television. But there is a counter-argument, supported by the success of Classic FM and implicit in the RPO's attempts to go audio-visual in their Royal

Albert Hall series. This is deconstructive of the seriousness of the world of concert classical music, and implies instead its specific, situational use. Classic FM's success is one sign of the death of abstract music and its replacement by music for use (which includes, of course, the accompaniment of the everyday: driving, washing up and just Walkman-ing around). In each case, the Proms must be made more multi-media sensitive, more able to cope with the blend of high technologies which form part of the musical future; or they will disappear into the vacant maw of static, touristic Heritage Culture.

Attempts, or rather suggested attempts, to reform the Proms have an irritating habit of avoiding these issues, concentrating instead on the symbolism of the Last Night or the (no doubt regrettable) absence of work by individuals or schools of composers. The vigorous, post-minimalist, Angry Youngish composer Steve Martland argued in a newspaper article at the end of the 1993 series that there should be more room for jazz and ethnic musics, perhaps in a shadow series such as 'New Proms' which would allow for more than mere tokenist gestures.[37] Martland insisted that these changes should be made to include people from black and Asian British cultures he felt were systematically excluded by the programming. Here again much negative energy was spent on the Last Night; no mention was made of technology and/or the problematic space of the Royal Albert Hall. Abolishing the Last Night would only create problems; unless Martland is happy to exclude the traditional audience by including new ones, the best we can do is to move towards another kind of last night, whose patriotism can be more inclusive, and whose irony can be more readily apparent. No doubt Sir John Drummond thought he was doing precisely this when he tried to change the temper of the Last Night in 1995. It may be that the work of the musicians I discuss in my final chapter will open the way to such a transformation. Until this happens, the Proms' representative role will remain exclusive.

## Notes

1   G. Lipsitz, *Dangerous Crossroads: Popular Music, Postmodernism and the Poetics of Place*, Verso, 1994, p. 5.

2   *Ibid.*

3   M. Bakhtin, *Rabelais and His World*, trans. Helene Iswolsky, Bloom-

ington, Indiana University Press, 1984; *The Dialogic Imagination*, trans. C. Emerson and M. Holquist, Austin, University of Texas Press, 1981.

4  P. Slack, ed., *Rebellion, Popular Protest and the Social Order in Early Modern England*, Cambridge, Cambridge University Press, 1984; D. Underdown, *Revel, Riot and Rebellion: Popular Politics and Culture in England 1603–1660*, Oxford, Oxford University Press, 1987.

5  P. Stallybras and A. White, *The Politics and Poetics of Transgression*, Methuen, 1987.

6  R. Sennett, *The Fall of Public Man*, Faber, 1984.

7  My thanks to Keri Powell for information on the Henley Festival.

8  See, for example, John Collins and Paul Richards, 'Popular Music in West Africa', in S. Frith, ed., *World Music, Politics and Social Change*, Manchester, Manchester University Press, 1989.

9  See W. Weber, *The Rise of Musical Classics in Eighteenth-Century England*, Oxford, Oxford University Press, 1992, chapter 4.

10  Personal testimony; M. Clarke, *The Politics of Pop Festivals*, Junction Books, 1982; R. Chernin, 'Rave in Danger', the *Independent*, 30 May 1996.

11  Clarke, *The Poliics of Pop Festivals*, pp. 21–2.

12  *Ibid.*, p. 77.

13  G. McKay, *Senseless Acts of Beauty: Cultures of Resistance since the Sixties*, Verso, 1996, p. 28.

14  McKay, *Senseless Acts of Beauty*, chapter 1; Clarke, *The Politics of Pop Festivals*, p. 157.

15  See my discussion of the football 'problem' in A. Blake, *The Body Language: the Meaning of Modern Sport*, Lawrence and Wishart, 1996, pp. 127–8.

16  McKay, *Senseless Acts of Beauty*, p. 109.

17  M. Hurd, *Rutland Boughton and the Glastonbury Festivals*, Oxford University Press, 1993; J.C. Powys, *A Glastonbury Romance*, Bodley Head, 1933; T.H. White, *The Once and Future King*, Fontana, 1958. Some connections are traced in A. Blake, 'T.H. White, Arnold Bax and the Alternative History of Britain', in D. Littlewood and P. Stockwell, eds, *Impossibility Fiction: Alternativity – Extrapolation – Speculation*, Amsterdam, Rodopi International, 1996, pp. 25–36.

18  Some coverage of the event still tends to the myopically critical. See a typical newspaper story of Hat Fair misbehaviour, 'Cathedral Drunks Fined after Bonfire Binge', *Hampshire Chronicle*, 16 August 1996.

19  G. Bruce, *Festival in the North: the Story of the Edinburgh Festival*, Robert Hale, 1975, p. 22.

20  For a brief account of the Night of the Proms concert tour, see M. Maes, 'Proms take Ampco across Europe', *ProSound News*, Decem-

ber 1995, p. 21.

21  R. Ponsonby, Foreword, *BBC Proms 1980*, p. 5.

22  R. Ponsonby, Foreword, *BBC Proms 1977*, p. 4.

23  D. Cox, *The Henry Wood Proms*, BBC Books 1980, p. 159.

24  *Ibid.*, p. 164.

25  *Ibid.*, p. 194.

26  R. Ponsonby, Foreword, *BBC Proms 1983*, p. 7.

27  J. Drummond, Foreword, *BBC Proms 1983*, 1993, p.6.

28  D. Harman, 'Handy Hints', *ibid.*, pp. 46–7.

29  In 1970 an attempt was made to involve the audience in a new work, Malcolm Williamson's 'The Wall' (Cox, *The Henry Wood Proms*, p. 197).

30  R. Simpson, *The Proms and Natural Justice*, Toccata Press, 1981.

31  Such as the hecklers: see the discussion in chapter 5. And note Donald Mitchell's view of Strauss's *Elektra* as politically correct Modernist music, in his *Cradles of the New*, Faber, 1995, pp. 216, 219, 220.

32  J. Drummond, *Foreword, BBC Proms 1994*, p. 4.

33  S. Walsh, 'Problem Solved?' *BBC Proms 1994*, pp. 107–8; this special case has been made *ad nauseam* over the years: compare R. Ponsonby, Foreword, *BBC Proms 1975*, p. 9. The BBC's own historian of the Proms, David Cox, will have none of this. He claims that Schoenberg and other twelve-tone composers will never be accepted by the general public (Cox, *The Henry Wood Proms*, p. 253).

34  J. Drummond, Foreword, *BBC Proms 1994*, p. 7.

35  Compare the incident of Priti Paintal and the orchestra, discussed in the Introduction.

36  Simon Croft, 'Lisa Stansfield', *Studio Sound*, November 1994, pp. 59–63.

37  S. Martland, 'Last Night of the Proms', *The Independent*, 10 September 1993.

# 5

# The muse of diversity

The traces, convergences and divergences followed here have created a system whose complexity precludes predictable outcomes. While all music in the Britain of the late 1990s has been strongly inflected by the political and commercial milieu of the post-1979 Conservative government, the effects of that Conservatism have not been uniform or unilinear. The paradoxes of Thatcherite Conservatism (the desire to destroy cultural patterns in the name of market forces while strengthening notions of patriotic pride) remain fruitful contradictions in British music, which has been reconstituted, throughout the twentieth century, through its interactions with America, the former colonies and the rest of the world. These changes have been expressed most completely in the changes in radio broadcasting which the Conservative regime has overseen; they have also been expressed in changing educational policies and practices. Indeed, the equation: enterprise, heritage, culture, which under Thatcherism supposedly equalled commodification, has a missing term, education, without which it won't add up.

The continuing presence of pop music and the music of the Asian and Caribbean communities on radio and in record stores, and the presence of the children of Commonwealth immigrants in the schools of British urban centres, have led gradually to the reformation of senior-school music-teaching away from music appreciation and classical composition and instrumental technique and towards the technologies and practices of popular music. The post-war curriculum leading to school examinations in music at the academic O- and A-levels (and their equivalents in Scotland), and the practical examination system conducted under the aegis of the joint examination board of the music colleges, had concentrated on the reproduction of classical music and its performers and appreciators. Composition was taught at school, if at all, only as a function of the rules of harmony and counterpoint which dominated European music in the eighteenth and nineteenth centuries. Increasingly, however, at the less academic qualification level of CSE, elements of popular music appeared on the curriculum.

Lucy Green's work on the structure of music education in the early 1980s reinforces the predictable point that the CSE syllabus was aimed at working-class children, many of whose teachers assumed that they had little or no musical ability, and who taught them aspects of popular music in a confirmation of that belief: pop was simple, commercial, easy to learn about and reproduce, where classical music was complex, imbued with liberal rather than commercial values, and whose reproduction required both effort and ability. Music-teaching, in other words, like so many other aspects of education, reproduced the class system.[1] It is perhaps surprising, then, that when the academic examination system was reformed in the 1980s and the differences between O-level and CSE were abolished, both the elitism of O-level music and its assessment in traditional examinations were qualified in a move towards the more inclusive curriculum of CSE.

The GCSE syllabuses introduced in 1985 stressed the learning of compositional and performance skills, including the use of synthesisers, samplers and recording equipment.[2] For pupils, this was in many ways a liberating departure. They could now perform and record their own music; they could present music in their own, vernacular styles, in a portfolio of their own recordings; they did not have to be skilled in the music of the European past in order to do so. This was welcomed by those who had campaigned for popular music to be heard in the classroom.[3] Green, however, argues that what may appear to be a liberating and confirmatory gesture is at best patronising, and at worst reproduces class and status once again:

> teaching pupils only about what is relevant and understandable merely affirms their social situation … and still perpetuates the universal appearance of a classical music which derives its cultural legitimacy precisely from the fact that it is neither relevant to nor understood by the majority of the populace.[4]

The point is well made, though I would argue that the non-teaching of popular music is categorically different from the teaching of it, and to argue that systems which ignore popular forms have the same outcome as systems which include them questions the role of education in any form of knowledge; but this lining up of musics against value systems and against class and power relations, whatever its importance, misses a trick. A crucial aspect of the turn to popular music is not its ideological value, its role in the making or confirming of children's identities, but its commercial value – its value to the music business as a whole. For the retailers of high-technology music equipment there were at last opportunities not only to sell their wares in the highly lucrative education market, but also to promote them to the consumers and musicians of the future; the Japan-based multinational Yamaha has been particularly insistent on doing this, through the Yamaha Music Foundation, a 'non-profit-making' organisation which is dedicated, in its own words, to 'helping children discover the everlasting joys of a life filled with music'.[5] It publishes song-books and textbooks for every level of school music-making, and provides teachers, classes and instruments; it sponsors concerts, recordings and competitions. All these help to raise the awareness of music, and of the various Yamaha products through which music can be made and, they would stress, enjoyed.

The motive behind such a company policy is clear and salutary. It reminds us that music can be and is bought and sold, that part of the story of music in twentieth-century Britain is of a reasonably successful multinational business, and that the impetus behind changes from an orthodoxy built around classics-based performance and appreciation to the composition and performance of popular music is as much commercially as aesthetically or culturally driven. Music is no longer an abstract set of theoretical propositions, but a commodified sign, to be exchanged in the market-place under the absolute signifier of Capital. The much-vaunted appearance, in 1990, of the BRIT School, the first music-based City Technology College (in Croydon, South London) and courses at degree level at the new Universities of Westminster and Bournemouth, for example, signals a new concern for the making of music for use. The Croydon college was sponsored by the British Record Industry Trust; the course at Westminster is called not 'Popular Music' (as with similar courses at Leeds and Salford) but, more clearly, 'Commercial Music': students learn to write music for film and television; they also learn about the self-marketing, contractual and accounting problems they will have to solve as freelance musicians or as runners of small businesses. Perhaps in their spare time they get to practise the clarinet. Music here, however excitingly high- (or low-) tech, is a means to an end, not an end in itself.

The implicit tensions in all this were highlighted when the Interim Report of the Working Group on the place of music in the national education curriculum was published in March 1991.[6] Enthusing in its multicultural brief, the committee's report assumed the equal value in education of musics as different as reggae and ragas, sambas and serialism. The skills of performance and composition were privileged over critical appreciation. The use of synthesisers and other electronic instruments, computer-based composition packages and multi-track tape recorders, African drumming techniques and jazz improvisation were placed alongside baroque counterpoint and sonata form. One composer from the European tradition, Mozart, was mentioned by name in a report which otherwise eschewed the naming of specific composers and works in favour of descriptive and generic terms.

There followed a furore in the pages of the broadsheet newspapers. The Working Group was arraigned for betrayal of the classical music tradition, for its substitution of multiculturalism for the values apparently inherent in the European tradition; some argued specifically for the 'Englishness' of the post-Elgarian tradition at the centre of music teaching in England (similar battles were fought, at around the same time, between multiculturalists, Europeanists and Little Englanders over other aspects of the curriculum, notably history, while the guardians of English Literature also fought to save their canonic texts from pollution by popular fiction). A series of letters and articles, notably in the *Daily Telegraph*, *The Times* and the educational press, rallied the intellectuals of both old and new right in defence of 'traditional' musical education, in other words, the abandoning of any idea of the creativity of the young in favour of the appreciation, and where appropriate also the reproduction, of the techniques and achievements of previous generations of male Europeans.[7] This musical tradition, according to its defenders, somehow encompassed the musical verities; others did not. Unsurprisingly, the authors of the anti-relativism polemic were among those engaged in the fight against musical Modernism in Radio Three programming which was discussed in chapter 1.[8] Their campaign resulted in a watering down of the Working Group's posi-

# PLEASE Mr Major, act to protect the musical future of our children.

## "I find it hard to understand why England is to be denied the enlightened music curriculum that is to be adopted by Wales." PIERRE BOULEZ

**21 FEBRUARY 1992**

Dear Prime Minister,

Mr David Pascall, the Chairman of the National Curriculum Council has hailed the national curriculum for music as an exciting development which will benefit all our children. But his Council's work so far has served only to jeopardise it.

Earlier this year, the specialist music curriculum working group's proposals were wholeheartedly endorsed by the Welsh Curriculum Council. By contrast, the NCC made no less than 60 amendments to them, and superimposed a list of detailed prescriptions. On 3 February the Secretary of State for Wales published Draft Orders which incorporate the working group's proposals in full, including the three attainment targets - performing, composing, appraising - which already form the basis of the curriculum in Scotland. Yet on Mr Pascall's advice, the Secretary of State for Education has produced Draft Orders built on two attainment targets, with a half-hearted "weighting" towards practical work, and a mass of statutory requirements.

How has this divergence come about? The Welsh have decided to adopt a straightforward and logical structure, which is clear, practicable and easy to understand, for parents as well as teachers. The NCC, on the other hand, appear to have been pursuing the chimera of "curriculum coherence". Yet there is no relationship between their ideas for music history and the requirements for general historical studies. Rather, the NCC have arbitrarily imposed statutory requirements for studying particular musical styles, forms and periods. They have undoubtedly made one sort of curriculum explicit. But what virtue or sense is there in compelling all pupils to study "symphony" or "oratorio"? Why not "concerto" or "opera"? And how will parents from non-Christian faiths react to compulsory doses of religious oratorio music for their 11 to 14-year old children?

Now, the bulk of the NCC's misconceived and arbitrary suggestions are enshrined in draft legislation for England. But it is not too late: consultation runs until 4 March. Mr Clarke can and must think again, for the sake of music as a whole. His Orders as they stand are a recipe for divisiveness and confusion, and risk undermining the achievements of the GCSE syllabus. The only sensible way forward is for him to adopt the working group's proposals in their entirety.

**Neil Hoyle**

Chief Executive, The Incorporated Society of Musicians
10 Stratford Place, London,W1N 9AE

**21 FEBRUARY 1992**

Dear Prime Minister,

The music profession has been united in its condemnation of the National Curriculum Council's decision to overturn much of the original Music Working Group's report on the contents of the National Curriculum. Assurances given recently by the Secretary of State for Education about the marking ratios in his revised structure have not allayed genuine concerns that the balance between practical and theoretical music has been sufficiently established.

The Secretary of State for Wales has now adopted the Working Group's original proposal with its three attainment targets: Performing, Composing and Appreciating. This model provides a better structure for teaching music and for reporting accurately children's progress in music to their parents.

It is our belief that the more prescriptive Draft Orders for England, if implemented in law, will alienate many thousands of youngsters who might otherwise have come to love Western classical music and a wide variety of music from other traditions.

We urge the Secretary of State for Education and Science to adopt Orders for England similar to those proposed for Wales.

**Ian Ritchie**

Chairman, Association of British Orchestras
Francis House, Francis St., London, SW1P 1DE

**Simon Rattle CBE, Alberni String Quartet, Thomas Allen, Norman Bailey CBE, Steuart Bedford, Alfred Brendel KBE, Jack Brymer OBE, Paul Crossley, Paul Daniel, John Dankworth, Sir Colin Davis, Peter Donohoe, Sian Edwards, Mark Elder CBE, James Galway, Lesley Garrett, Evelyn Glennie, Jane Glover, Sir Charles Groves, Richard Hickox, Elgar Howarth, Nicholas Hytner, Yvonne Kenny, Cleo Laine, Philip Langridge, Robert Lloyd, Benjamin Luxon CBE, Colin Matthews, Sir Peter Maxwell Davies, Jonathon Miller, Ann Murray, Roger Norrington CBE, Dennis O'Neill, Nigel Osborne, David Pountney, Andre Previn, Joan Rodgers, Mstislav Rostropovich, Sir Georg Solti, Michael Tilson Thomas, Roger Vignoles, Judith Weir, Willard White, John Williams.**

**21 FEBRUARY 1992**

Dear Prime Minister,

I have followed the polemic surrounding the English National Curriculum for Music with interest.

Music is not the narrow field defined in the Draft Orders. Composers of today draw on the full diversity of culture available to them. Those learning should be exposed to practical experience of an equally wide variety of music.

To expect all children by the age of 11 to "understand the distinctive characteristics of medieval, renaissance, classical, romantic, recent and contemporary music" is totally unrealistic. To require by law that every 14-year-old in the land shall study "symphony and oratorio" is ludicrously arbitrary.

One cannot legislate for the taste of a nation. I join my colleagues who have already written to you in protesting that the Draft Orders for Music will do little to preserve your musical tradition. On the contrary, their narrow, prescriptive nature will drive many children away.

Teachers should be free to devise a curriculum suitable for each child within a challenging and flexible framework. I find it hard to understand why England is to be denied the enlightened curriculum that is to be adopted by Wales.

**Pierre Boulez**

Welsh National Opera,
Cardiff.

**Over 80% of those who responded to proposals for the National Curriculum in Music wanted the same practical, non-prescriptive curriculum for English children as is to be adopted in Wales.**

**The most respected professional musicians working in Britain have repeatedly warned that plans for music in England will be disastrous for thousands of children.**

**This space was donated by Andrew Lloyd Webber who writes, "Over twenty years ago I composed "Joseph and the Amazing Technicolor® Dreamcoat" for a school performance. It was my first piece to be publicly performed and the consequence of its joyous, yet rough and ready premiere, was directly responsible for my career getting off the ground.**

**Children should perform, compose, sing and then come to the theory of music through love of music".**

**Figure 1** A spectrum of musicians in search of reproduction. Lord Lloyd Webber and Pierre Boulez join forces to argue for the teaching of musical performance and composition. The advertisement appeared in *The Independent*, 24 February 1992.

tion,[9] and of the place of music in national education, with the mixture far more dilute for England than for Wales or Scotland, where the three areas of attainment – composing, performing and appraising – were adopted without demur, as the accompanying advertisement illustrates.

Meanwhile, as I have argued elsewhere,[10] *de facto* this argument has been won by the multiculturalists, if in a way which might worry Lucy Green. In the East London boroughs of Tower Hamlets and Newham, schools with a majority Bengali population provide lessons in tabla, tanpura, harmonium and other South Asian instruments; children are taught to sing through the work of Rabindranath Tagore, in the popular singing style known as 'Rabindrasangheet'. Most of the children who take to these lessons, however, have ambitions beyond classical or folk styles – many wish to pursue music in order to perform bhangra or Hindi film music.[11] Here as elsewhere, music education does not follow an Anglocentric conservative agenda.

The conservatives' moral panic over the disappearance of 'their' musical tradition is no doubt amplified by the extreme fragility of the very notion of an established, autonomous tradition of music-making. Whatever its internal hierarchical structure, the power, status and authority of the European composed music tradition is one with which musics and musicians from 'outside' the culture continually negotiate – with those 'inside' it also parties to the negotiation. Sometimes, perhaps through ignorance, the critics of the new curriculum have lavished their approval on composers who have based much of their music on a direct engagement with popular musics. This can be, and sometimes is, justified with reference to the particular type or status of the music engaged with. In the case of a composer like Bax, beloved of the traditionalists, his use of Irish 'folk' models is clear: listen, for instance, to the opening of the final movement of his third symphony (1929), with the violas playing a fiddle tune and the side-drum providing a reasonably effective version of a bhodran drum accompaniment. This is not a direct copy (Bax insisted that he only once used an actual folk-tune);[12] nor is it pastiche – the passage in question is an integrated part of a symphonic argument. But the music would have been impossible without the Irish folk tradition.

This dialogue with the popular is not, however, confined to music which identifies with a specific popular tradition. Even the most

extreme avant-garde compositions of the 1950s are not hermeti-
cally-sealed products of an autonomous European tradition, but of
dialogue. Stockhausen's *Gruppen* ('Groups') for three orchestras
(1957), for example, displays the mathematical fastidiousness of
'total serialism', with pitches, dynamics and sound dispersal all controlled by algorithms. The work can be analysed, and taught, as
such. It can, however, be equally well taught as a Romantic tone-
poem, whose overall shape involves that genre's dialectical movement to climax, release and a cadence which even its most
committed Modernist commentator called 'a romantically dying
solo horn'.[13] In other words, not the individual sounds and combi-
nations of sounds, but for all the absence of tonal harmony, their
overall shape and distribution, the very *narrative* of the piece, are
reminiscent of examples of Romantic expressivity such as the pre-
lude to Wagner's opera *Tristan und Isolde* (1857). Yet *Gruppen* can
also be taught as an example of the engagement of the 'classical'
with the popular. *Gruppen*'s orchestration (which includes in this
case electric guitar, saxophones and many drums) owes as much to
the then current popularity of rock'n'roll, the big-band jazz of the
Stan Kenton orchestra and the jazz piano trio, as to the symphonic
tradition. Indeed, the 'innovations in modern music orchestra'
which toured and recorded with Kenton in the early 1950s and can
be heard on the 1951 *City of Glass* album, inhabits a very similar
soundscape, its timbre-signature dominated by the drumkit's tom-
toms and an interjectory arrangement style using the various families of instruments in blocks, which anticipates Stockhausen's
'moment-form'.

This popular-learned multilogue has always happened; musical
hegemony is perpetually in flux, with the arrival of new rhythmic
and harmonic processes, new instruments and new performing and
recording techniques, changing the accepted parameters of composition and performance. Many innovations in 'classical music' have
involved the acceptance of a popular musical form or practice. Walton and Tippett were doing nothing radically new in incorporating
African–American rhythms and harmonies into their music.
Arguably the whole symphonic tradition is based on the continuing
dialogue between musical processes drawn from church music, popular songs and dance musics, and military music. It is unsurprising,
therefore, that the explosion of new musics resulting from urban
interaction has also produced new voices within composed musics

which re-create British classical music along these multicultural
lines, while simultaneously undermining the always fragile Art/Pop-
ular division.

## Is there a British classical music in the 1990s?

Using again the analytical shorthand with which the traditional,
modern and Modernist approaches were delineated in Chapter 1 is
no longer possible. A fourth term must be added to the list: the postmodern.

The term 'postmodern' is really useful here, but I should make my
use of it clear. Postmodernism can be seen as a mode of interpretation, and has become an object of cultural theory, to be feared and
reviled by those for whom either the narrative of history or the
abstract truths sought in and by the human mind since the Enlightenment give meaning to life; for some of its most rigorous critics,
postmodernity is the latest phase in that greatest of all historic
conspiracies, capitalism – and therefore the latest incarnation of
Absolute Evil.[14] Others welcome it as a way of seeing a world which
is no longer stratified by class and nationality but by global problems
of production, consumption and communication, by local problems
of work and community, and by personal ones of health, lifestyle
and identity. Many of the positive commentators on postmodernity
welcome new artistic forms such as magic realism and cyberpunk
fiction as in effect the new 'realism' of this particular moment, and
similarly react positively to new musics: for example, ambient techno's infiltration into the New Age philosophy and related thought is
taken to reflect the new cultural realities.[15]

For the purposes of this book, however, 'postmodernism' is a set
of intellectual and artistic practices characterised by a refusal of
hierarchy and teleology, and postmodern composers are those who
work within this frame. Postmodernism in this sense acknowledges
no single set of correct values and no single narrative of historical
or aesthetic correctness; partly because of this, it is concerned with
the spatiality as much as the temporality of artistic work. In music,
which is always constrained by the passing of time in performance
or listening, the concern can be seen in the denial or modification,
not of tonality itself, but of the narrative processes of tonality, that
musical equivalent of the dialectic (in sonata form, but, as I
remarked above, also a ghost present at a musical feast such as

*Gruppen*) which has produced, through Marxism, one powerful interpretation of the meaning of history.

Traditional music in the sense of the Elgarian, the neo-Tudor, or the neo-folkish, has almost died as a mode of current composition, but its legacy has been revived in very different ways by different composers who have worked through Modernism, emerged on the other side, and draw from an eclectic range of sources including folk and other traditional musics and the European symphonic/tonal tradition, in order to get there and/or continue to make music on the other side. The last vestiges of a relatively traditional Romantic tonality are to be found in the continuing work of George Lloyd (b. 1913); other composers who have stuck to tonality and its consequences have included the autodidact and former BBC producer Robert Simpson. The use of tonal techniques has largely replaced atonality and other aspects of Modernism in the work of Sir Peter Maxwell Davies, now a composer of symphonies and concerti (with an increasingly Baxian–Celtic inflection) rather than experimental music–theatre. Like Davies, now an honorary Scot, the Scottish composer Judith Weir has drawn on local folk-music in her large- and small-scale works, including the outstanding opera/musical *A Night at the Chinese Opera* and the brief folk-story-derived opera commissioned by English National Opera and premiered in 1994, *Blond Eckbert*. Weir's other music, while experimental in many ways, is usually tonally located, and often ironically witty; while acknowledging the continuing presence of the European composed music tradition, she also uses and plays with folk and other popular sources, as for example in the piece for piano and strings 'Airs from Another Planet' – a postmodern piece using Scottish folk-music, while referring in its title to a classic of Modernist music, the second string quartet by Arnold Schoenberg; and sounding nothing like either.

Another area of work popular at present is that derided by its no-nonsense critics as 'faith minimalism'. This is a postmodern term if ever there was one, since minimalism's targets included organised religion as much as the arrogance of Modernism. Composers like Terry Reilly in the California of the 1960s, Philip Glass and Steve Reich in the New York of the late 1960s and Louis Andriessen in the Holland of the 1970s, made a music which set out quite deliberately to deny the tenets of Modernism. Their music used tonal harmony as a functional rather than a structuring device, offering instead

structures using simple tonal chords, and based on small-scale accu-
mulative rhythmic and/or harmonic change, in Reich's case based
on his studies of West African music. Born in the late 1960s counter-
cultural moment, this music quickly acquired a cachet as music for
meditation rather than 'rational' listening; the massive popularity of
Glass's music in particular, which has been in pop charts as well as
opera-houses and the concert-hall, has furthered the cause of the
succeeding generation. Post-minimalist composers like John Adams
and Michael Torke in the USA, and Steve Martland and Michael
Nyman in Britain, have reintroduced aspects of the dialectics of
tonality (the use of opposing tonal centres within a composition to
further the musical narrative) as well as working with some of the
instruments and amplification of rock (a practice which had been
started by Reilly and Glass).

'Faith minimalism', using the large-scale but very simple musical
structures of minimalism not to accompany the ritual but to express
the theological beliefs of forms of Christianity, has become one of
the success stories of late twentieth-century classical music. The
Estonian Arvo Part and the Pole Henryk Gorecki are among the
leading exponents of this style, as is the English composer John
Tavener. Like Maxwell Davies, Tavener started his composing
career in the 1960s as a Modernist, but an experimentalist who, like
the Pole Penderecki, disliked Modernism's absolute principles, and
always had a place for tonal music within the mix of new techniques, serialism and other mathematical procedures, and noise. His
first successes were with a short cantata, *The Whale*, and the rather
longer *Celtic Requiem*, both works requiring (usually amateur)
choral forces to use new vocal techniques. *Celtic Requiem* also featured a bass guitar and electric guitar in the orchestra. The resultant
eclectic heterophony, mixing speech, Celtic laments and modernist
sound clusters, impressed Paul McCartney and John Lennon
enough for them to have both works recorded and released on the
Beatles' Apple label. Another Tavener composition, 'In Alium', was
the new music hit of the 1968 Proms season.

Perhaps his conversion to Orthodoxy, perhaps a long illness, perhaps the times, perhaps all three, have led to a change in musical
direction for Tavener, whose music is now simple, tonal, repetitive
and clear – a long remove from the polystylism of his music of the
1960s. His long cello concerto, 'The Protecting Veil', was one of the
highlights of the 1991 Proms concert series (and has since been per-

formed there twice again), and in the following year a best-selling CD of the work was shortlisted for the 1992 Mercury Music Prize. The year of faith minimalism's greatest success so far was 1993, which saw the triumph of Gorecki's long, eloquent and miserable Third Symphony, the 'Symphony of Sorrowful Songs', referred to in chapter 1, and 1994 saw the premiere, again at the Proms, of another long, if less meditative, piece by Tavener, 'The Apocalypse', and the oddball CD success of the vocal group the Hilliard Ensemble's medieval religious music accompanying the saxophone improvisations of Jan Garbarek (a recording made in a monastery, naturally).

As we saw in chapter 4, the success of all this 'new simplicity' has finally forced the post-war, post-1960s establishment on to the defensive. An article in the *BBC Music Magazine* for July 1994 echoed the plaintive defensiveness of John Drummond's introduction to the 1994 Proms guide. Noting a recent article by the composer Robin Holloway in the *Spectator*, a right-wing magazine of social commentary, the editor of the *BBC Music Magazine* commented on a draft policy statement circulated by the artistic programmes director of the Royal Liverpool Philharmonic Orchestra, Duncan Grant. This document alerted programme-makers to the existence of new music which was neither difficult nor unattractive, and which crossed over into the worlds of pop, film and theatre – and recommended their programming it. 'Perhaps it just doesn't stand up on its own merits?', queried the magazine with undignified sarcasm, describing this document as 'a more subtle but perhaps more sinister sign of the times' even than the 'hecklers'' activities at a performance of Sir Harrison Birtwhistle's Modernist opera *Gawain*.[16]

The episode referred to here proved both that Modernism, too, is alive and, if not well, still bankrolling the grants, and that some people are unhappy with the situation. Convinced that British audiences hated Modernist music but were too polite to say so, Frederick Stocken, a young composer of tonal music, advertised in the *Spectator* asking for people who wanted to show disapproval at new music concerts to contact him. From this advertisement 'the hecklers' were formed: a group of right-wing, right-minded and right-thinking young people who would boldly yell where none had yelled their disapproval before. Armed with a great deal of advance publicity, a couple of dozen of them then visited the Royal Opera

House in order to see a production they did not wish to see, as it were (Birtwistle's *Gawain*), and afterwards happily booed away, their protests comfortably drowned by the applause of the majority of the full house. There was much commentary in the broadsheet press, and Stocken appeared on the BBC's commentary programme *Newsnight*, opposite an angry and depressed Modernist composer, George Benjamin. The run of the opera, albeit at prices considerably lower than the Covent Garden norm, thereafter sold out.[17]

The hecklers' target was musical Modernism, especially public subsidy for Modernism; the apparent objectivity of their arguments was compromised somewhat as it emerged that the fervent wish of some of the leaders of this campaign was not *against* public subsidy as such, but *for* subsidy for their own, tonal, and consciously derivative works. Lists of approved models for composition were declaimed, usually ending chronologically with Mahler. 'They wrote beautiful music, why can't we?' was the argument, supplemented by the assertion that if more Mahler-type symphonies were written, people would flock to hear them. Hardly a compelling case, though on the eve of (rare) performances by a composer associated with the hecklers, Keith Burstein, the manager of the orchestra involved, the New Queen's Hall Orchestra (which specialises in early twentieth-century music), claimed that Burstein's music was 'grateful to the ear and more tolerable to the player than so-called modern music'.[18] But the young fogeys were not distinguished by their analytical knowledge of the Modernist music they were so keen to oppose; indeed, it seemed that their ears needed syringing as a matter of urgency. They confused the Modernists of the older generation, such as Birtwistle, both with the anoraks of new complexity, like Brian Ferneyhough, Roger Redgate, James Dillon, Christopher Fox and Chris Dench (which is perhaps understandable) and with the aggressive, jazz/rock influenced and usually thoroughly tonal music of composers like Mark-Anthony Turnage (which is not). The hecklers lacked the analytical skills, the ears probably, to differentiate among any musics which did not sound as if they were written in the eighteenth, nineteenth or very early twentieth centuries by mainstream German or Austrian composers. The need for careful and comprehensive musical education has never been clearer than in the confusion of this debate.

This analytical naivety does not mean that aspects of the hecklers' case were wrong in themselves, as members of the music-critical establishment fell over themselves to suggest, as they defended their favourite anti-tunesmiths. The heckler/fogey concern is part of the general directional crisis in 'classical music' which includes the continuing decline in numbers, and rising age profile, of the concert audience (outside the Proms), the failure of the Arts Council or anyone else to rationalise the orchestral scene in London and the commercial success of Classic FM, with its pop-style charts dominated by themed CDs which undercut the primacy of the composer's text as the sacred basis for the worship of European music.

Modernism, and its relative unpopularity, remains a very real problem within this scenario, although in some ways it could also be seen as part of the solution. Take the 'new complexity' of Ferneyhough and others As a series of compositional techniques, this involves the maximum control by the composer over the performed events. All the minutiae of notation are called into play, as not only pitch and dynamic levels, but also vibrato, attack, sustain and decay are indicated as precisely as possible. A percussion-player might be asked not just to play a certain rhythm on a side-drum, but to use sticks of a particular wood on a side-drum of a particular size and make, with precisely loosened snares, mounted at a precise angle on a particular type of stand. Some Modernist scores include pages of written commentary to help the performers realise the composer's ideas in this very precise way. Notation has been approaching this point of control since the eighteenth century, the point which, as I indicated in chapter 1, encompassed the gentlemanly performer's alienation from the strict disciplines of orchestral playing, and the end of improvisation by orchestral players. The paradox is that for all the reappearance of some forms of composition through chance, improvisation and choice in 1960s scores by Cage, Stockhausen and even Boulez, the position of the classical orchestral performer since the rise of the conductor has become ever more disciplined, proletarian, and alienated. The new complexity takes to extremes this development, fetishising both the power of the composer and the powerlessness of the performer.

It also, simultaneously, undermines this relationship. This proletarianisation of the performer is a deeply alienating experience, and alienation will produce disaffected or deliberately inaccurate playing. Poor performances by uninvolved players are a common complaint against orchestral musicians, and especially against British orchestral musicians. The orchestral musician is particularly liable to such a charge, and is particularly liable to be so alienated. As we have seen, the treatment of musicians by the public and by the composer has reflected the values of bourgeois society. Individual performers, even of new music, are often feted as 'great' interpreters, in a way which, since Modernism, the general public often substitutes for great living composers (the principal difference between the celebration of a solo pianist of the present, like Maurizio Pollini, and one from the nineteenth century, such as Liszt, is that it was part of the deal that Liszt was himself a composer and improviser, whereas Pollini is merely expected to play, brilliantly, other people's music). Small ensembles, especially the string quartet, are also, sometimes, granted this status. In Britain, however, the large ensemble is not.

This situation often produces alienated performances (though it has also found performers of heroic virtuosity); the relationship between composer and interpreter reaches a crisis, unsurprisingly, when players are asked to do the impossible. Sometimes this is the physically impossible – for example to play extremely fast, rhythmically complex passages inside which they are asked to observe extreme differences of attack or intensity; or to play very short notes within which there are noticeable changes in volume.[19] Or they are asked to use their instruments in ways which are physically possible but potentially damaging to performer, instrument, or both. Not every orchestral violinist wishes to hit the fragile body of her £20,000 instrument hard with the wrong side of the bow. Not every trumpeter wishes to push the mouthpiece further into the main tube of the instrument, a potentially damaging act which will certainly affect intonation. Both activities will produce sounds otherwise unobtainable in live performance, but at potential danger to the instrument itself. In the 1970s, several orchestras threatened to strike rather than perform the music of the Polish composer Krzystof Penderecki, which made demands of this sort. Since then, Penderecki's style has changed; he is now an exponent of new tonality and conventional playing techniques, no doubt to the relief of orchestral musicians everywhere.

Both these problems, the physically impossible and the abuse of instruments, imply that the performing musician is a being with neither will nor emotion. It is unlikely that composers who make excessive demands are sadists exactly, but the problem here has clear sexual analogies: they see the musician as a transparent vessel through which their desires may be realised, in precisely the way in which some people use others as sex-objects. Another comparison, with authoritarian bourgeois employers, unable to see workers as more than 'hands' – identified brilliantly by Thomas Carlyle in his 1839 essay 'Chartism' – is apt.[20] Here, for instance, composer James Dillon expounds his authoritarian position in an interview with Ben Watson which portrays him as a musical radical:

> He explains how in the orchestral piece *Helle Nacht*, his score demands concentration from every member of the orchestra. He'll ask the fourteenth, second-desk violin to do some really taxing work. 'If a player hates it, doesn't want that kind of responsibility, what can I do? I'm willing to stand up in front of these hundred musicians and justify it when some jerk at the back of the orchestra – not necessarily the violinist, by the way – starts making comments. I will explain that I don't want this guy sat there playing the same arpeggios for five minutes and reading a motoring magazine. I want him to engage with the music on the same level as a soloist.'[21]

He adds, curiously, 'It's idealistic.' The position of the performing musician (as anything other than a machine for performance) is too often not considered; composers are taught about the ranges and capabilities of instruments, not of instrumentalists.[22] In the orchestral mode of musical production, whatever the text produced, its production may involve alienated wage-slavery; all the worse when 'some jerk' is made to play something he or she regards as physically or aesthetically objectionable. 'You feel trapped' is one orchestral musician's response.[23] The music of new complexity, the outcome of two hundred years' subordination of musicians, has no place in the orchestral repertoire; it is a *sul ponticello* too far.

This does not deny a place for a music of vast complexity, in which almost innumerable events jostle for the attention, and long-, short- and medium-term musical processes occur at bewildering frequency (which happens in some jungle/drum'n'bass, to general rejoicing). But people shouldn't be asked, and certainly shouldn't be contractually forced, to attempt to play them. One eccentric solution to the problem, by the Mexico-based composer Conlon Nancarrow, has been to write difficult music for that mechanical marvel of the early twentieth century, the player-piano (though recently his music has been performed successfully, by, among others, pianist Joanna MacGregor, the Arditti String Quartet, and Ensemble Modern). There exists, of course, a more common means through which music of massive complexity may be made, and may be made reliably; it involves the use of computers and electronic musical instruments, and it has been itself an important and developing field in the making of music since the 1950s – when Modernist composers like Stockhausen, Boulez and Berio began to experiment with oscillators and filters, tapes and tape-recorders, notably in the Cologne radio studio. Whereas in the 1960s and for twenty years thereafter these developments were based on mainframe or minicomputers with software specific to each computer and usually to each university music department, the development of the personal computer (in all its forms, Apple Macintosh, IBM PC clone and even the humble Atari) has meant both usable stand-alone software, currently vital to the music industry, and the development of networked software and data exchange. The latter is important to the classical composer, especially to the composer of complex music, because of the limitations of the former, sequencing software which is relatively crude, slow and limited in many cases by its primary purpose, which is the production of pop music. It is very difficult, for instance, to produce rhythmically complex music using conventional sequencing or score-writing software.

Through a development such as the composers' desk-top project,[24] currently run in the UK from York University, musical processes requiring many more simultaneous musical events and processes, and therefore faster processing and communication speeds, are possible. This prevents the torture of musicians; and it enables composers to exchange musical information, to co-operate in composition, in a way which also undercuts the ideal of Romanticism. The artist can now both starve in a garret (or take on whatever other narcissistic model of the Romantic Artist he or she chooses) and compose music collectively. New complexity will survive, and may perhaps thrive, in this environment.

This does not mean that all music made in music departments using computers will or should be high-resolution new complexity. The ubiquity of computers in the preparation of information, including traditional scholarship and the preparation of musical scores, will pull computer music back into more conventional worlds, while the development of multi-media applications will take the university studio into the worlds foreshadowed by Future Sound of London and the other prophets of audio-visual tomorrows. However important the differences, we have here yet more new popular/classical interactions. The interactive composition of music using software on personal computers will of necessity change the way music is seen, taught and appreciated within the academy; it will remove one more aspect of the continuing barrier between 'high' and 'low' versions of music.

Where does this leave the hecklers and other opponents of the twentieth century? They are not simply anachronisms. One of my key arguments is that modernity has often been experienced through the creation of traditions. At the start of the book I referred to one important aspect of the Britain of the 1980s, wedded both to ideologies of change and to the maintenance of idealised notions such as 'family values': this was the creation of 'Heritage Culture', a reworking of certain aspects of the past, including the very notion of the traditional, within the commercial imperatives of the day. Heritage Culture was spectacular, available, displayed, and valuable. It presented Britain as a land of country houses, pretty rural cottages, tidy dwellings for the working class (who were the salt of the earth) and neat Victorian town-houses, all to be restored to some notional original state (plus central heating) and inhabited by the aspirational bourgeoisie. The emphasis on the Victorian (as in Mrs Thatcher's calling on 'Victorian Values') was also important in the creation of a past Great Britain, at the height of its imperial glory and economic prosperity; this is the centre for much 'heritage culture'. The hecklers and their friends wish to re-create music made *at this time*; not necessarily music made in Britain, but in Europe, by Mahler and others, before the First World War. This is their contribution, paradoxically, to a version of Britishness which insists on its own independence, its own identity, and which refuses the prospect of a federal Europe because it undermines this fragile sense of identity.

Thatcherism was about broadcasting, not narrowcasting, seeking always to widen the appeal of cultural products (such as the Conservative Party itself), and succeeding in the quest for the crucial vote of the skilled manual worker. This, it should not be forgotten, was itself the populist model which some Tory ministers then tried to impose on the arts and education. Such people, ministers or manual workers, have very little interest in the re-creation of the high culture of the late nineteenth century, whether musical or otherwise. They might listen to Classic FM, or indeed to Radio Three, but that does not imply a demand for new Mahler symphonies, or any other form of concert music. Meanwhile, advertising and programme-making both in radio and television are increasingly under the domination of middle-class people brought up in and after the 1960s, and for most of whom, whatever their social background, the world created by pop music means that they have little belief in old 'high' culture as an autonomous realm, replete with value. The hecklers, for all the force of their arguments against state subsidy for Modernism, and their creation of tradition, will find it difficult to place themselves in this world.

But this is the world now inhabited by most young 'classical' composers, whose work I would describe as 'postmodern'. Many work with jazz and rock instruments, and with computers and samplers, and while they still write complex music meant for the concert-hall, many have quite deliberately tried to knock down the remaining steps of the high/low barrier. Their attempts have occasionally been reciprocated. The Manchester-based pop and dance-music label Factory launched its own 'classical' subdivision in 1989, headlining as its star attraction the aggressive, jazz-influenced minimalism of Steve Martland (though it neglected to pay royalties, and went bust with the rest of Factory in 1993). Decca's Argo label has also been relaunched in an attempt to catch this particular niche market, presenting to an eager world the work of Michael Nyman and the pop-playing postmodernist Balanescu String Quartet, among others. The sound-world created for these discs, using multi-track recording techniques, is deliberately different from the staight-to-stereo approach used in more orthodox classical recordings.[25]

There is increasing convergence of sound-worlds, of audiences, and indeed of appreciation of this by taste-formers such as advertisers and journalists. The illustration reproduced here advertises a new production of Richard Strauss's opera *Elektra* as 'by the creators of the Pet Shop Boys' world tour': the potential opera-goer is assumed to be familiar with the latter. Similarly, when in a newspaper review a new recording of 'Three Screaming Popes', a piece by the composer Mark-Anthony Turnage, is described as 'acid-house Bartok with attitude',[26] the implication is that the reader can decode references to rap, rave and the folk-derived Modernism of the Hungarian composer, and imagine the resulting sound.

Whatever the difficulties of the newspaper-reading public in this regard, there is no doubt that many composers are hearing their

**Figure 2** A display of postmodern credentials. Chris Travers, then director of marketing at Welsh National Opera, produced this poster for their 1992 tour. Reproduced by kind permission of Welsh National Opera.

music in this way. The Belize-born composer Errollyn Wallen is a graduate of Goldsmith's College and King's College, London and was schooled in Modernist composition, but with a family background in popular music and jazz, found it easy to construct her own musical path from all three positions. Her early 1990s band

Ensemble X consisted of session musicians (often including her brother, jazz trumpeter Byrom Wallen) who work happily in either jazz, commercial music or classical music traditions, which is just as well, as her compositions demand equal facility among all the possible permutations of these styles: strict observance of complex notation at one extreme, improvisatory solos at the other, with in between the ability to interpret a written part with the right, but unwriteable, groove or swing. Ensemble X refused to be bound within any notion of musical particularity: 'We don't break down barriers in music ... we don't see any.'[27] Wallen has written a short opera; a percussion concerto premiered on BBC television at the finals of the 1994 Young Musician of the Year contest; she has toured with saxophonist Courtney Pine and soul diva Juliet Roberts; she has her own quartet which performs her songs, which are soul/jazz/twentieth-century French confections, always written in the shadow of her musical mentor, Johann Sebastian Bach. Future projects include a musical about the doll Black Barbie. No barriers there.

Eleanor Alberga is another black woman whose music acknowledges and works within the rhythms of Caribbean music as well as the harmonic processes of European and American classical music. Jamaica-born of Scottish, Portuguese, Jewish and African–Caribbean ancestry, she trained at the Royal Academy of Music as a concert pianist, and is virtually self-taught as a composer, having started to write short pieces for dance while working as a rehearsal and performance pianist with the London Contemporary Dance Theatre (alongside Michael Nyman and the successful television music composer Barrington Pheloung, among others). Acknowledging the influence of Bartok, a composer who both collected and reworked folk-song, Alberga has worked with an African dance group and the Jamaican Folk-singers, agreeing that to do so has been a process of identity construction through cultural history: 'I am always seeking, to be corny, to find my roots.'[28] While she has also been drawn to the rather tame processes of English minimalism partly through the influence of Michael Nyman, a far less abrasive minimalist writer than the Dutch-trained Steve Martland, her personal voice continues to add layers of rhythmic and harmonic complexity to the apparent simplicities of minimalist process – and as she says, minimalism, which in Steve Reich's case at least derives fairly directly from African music, is a part of her search for roots.

But she is also aware of contemporary popular music, citing dub and other reggae-derived music as a continued influence. In her setting of Roald Dahl's rewriting of the Snow White story (commissioned by the Roald Dahl foundation as one of a series of musical versions of the writer's *Revolting Rhymes*), she has used the 'almost frenetic, over-the-top, rhythmic driving music' of rave, using the gong-gongs and wood blocks of the orchestral percussion section for an analogue of the hi-hat pattern, locking the whole orchestra into a fast repetitive groove: 'It's all in 4/4 and there's always someone playing on the beat.'[29]

In a slightly different direction, Priti Paintal's ensemble Shiva Nova attempts, as the name suggests, to cross between Asian and European models of musical construction and realisation: a 'classical' homology with the popular music of Najma Akhtar and Sheila Chandra.

Whatever the closed world of the Society for the Promotion of New Music may think, these examples are not the exception, but the rule. Belatedly, much 'new music' made by trained composers (for dance, for theatre, for television and film, as well as for the concert-hall) now acknowledges once more the engagement with the popular which has characterised previous musical renewals: the continuities are with Walton's and Tippett's modernity, rather than Webern's and Lutyens's Modernism. Young(ish) composers like Wallen, Steve Martland and John Lunn now work within the realms of reprocessing: Lunn's string quartet 'Strange Fruit' (1988), inspired by the Billie Holiday song of the same name, for example, is a creative reworking of an established form which owes as much to the repetitive drive of African–American musics as to the constant development of ideas finally legitimised by Beethoven. While the term 'postmodern' is as hackneyed a word in music as in any other of the arts – and while it can as easily be applied to the work of Charles Ives and Gustav Mahler as to any contemporary musician – it can serve here as a convenient label for the efforts of most of these younger composers. Certainly the open engagement with popular styles, and the questioning of any fixed hierarchies of value, often make their efforts explicitly post- and implicitly anti- Modernist. Festivals organised in London in the early 1990s by the pianist and composer Joanna MacGregor emphasised how far we have moved from both the traditionalist and Modernist traditions by programming jazz, minimalist and postmodernist musics, in an echo of her career which has seen her working with Django Bates's jazz groups as well as playing Gershwin and Messiaen at the Proms.

Even the long-running Proms music festival itself also demonstrated this, as discussed in chapter 4. In 1991 there were first performances of pieces by Martin Butler (openly acknowledging the influence of Latin-American musics) and Mark-Anthony Turnage (with an acknowledged debt to jazz, specifically that of Miles Davis), and in 1992 an evening of music by Rossini arranged for big band by the jazz composer Mike Westbrook, premieres of a saxophone concerto by Richard Rodney Bennett originally written for Stan Getz and a percussion concerto by James Macmillan written for the young virtuoso Evelyn Glennie – a piece based on a plainchant melody but with world-wide rhythmic influences; 1993 saw a late-night concert by the Wynton Marsalis band, offering their historicist reading of the African–American tradition, and 1995 a more eclectic look at the jazz traditions from the (British) Julian Joseph band, featuring the alto sax-player Peter King.

One further barrier began to fall in the early 1990s, as post-Modernist writing for string ensemble was heard as a part of rock music. Arguably *the* sign of the 'high', as opposed to the popular, the small group of stringed instruments (including trios, quintets, sextets and octets, but more usually the string quartet) is an ensemble seemingly terminally appropriated by cultural elitism. It is taken for granted that training, performance, composition and even listening to the quartet and other small string ensembles require the skills of the music academy and its subaltern studies, A-levels and the like. The generic term for small-ensemble classical musics, 'chamber music', is redolent of this elitism, implying the world of eighteenth-century patronage. Where Beethoven or Tchaikovsky may be to some extent popular musicians as symphonists, as quartet writers they remain firmly within the boundaries of trained appreciation; similarly, the orchestral music of contemporary composers like Bartok and Shostakovich is better known than their chamber music.

String ensembles have never been perfect strangers to popular music; the lush sound of a large string orchestra has accompanied countless singers, and was important to early 1970s soul via Norman Whitfield's arrangements for the Temptations ('Papa was a Rolling Stone', for example: this is a post-minimalist symphonic movement, lasting twelve minutes on the original album version of 1968). Though the intimate sound of the smaller ensemble is rare, it has been heard: the nostalgic push of George Martin's arrangements for the Beatles, 'Yesterday', 'Eleanor Rigby' and 'She's leaving home' are perhaps the best-known examples. There were attempts in the moment of 'progressive rock' to marry strings and rock band, perhaps least unsuccessfully with the progressive rock band Barclay James Harvest and the more pop-based Electric Light Orchestra. More recently Jimmy Somerville has toured with a small string group as an integral part of the band, and classical strings have appeared regularly, if as novelty acts, accompanying pop acts such as Tears For Fears (1993), in which Roland Olazorbal appeared surrounded by nine cellists. So the appearance of a string sextet as sole accompanist to one of the tracks on P.J. Harvey's 1993 album *Rid of Me*, otherwise glorying in its self-propelling drums, bass and guitar sound, is not new of itself. What was surprising about this was the intensity of the arrangement, a Modernist emphasis (by the band's drummer, Rob Ellis) owing far more to Bartok than to George Martin – Ellis has since produced more of the same on a solo album.[30] Early 1993 also saw singer/songwriter Elvis Costello (an Irish Londoner) and the Brodsky String Quartet collaborate to produce *The Juliet Letters*, an album and concert tour; again the arrangements crossed virtually every available musical boundary.

These are not isolated examples: Lunn's 'Strange Fruit', mentioned above, is far from alone in its obvious homage to popular music. The 1990s have seen the emergence of what could be called the postmodern string quartet, with so many pieces being created that there are now several ensembles dedicated to working against both the traditional quartet repertoire and its Modernist equivalents. Alex Balanescu, a Romanian Londoner, who amongst other credits has commissioned a concerto for violin and jazz ensemble by the American jazz composer Carla Bley, has played in both the Arditti String Quartet, which is dedicated to the performance of complex Modernist musics, and his own Balanescu Quartet, which follows the example of the American Kronos Quartet and plays pop arrangements as part of its standard repertoire. A typical release by this ensemble featured music by David Byrne (of Talking Heads); John Lurie (the actor and saxophone-playing leader of the American postmodern jazz band The Lounge Lizards); and Robert Moran and Michael Torke, leading American post-minimalist composers.[31] The Brodsky Quartet and the Smith Quartet are other ensembles at home in this area.

What we have, then, is convergence, and at a faster rate than at any time since the classical music tradition was created. Given that music remains a compulsory school subject, and that its teaching crosses the boundaries of cultures and technologies, this convergence will continue. Complex music for the concert-hall and the hi-fi system will still, no doubt, be made; but the differences between this and other musics – jazz, ethnically-specific musics, the musics of the dance-floor – will be those of emphasis and scale, rather than source-material and process. The history of cultural interaction now being acknowledged in new music at the Proms series joins 'Land of Hope and Glory' in an ironic celebration of post-imperial global cultural and economic relations; and of the positive cultural transformations music continues to set against the maelstrom, the continuing cultural and ecological destructions of modernity. In the music of the current generation of composers, we have an acknowledgement of and a contribution to those positive transformations, a music for our times.

Convergence, though, is not unidirectional. In British jazz, for example, since Spike Hughes's glorious failure to register jazz as art in 1930s Britain, jazz has become concert music, yet it has ceased to be a cordoned-off area. The jazz/r'n'b/soul connections are preserved (in very dilute form) in the programming of the radio station Jazz FM. Through hybrids such as jazz–rock, jazz–funk and acid jazz, it has remained entertainment/dance music while simultaneously claiming its own space in the concert-hall. And there are many classical/jazz hybrids. Part of the musical language of composers from Walton to Richard Rodney Bennett, it has more recently been the starting-point for Julian Joseph's emergent career as a composer.

The late 1980s, as pointed out in chapter 2, saw a cyclical upswing in jazz's public profile. While that moment of 'jazz-revival' high fashion passed within two years, a number of long-term careers in jazz have been launched. Pine, Williamson, Philip Bent, Orphy Robinson and others have collaborated with American and European musicians and have produced music in dialogue with the American jazz tradition. Indeed, arguably the most significant achievement of this new group of musicians is the insistence on its African–American roots, and their exploration of the legacy, notably of late-1950s 'hard bop', revalorising this as great music created largely by black people – and taught as such, by Gail

Thompson among others, to future generations of musicians. A musical style created in the USA in the late 1950s and early 1960s (the moment of Civil Rights) when re-created in the Britain of the late 1980s and 1990s demanded recognition as part of a Great Tradition; for British blacks, this music of the Black Atlantic was Heritage Culture, a proud re-creation of the past as intense and important in the formation of black identities within modern Britain, as the re-creation of the cottage-garden past by middle-class white professionals which was discussed at the start of this book.[32]

However, this is not a static position: black British jazz has moved outwards from the core of hard-bop 'Heritage Culture' and begun to explore the musics of Africa, the Caribbean, Latin America and Europe within a move towards a less aggressive and perhaps more commercial status. Bandleaders Orphy Robinson and Steve Williamson have all incorporated aspects of 'World Music'; the latter in particular also with a positive regard for the innovations in dance music of the Acid House era and beyond in a way which echoes American alto sax-player Steve Coleman's 'M-Base' movement, a very hard-edged funk. Orphy Robinson is clearly influenced by English and Scottish folk-musics, and has said so in interview. The liner notes for Robinson's band Annavas's 1992 album *When Tomorrow Comes* are explicit:

> The Annavas Project was conceived as a means of fusing together the many strands of music that have influenced me whilst growing up in London – a rich musical language, out of the many different cultural backgrounds that have left their imprint, whether spiritually or physically. Jazz, classical music, funk, Latin, reggae, folk, African – too many to mention.[33]

The instrumentation in this band includes orchestral flute and cello and kora (a harp-like West African instrument) along with electric keyboards, bass, percussion and Robinson's vibes and marimba (also African in origin). The music on *When Tomorrow Comes*, constantly experimenting with time-signature as well as modes and tonalities, includes the folk-dance-based 'Jigsaw' and the equally aptly titled 'Bach to 1st Bass'. Another black British musician, Julian Joseph, has also used his college education to work on the connections between the structures of jazz and those of classical music, bringing his big band to the 1995 Proms, small-band jazz to the Wigmore Hall recital-room, and signing a deal to record specifically not jazz but composed music. Courtney Pine, meanwhile, produced *Closer to Home* (1990; remixed and re-released 1992), an album of Caribbean musics, mainly reggae.[34] Black British jazz musicians have confidently moved out from the hard bop African–American base; they, too, have joined the convergence.

So, from a different angle, has the white saxophonist and composer John Surman, the producer of that Annavas album. Surman's career began with the 1960s jazz revival, soon moved to the experimental use of synthesisers and solo performance, and has, despite his clearly articulated reservations, used folk-musics as a basis for improvisation and composition – one piece, premiered at the Salisbury Festival in 1996, was 'Proverbs and Songs', for amateur chorus, small orchestra and jazz ensemble. Here both in the physical setting for the piece and its use of the chorus, the jazz musician has become Anglicised, localised, taken into a soundscape very different from its African–American origins.

It would, however, be invidious to end with the music of the concert hall and home hi-fi, from whatever direction it originates. Music has, of course, been continually affected by changing technologies. The development of transport and distribution, recording and broadcasting technologies has enabled certain mass-produced musics to become global phenomena and also enabled local musics to become globally connected. The potential within new technology to liberate music from the musician, to enable those without the skills of the performer or the trained composer to create, record and market listenable music may yet make the concert-hall's pursuit of the exceptional redundant. The output of one such non-musician band, Future Sound of London, draws out some potentially interesting points of development. Typical of the new generation of high-technology producers, they (two people) are not 'musicians' in the sense of public instrumental or vocal proficiency, or even the shared non-proficiency of skiffle or punk. Their music is made for CD, for broadcast and for the internet. They are non-stars, refusing the definition of the Romantic Artist which has been shared by rock musicians since the emancipation of their kind which was confirmed in Britain by the emergence of the Lennon–McCartney writing partnership. Like the Beatles in their last years and unlike most musicians whose careers depend on public visibility, they maintain no public profile. Yet their ideas about the future imply a new visibility for music. Their vision of the future of music is precisely a vision: a music which is integrated back into the specular, which is created within high-technology multi-media in which the sonic and the graphic interact, and which is part of the visual–aural network. It could be that at the end of the twentieth century the abstraction of music which was surgically performed within bourgeois society in the eighteenth century will have been reversed, and sound and vision will take up a new relationship. The two were unstitched by the emerging notion of the 'classical'; they may be stitched back together by this movement within the 'popular'. Through the desire for multi-media experience, the land without music may be both heard, and envisioned, anew.

## Notes

1 L. Green, *Music on Deaf Ears*, Manchester, Manchester University Press, 1987.
2 Discussed in A. Blake, *The Music Business*, Batsford, 1992, pp. 97–101.
3 See, for example, G. Vulliamy and E. Lee, *Popular Music in Schools*, 2nd edn, Cambridge, Cambridge University Press, 1980; Vulliamy and Lee, *Pop, Rock and Ethnic Music in Schools*, Cambridge, Cambridge University Press, 1982.
4 Green, *Music on Deaf Ears*, p. 119.
5 Quoted in Blake, *The Music Business*, p. 103.
6 *Interim Report of the National Curriculum Music Working Group*, HMSO, March 1991; *Final Report of the National Curriculum Music Working Group*, HMSO, October 1991.
7 See, for example, R. Morrison, 'A Generation Drummed Out', *The Times*, 13 February 1991; R. Scruton, 'Rock Around the Classroom', *The Daily Telegraph*, 10 February 1991; M. Kennedy, 'Throw this Report Straight Out of the Window, Mr Clarke', *The Daily Telegraph*, 14 February 1991; A. O'Hear, 'Out of Sync with Bach', *The Times Educational Supplement*, 22 February 1991; A. O'Hear, 'Tone Deaf to Tradition', *The Daily Telegraph*, 28 February 1991; G. Chew, 'Putting Beethoven before Chuck Berry', *The Guardian*, 5 March 1991.
8 See the reports and letters in *The Independent*, of the 18, 23, 28 and 29 January and of 24 February 1992.
9 See *Final Report of the National Curriculum Music Working Group*, HMSO, October 1991.
10 A. Blake, 'The Echoing Corridor: Music in the Postmodern East End', in *Soundings*, vol. 1, no. 1, autumn 1995, reprinted in T. Butler and M. Rustin, eds, *Rising in the East: the Regeneration of East London*,

Lawrence and Wishart, 1996.

11  G. Farrell, 'South Asian Music Teaching in Change', unpublished paper delivered to the conference *Music, Performance and Identity*, held under the auspices of the International Council for Traditional Music at King's College, Cambridge, 7 December 1994.

12  A. Bax, ed. L. Foreman, *Farewell My Youth*, Aldershot, Scolar Press, 1992, p. 41.

13  R. Smalley, 'Stockhausen's *Gruppen*', *Musical Times*, April 1970, p. 379.

14  The classic essay in this idiom is F. Jameson, *Postmodernism, or the Cultural Logic of Late Capitalism*, Verso, 1991.

15  See, for example, D. Toop, *Ocean of Sound: Aether Talk, Ambient Sound and Imaginary Worlds*, Serpent's Tail, 1995.

16  F. Maddocks, 'Mersey Beat with Minimal Effort?', *BBC Music Magazine*, July 1994, p.8.

17  Disapproval has always been more readily heard abroad. In 1961 a BBC Symphony Orchestra broadcast from Italy of the communist Modernist Luigi Nono's *Intolleranza* was booed by the audience; but a performance of Vaughan Williams's (traditional but would-be Modernist) fourth symphony was also booed at the same festival; see A. Briggs, *A History of British Broadcasting*, Oxford, Oxford University Press, 1995, vol. 5, p. 234.

18  See the report in *The Independent*, 24 September 1994.

19  The problems here are discussed by J. Fulkerson, 'Morty Feldman is Dead', in J. Paynter, T. Howell, R. Orton and P. Seymour, eds, *The Routledge Companion to Contemporary Musical Thought*, Routledge, 1992, vol. 2, pp. 751–61.

20  T. Carlyle, 'Chartism', in Carlyle, *Selected Writings*, Harmondsworth, Penguin, 1971.

21  James Dillon, interviewed by B. Watson, 'Mighty Atom Smasher', *The Wire*, no. 150, August 1996, p. 39.

22  Compare the recurring despair over inadequate performances, with no reflection on the role or humanity of the performer(s), by the composers in P. Griffiths, *New Sounds, New Personalities: British Composers of the 1980s*, Faber, 1985. Brian Eno's thoughts on the issue are illuminating; see E. Tamm, *Brian Eno, his Music, and the Vertical Colour of Sound*, Faber, 1989, pp. 57–61.

23  Quoted in P. Martin, *Sounds and Society*, Manchester, Manchester University Press, 1995, p. 213.

24  A brief account is R. Orton, 'Musical, Cultural and Educational Interpretations of Digital Technology', in J. Panter, T. Howell, R. Orton and P. Seymour, eds, *The Routledge Companion to Contemporary Musical Thought*, Routledge, 1992, vol. 2, pp. 319–28.

25  Decca producer Andrew Cornall, interviewed by S. Sillitoe, 'Classical Views', *Studio Sound*, May 1996, pp. 90–2.

26  *The Independent*, 29 August 1992.

27  Ensemble X concert programme, 24 July 1991.

28  Eleanor Alberga interviewed on Radio Three by Robert Sandall, 9 November 1994.

29  *Ibid.*

30  R. Ellis, *Soundtrack to Spleen*, Swarf Finger label, 1996.

31  Music by David Byrne, Robert Moran, John Lurie and Michael Torke, played by the Balanescu Quartet, Argo CD 436 565–2, 1992.

32  Compare the 1989 postlude to Hobsbawm, *The Jazz Scene*, p. 289.

33  Sleeve-notes to the Orphy Robinson album *When Tomorrow Comes*, Blue Note International CDP 7985812; compare, Henry Threadgill, interviewed by Ben Watson, BBC Radio Three, 18 May 1992; Robinson interview, *The Wire*, July 1992; Incognito, interviewed in *Music Technology*, vol. 5, no. 10, September 1991.

34  For comment on this see the *Independent*, 22 August 1991; *The Wire*, July 1992. One problem here is the attempt to win over an American audience: sleeve-notes for Pine's albums are Americanised, and posters for his 1993 tour carried a pastiche photo of Pine as Charlie Parker.

# Select bibliography

Place of publication is London unless otherwise stated.

Adorno, T., *Philosophy of Modern Music* [1941], Sheed and Ward, 1973.

Adorno, T., *Introduction to the Sociology of Music* [1962], New York, Seabury Press, 1976.

Adorno, T., 'On Popular Music', in S. Frith and A. Goodwin, eds, *On Record*.

Adorno, T. and M. Horkheimer, 'Enlightenment as Mass Deception', in their *Dialectic of Enlightenment*, Allen Lane, 1973.

Aizlewood, J., ed., *Love is the Drug: Living as a Pop Fan*, Harmondsworth, Penguin, 1994.

Appleyard, B., *The Culture Club: Crisis in the Arts*, Faber, 1984.

Attali, J., *Noise*, trans. B. Massumi, Manchester, Manchester University Press, 1985.

Bailey, P., *Leisure and Class in Victorian England*, Routledge Kegan Paul, 1978.

Bailey, P., ed., *Music Hall, the Business of Pleasure*, Milton Keynes, Open University Press, 1987.

Bakhtin, M., *The Dialogic Imagination*, trans. C. Emerson and M. Holquist, Austin, University of Texas Press, 1981.

Bakhtin, M., *Rabelais and His World*, trans. Helene Iswolsky, Bloomington, Indiana University Press, 1984.

Bannerjee, S. and G. Baumann, 'Bhangra 1984–8: Fusion and Professionalisation in a Genre of South Asian Dance Music', in P. Oliver, ed., *Black Music in Britain*.

Barnard, S., *On the Radio*, Milton Keynes, Open University Press, 1989.

Barrell, J., *English Literature in History 1730–80: an Equal Wide Survey*, Manchester, Manchester University Press, 1983.

Barthes, R., 'The Grain of the Voice', *Image–Music–Text*, ed. S. Heath, Fontana, 1977.

Bax, A, ed. L. Foreman, *Farewell My Youth*, Aldershot, Scolar Press, 1992.

Beadle, J.J., *Will Pop Eat Itself?*, Faber, 1993.

Beedell, A.V., *The Decline of the English Musician 1788–1888*, Oxford, Oxford University Press, 1992.

Benjamin, W., 'The Work of Art in the Age of Mechanical Reproduction', in Benjamin, ed. H. Arendt, *Illuminations*, New York, Schocken, 1969.

Berman, M., *All that is Solid Melts into Air*, Verso, 1983.

'Björk meets Stockhausen', *Dazed and Confused*, no. 23, August 1996, pp. 42–6.

Blake, A., 'The Death of a Hero?', *Magazine of Cultural Studies*, no. 1, March, 1990, 32–5.

Blake, A., *The Music Business*, B.T. Batsford, 1992.

Blake, A., 'Summer's Lists', *New Statesman and Society*, 7 June 1994.

Blake, A., 'Village Green, Urban Jungle', *New Statesman and Society*, 12 August 1994.

Blake, A., 'Britische Jugend: Gibt es noch/British Youth: Does it Still Exist?', in N. Bailer and R. Horak, eds, *Jugendkultur Annäheurungen*, Vienna, Wiener Universitätsverlag, 1995, pp. 206–38.

Blake, A., 'Re-Placing British Music', in M. Nava and A. O'Shea, eds, *Modern Times: Reflections on a Century of English Modernity*, Routledge, 1995, pp. 208–38.

Blake, A., 'The Echoing Corridor: Music in the Postmodern East End', in T. Butler and M. Rustin, eds, *Rising in the East: the Regeneration of East London*, Lawrence and Wishart, 1996, pp. 197–214.

Blake, A., 'Listen To Britain: Music, Advertising and Postmodern Culture', in M. Nava, A. Blake, I. MacRury and B. Richards, eds, *Buy This Book: Advertising and Consumption since the 1950s*, Routledge, 1996, pp. 224–38.

Blake, A., 'T.H. White, Arnold Bax and the Alternative History of Britain', in D. Littlewood and P. Stockwood, eds, *Impossibility Fiction*, Amsterdam, Rodopi International, 1996, pp. 25–36.

Blom, E., *Music in England*, Harmondsworth, Penguin, 1942.

Bloomfield, T., 'Negative Dialectics in Pop', *Popular Music*, vol. 12, no. 1, January 1993.

Boulton, D., *Jazz in Britain*, W.H. Allen, 1958.

Boyes, G., *The Imagined Village: Culture, Ideology and the English Folk Revival*, Manchester, Manchester University Press, 1993.

Brackett, D., *Interpreting Popular Music*, Cambridge, Cambridge University Press, 1995.

Bradley, D., *Understanding Rock'n'Roll: Popular Music in Britain 1955–1964*, Buckingham, Open University Press, 1992.

Bratton, J.S., ed., *Music Hall: Performance and Style*, Milton Keynes, Open University Press, 1989.

Brett, P., ed., *Benjamin Britten: Peter Grimes*, Cambridge, Cambridge University Press, 1983.

Briggs, A., *A History of Broadcasting in the United Kingdom*, 5 vols, Oxford, Oxford University Press, 1965–95.

Bruce, G., *Festival in the North: the Story of the Edinburgh Festival*, Robert Hale, 1975.

Buett, P., E. Wood and G.C. Thomas, eds, *Queering the Pitch: the New Gay and Lesbian Musicology*, Routledge, 1994.

Cannadine, D., 'The Theory and Practice of the Victorian Leisure Class', *The Historical Journal*, vol. 21, no. 2, 1978, pp. 445–67.

Carpenter, H., *Benjamin Britten*, Faber, 1992.

Chambers, I., *Urban Rhythms: Pop Music and Popular Culture*, Macmillan, 1985.

Chanan, M., *Musica Practica: the Social Practice of Western Music from Gregorian Chant to Postmodernism*, Verso, 1994.

Chanan, M., *Repeated Takes: a Short History of Recording and its Effects on Music*, Verso, 1995.

Chion, M., trans. C. Gorbmann, *Audio-Vision: Sounds on Screen*, New York, Columbia University Press, 1994.

Citron, M., *Gender and The Musical Canon*, Cambridge, Cambridge University Press, 1993.

Clarke, D., *The Penguin Encyclopaedia of Popular Music*, Harmondsworth, Penguin, 1989.

Clarke, D., *The Rise and Fall of Popular Music*, Harmondsworth, Viking Penguin, 1995.

Clarke, M., *The Politics of Pop Festivals*, Junction Books, 1982.

Cohen, Sara, *Rock Culture in Liverpool: Popular Music in the Making*, Oxford, Oxford University Press, 1991.

Cohen, Stan, ed., *Images of Deviance*, Harmondsworth, Penguin, 1970.

Cohen, Stan, *Folk Devils and Moral Panics: the Creation of the Mods and Rockers*, McGibbon and Kee, 1972.

Cole, H., *The Changing Face of Music*, Victor Gollancz, 1978.

Colley, L., *Britons: Forging the Nation 1707–1837*, Yale University Press, 1992.

Collins, J. and P. Richards, 'Popular Music in West Africa', in S. Frith, ed., *World Music, Politics and Social Change*, Manchester, Manchester University Press, 1989, pp. 12–46.

Colls, R., and P. Dodd, eds, *Englishness: Politics and Culture 1880–1914*, Croom Helm, 1986.

Cotterell, R., ed., *Jazz Now*, Quartet, 1976.

Cox, D., *The Henry Wood Proms*, BBC Books, 1980.

Culshaw, J., *Putting the Record Straight*, Secker and Warburg, 1984.

Cunningham, H., *Leisure in the Industrial Revolution 1780–1880*, Croom Helm, 1980.

Dannen, F., *Hit Men: Power Brokers, Fast Money and the Music Business*,

Vintage, 1991.

Darnton, C., *You and Music*, Harmondsworth, Penguin, 1940.

Davis, S., *Hammer of the Gods: the Led Zeppelin Saga*, Sidgwick and Jackson, 1985.

Denison, J., 'Reflections on an Orchestral Theme for London', in J. Pick, ed., *The State and the Arts*, Eastbourne, John Offord, 1980, pp. 99–107.

Durant, A., *Conditions of Music*, Macmillan, 1984.

Dyer, R., 'In Defence of Disco', in S. Frith and A. Goodwin, eds, *On Record*, Routledge, 1990, pp. 410–18.

Eagleton, T., *The Function of Criticism*, Verso, 1984.

Ehrlich, C., *The Musical Profession in Britain since the Eighteenth Century*, Oxford, Oxford University Press, 1985.

Emmerson, S., ed., *The Language of Electroacoustic Music*, Macmillan, 1986.

Eno, B., *A Year with Swollen Appendices*, Faber, 1996.

Finnegan, R., *The Hidden Musicians: Music Making in an English Town*, Cambridge, Cambridge University Press, 1989.

Fiori, U., 'Popular Music: Theory, Practice, Value', in *Popular Music Perspectives 2*, Exeter, Exeter University Press, 1985, pp. 13–23.

Flinn, C., *Strains of Utopia*, Princeton University Press, 1992.

Foreman, L., ed., *From Parry to Britten: British Music in Letters 1900–1945*, B.T. Batsford, 1987.

Foreman, L., *Bax: a Composer and His Times*, 2nd edn, Aldershot, Scolar Press, 1988.

Frith, S., 'Why do Songs have Words?', in A. Levene-White, ed., *Lost in Music: Culture, Style and the Musical Event*, Routledge, 1987, pp 77–106.

Frith, S., *Music for Pleasure*, Cambridge, Polity Press, 1988.

Frith, S., 'Playing with Real Feeling – Jazz and Suburbia', in Frith, *Music for Pleasure*, pp. 42–58.

Frith, S., 'Anglo-America and its Discontents', *Cultural Studies*, vol. 5, no. 3, October 1991, pp. 263–9.

Frith, S., *Music and Copyright*, Edinburgh, Edinburgh University Press, 1993.

Frith, S., 'Popular Music and the Local State', in Frith, L. Grossberg, J. Shepherd and G. Turner, eds, *Rock and Popular Music: Politics, Policies, Institutions*, Routledge, 1993, pp. 14–23.

Frith, S. and A. Goodwin, eds, *On Record: Rock, Pop and the Written Word*, Routledge, 1990.

Fulkerson, J., 'Morty Feldman is Dead', in J. Paynter, T. Howell, R. Orton and P. Seymour, eds, *Routledge Companion to Contemporary Musical Thought*, vol. 2, pp. 751–61.

Gammond, P., *The Oxford Companion to Popular Music*, Oxford, Oxford

University Press, 1991.

Garfield, S., *Expensive Habits: the Dark Side of the Music Industry*, Faber, 1988.

Garner, K., *In Session Tonight: the Complete Radio 1 Recordings*, BBC Books, 1993.

Garratt, S. 'All of Me Loves All of You: the Bay City Rollers', in Aizlewood, ed., *Love is the Drug*, pp. 72–85.

Gill, J., *Queer Noises*, Cassell, 1995.

Gilroy, P., *The Black Atlantic: Modernity and Double Consciousness*, Verso, 1993.

Glock, W., *Notes in Advance*, Oxford, Oxford University Press, 1991.

Goodwin, A., *Dancing in the Distraction Factory: Music, Television and Popular Culture*, Routledge, 1993.

Gorbmann, C., *Unheard Melodies: Narrative Film Music*, Bloomington, Indiana University Press, 1987.

Gottlieb, J. and G. Wald, 'Smells like Teen Spirit: Riot Grrls, Revolution and Women in Independent Rock', in A. Ross and T. Rose, eds, *Microphone Fiends*, pp. 250–74.

Green, L., *Music on Deaf Ears: Music, Meaning and Ideology in Education*, Manchester, Manchester University Press, 1988.

Griffiths, P., *New Sounds, New Personalities: New Music of the 1980s*, Faber, 1985.

Grossberg, L., 'Is Anybody listening? Does Anybody Care? On the State of Rock', in A. Ross and T. Rose, eds, *Microphone Fiends*, pp. 41–58.

Hall, S. and T. Jefferson, eds, *Resistance Through Rituals*, Hutchinson, 1976.

Hamm, C., *Putting Popular Music in its Place*, Cambridge, Cambridge University Press, 1995.

Harker, D., *One for the Money: Politics and Popular Song*, Hutchinson, 1980.

Harker, D., *Fakesong: the Manufacture of British 'Folksong' from 1700 to the Present Day*, Milton Keynes, Open University Press, 1990.

Harries, M. and S. Harries, *A Pilgrim Soul: the Life of Elizabeth Lutyens*, Faber, 1989.

Harris, E.T., 'Handel's Ghost: the Composer's Posthumous Reputation in the Eighteenth Century', in J. Paynter, T. Howell, R. Orton and P. Seymour, eds, *Routledge Companion to Contemporary Musical Thought*, vol. 1, pp. 208–25.

Harrod, R.F., *The Life of John Maynard Keynes* [1951],Harmondsworth, Penguin, 1972.

Hatch, R. and D. Millward, *From Blues to Rock: an Analytical History*, Manchester, Manchester, University Press, 1987.

Hebdige, D., *Subculture: the Meaning of Style*, Methuen, 1979.

Heckstall-Smith, D., *The Safest Place in the World: a Personal History of British Rhythm and Blues*, Quartet, 1988.

Hind, J. and S. Mosco, *Rebel Radio*, Pluto Press, 1985.

Hobsbawm, E. (writing as Francis Newton), *The Jazz Scene* [1959], Weidenfeld and Nicolson, 1989.

Hobsbawm, E. and T. Ranger, eds, *The Invention of Tradition*, Cambridge, Cambridge University Press, 1982.

Howes, F., *The English Musical Renaissance*, Secker & Warburg, 1966.

Hurd, M., *Rutland Boughton and the Glastonbury Festivals*, Oxford, Oxford University Press, 1993.

Hyde, D., *New Found Voices: Women in Nineteenth Century English Music*, Canterbury, Tritone Music Publishers, 1991.

Jameson, F., *Postmodernism, or the Cultural Logic of Late Capitalism*, Verso, 1991.

Jones, S., *Black Culture, White Youth*, Macmillan, 1987.

Jordan, T., 'Collective Bodies: Raving and the Politics of Gilles Deleuze and Felix Guattari', *Body and Society*, vol. 1, no. 1, pp. 125–44.

Kent, N., *The Dark Stuff: Selected Writings on Rock Music 1972–1993*, Harmondsworth, Penguin, 1994.

Kerman, J., *Musicology*, Fontana, 1985.

Kernfeld, B., ed., *The New Grove Dictionary of Jazz*, Macmillan, 1994.

Kohn, M., *Dope Girls*, Lawrence and Wishart, 1993.

Kozinn, A., *The Beatles*, Phaidon, 1995.

Kozinn, A., 'Beatles as Classics', *BBC Music Magazine*, October 1995, pp. 33–7.

Laing, D., 'Sadeness, Scorpions and Single Markets: National and Transnational Trends in European Popular Music', *Popular Music*, vol. 11, no. 2, 1992, pp. 127–40.

Laing, D., 'Scrutiny to Subcultures: Notes on Literary Criticism and Popular Music', *Popular Music*, vol. 13, no. 23, January/February 1994, pp. 209–22.

Lambert, C., *Music Ho! A Study of Music in Decline*, Faber and Faber, 1934.

Lanza, J., *Elevator Music*, Quartet, 1995.

Lapsley, R. and M. Westlake, *Film Theory: an Introduction*, Manchester, Manchester University Press, 1988.

Larkin, C., ed., *The Guinness Encyclopaedia of Popular Music*, Guinness Publishing, 1994.

Lebrecht, N., *The Maestro Myth*, Simon and Schuster, 1991.

Lebrecht, N., *When the Music Stops: Managers, Maestros and the Corporate Murder of Classical Music*, Simon and Shuster, 1996.

Lee, E., *Music of the People: a Study of Popular Music in Great Britain*, Barrie and Jenkins, 1970.

Leppert, R., *Music and Image: Domesticity, Ideology and Socio-Cultural Formation in Eighteenth Century England*, Cambridge, Cambridge University Press, 1988.

Leppert, R., *The Sight of Sound: Music, Representation and the History of the Body*, University of California Press, 1995.

Leppert, R. and S. McLary, eds, *Music and Society: the Politics of Composition, Performance and Reception*, Cambridge, Cambridge University Press, 1987.

Light, A., *Forever England: Femininity, Literature and Conservatism between the Wars*, Routledge, 1991.

Lipsitz, G., *Dangerous Crossroads: Popular Music, Postmodernism and the Poetics of Place*, Verso, 1994.

Lister, D., *Bradford's Rock'n'Roll*, Bradford, Bradford Libraries and Information Service, 1991.

McClary, S., *Feminine Endings*, Minnesota, University of Minneapolis Press, 1991.

MacDonald, I., *Revolution in the Head: the Beatles' Records and the Sixties*, Fourth Estate, 1994.

McKay, G., *Senseless Acts of Beauty: Cultures of Resistance since the Sixties*, Verso, 1996.

MacKinnon, N., *The British Folk Scene*, Buckingham, Open University Press, 1993.

McNab, M., 'Computer Music: Some Aesthetic Considerations', in S. Emmerson, ed., *The Language of Electroacoustic Music*, pp. 141–54.

McRobbie, A., 'Settling Accounts with Subcultures', in S. Frith and A. Goodwin, eds, *On Record*, pp. 66–80.

McVeigh, S., *Concert Life in London from Mozart to Haydn*, Cambridge, Cambridge University Press, 1993.

Marcus, G., *Lipstick Traces: a Secret History of the Twentieth Century*, Secker and Warburg, 1985.

Martin, G., *Summer of Love: the Making of Sergeant Pepper*, Pan, 1995.

Martin, P., *Sounds and Society*, Manchester, Manchester University Press, 1995.

Medhurst, A., 'It Sort of Happened Here: the Strange, Brief Life of the British Pop Film', in J. Romney and A. Wootton, eds, *Celluloid Jukebox*, British Film Institute, 1995, pp. 60–71.

Meller, H., *Leisure and the Changing City*, Routledge Kegan Paul, 1976.

Mellers, W., *Music and Society*, 2nd edn, Dennis Dobson, 1950.

Mellers, W., *Vaughan Williams and the Vision of Albion*, Barrie and Jenkins, 1989.

Melly, G., *Revolt into Style*, Harmondsworth, Allen Lane, 1969.

Merwe, P. van der, *Origins of the Popular Style: the Antecedents of Twentieth-Century Popular Music*, Oxford, Oxford University Press, 1989.

Middleton, R., *Studying Popular Music*, Milton Keynes, Open University Press, 1990.

Mitchell, D., *Cradles of the New*, Faber, 1995.

Moore, A.F., *Rock, the Primary Text*, Buckingham, Open University Press, 1993.

Motion, A., *The Lamberts*, Faber, 1986.

Mulhern, F., *The Moment of Scrutiny*, New Left Books, 1979.

Murray, C.S., *Crosstown Traffic: Jimi Hendrix and Post-War Pop*, Faber, 1989.

Nava, M., *Changing Cultures: Feminism, Youth and Consumeris*, Sage, 1992.

Nava, M. and A. O'Shea, eds, *Modern Times: Reflections on a Century of English Modernity*, Routledge, 1995.

Negus, K., *Producing Pop*, Edward Arnold, 1992.

Nettel, R., *Music in the Five Towns 1840–1914*, Oxford, Oxford University Press, 1944.

Nettel, R., *A Social History of Traditional Song*, Adams & Dart, 1969.

Newman, E., *Wagner: a Biography*, 4 vols, Cambridge, Cambridge University Press, 1978.

O'Brien, L., *She-Bop: the Story of Women in Popular Music*, Harmondsworth, Penguin, 1995.

Oliver, P., ed., *Black Music in Britain*, Milton Keynes, Open University Press, 1991.

Orton, R., 'Musical, Cultural and Educational Interpretations of Digital Technology', in J. Paynter, T. Howell, R. Orton and P. Seymour, eds, *Routledge Companion to Musical Thought*, vol. 2, pp. 319–28.

Palmer, R., 'The Church of the Sonic Guitar', in A. de Curtis, ed., *Present Tense: Rock & Roll Culture*, Duke University Press, 1992, pp. 16–36.

Palmer, T., *All You Need is Love*, Futura, 1976.

Parker, M., 'Reading the Charts', *Popular Music*, vol. 10, no. 2, pp. 205–18.

Paynter, J., *Music in the Secondary School Curriculum*, Cambridge, Cambridge University Press, 1982.

Paynter, J., T. Howell, R. Orton and P. Seymour, eds, *Routledge Companion to Contemporary Musical Thought*, 2 vols, Routledge, 1992.

Peacock, A. and R. Weir, *The Composer in the Market Place*, Faber, 1975.

Pearsall, R., *Edwardian Popular Music*, Newton Abbot, David and Charles, 1975.

Pearsall, R., *Popular Music of the Twenties*, Newton Abbot, David and Charles, 1976.

Pick, J., ed., *The State and the Arts*, Eastbourne, John Offord, 1980.

Pickering, M. and T. Green, eds, *Everyday Culture: Popular Song and the Vernacular Milieu*, Milton Keynes, Open University Press, 1987.

Pirie, P., *The English Musical Renaissance*, Gollancz, 1979.

Porter, R., ed., *Myths of the English*, Cambridge, Polity Press, 1992.

# Index